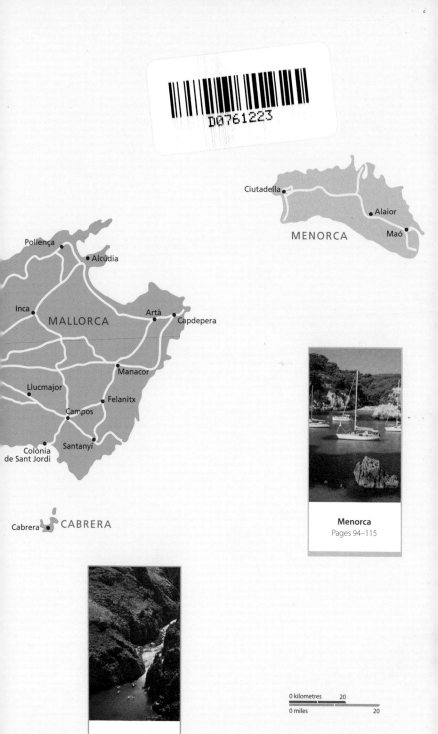

Ciutadella

Alaior

Maó

MENORCA

Pollença

Alcúdia

Inca

MALLORCA

Artà

Capdepera

Manacor

Llucmajor

Felanitx

Campos

Santanyí

Colònia
de Sant Jordi

Cabrera CABRERA

Menorca

Mallorca

0 kilometres 20

0 miles 20

DK EYEWITNESS TRAVEL

Mallorca
Menorca & Ibiza

DK EYEWITNESS TRAVEL

Mallorca
Menorca & Ibiza

Main Contributor **Grzegorz Micula**

Produced by Wydawnictwo Wiedza
i Życie S.A., Warsaw

Senior Graphic Designer Paweł Pasternak

Editors Robert G. Pasieczny,
Anna Moczar-Demko

Graphic Design Paweł Kamiński,
Piotr Kiedrowski

Typesetting and Layout Paweł Kamiński,
Piotr Kiedrowski, Elżbieta Dudzińska

Cartography Magdalena Polak

Photography Bartłomiej Zaranek

Illustrations Bohdan Wróblewski,
Michał Burkiewicz, Monika Żylińska

Contributors Grzegorz Micuła, Katarzyna
Sobieraj, Robert G. Pasieczny,
Eligiusz Nowakowski

Consultant Carlos Cassas Marrodan

For Dorling Kindersley
Translator Magda Hannay

Editor Matthew Tanner

Senior DTP Designer Jason Little

Production Controller Sarah Dodd

Printed in Malaysia

First American edition, 2004
18 19 20 21 10 9 8 7 6 5 4 3 2 1

Published in the United States by DK
Publishing,
345 Hudson Street, New York, New York
10014

**Reprinted with revisions 2006, 2008,
2010, 2012, 2014, 2016, 2018**

Copyright © 2004, 2018 Dorling Kindersley,
London
A Penguin Random House Company

Published in Great Britain by Dorling
Kindersley Limited.

ISSN 1542-1554
ISBN 978-1-46546-828-4

Floors are referred to throughout
in accordance with British usage; ie the
"first floor" is the floor above ground level.

MIX
Paper from
responsible sources
FSC™ C018179

Introducing the Balearic Islands

Aerial view of the Sa Penya district of
Eivissa, on the island of Ibiza

The majestic Es Pontas, a natural arch in Santanyí, Mallorca

**The information in this
DK Eyewitness Travel Guide is checked regularly.**
Every effort has been made to ensure that this book is as up-to-date as possible
at the time of going to press. Some details, however, such as telephone numbers,
opening hours, prices, gallery hanging arrangements and travel information are
liable to change. The publishers cannot accept responsibility for any consequences
arising from the use of this book, nor for any material on third party websites, and
cannot guarantee that any website address in this book will be a suitable source of
travel information. We value the views and suggestions of our readers very highly.
Please write to: Publisher, DK Eyewitness Travel Guides, Dorling Kindersley,
80 Strand, London, WC2R 0RL, UK, or email: travelguides@dk.com.

◄ **Title page** Boats anchored in Esteny d'es Peix, Formentera   **Front cover main image** La Seu, Palma's cathedral, overlooking
the harbour, Mallorca   **Back cover main image** Cala del Pilar, Menorca

Contents

Dancers in traditional costume at a folkloric event in Ibiza

The Neo-Gothic façade of the church of Sant Bartomeu in Sóller, Mallorca

La Granja, Mallorca

HOW TO USE THIS GUIDE

This guide will help you to make the most of your visit to the Balearic Islands. The first section, Introducing the Balearic Islands, locates the islands geographically and gives an outline of their rich history and culture. Individual sections describe the main historic sights and star attractions on each of the four populated archipelago islands.

Help with accommodation, restaurants, shopping, entertainment and many recreational activities can be found in the *Travellers' Needs* section, while the *Survival Guide* provides useful tips on everything you need to know, from money and language to getting around and seeking medical care.

The Balearic Islands Island by Island

In this guide, each of the islands has been given its own chapter. Within each chapter there is an introduction, a Regional Map, and a detailed listing of all the best sights.

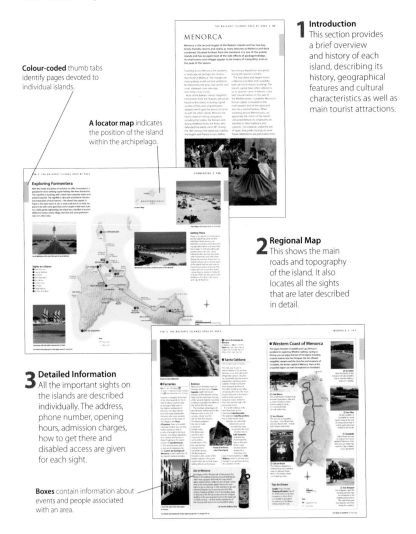

Colour-coded thumb tabs identify pages devoted to individual islands.

A locator map indicates the position of the island within the archipelago.

1 Introduction
This section provides a brief overview and history of each island, describing its history, geographical features and cultural characteristics as well as main tourist attractions.

2 Regional Map
This shows the main roads and topography of the island. It also locates all the sights that are later described in detail.

3 Detailed Information
All the important sights on the islands are described individually. The address, phone number, opening hours, admission charges, how to get there and disabled access are given for each sight.

Boxes contain information about events and people associated with an area.

4 Major Towns
At least two pages are devoted to each major town, with a detailed description of the historic remains and local curiosities that are worth seeing.

A Visitors' Checklist provides tourist and transport information, including opening hours of tourist attractions, admission charges, and details of local festivals and market days.

A town map shows the location of all the main sights within the town centre and provides tourist information on post offices and car parks.

5 Street-by-Street Map
This gives a bird's-eye view of a particularly interesting sightseeing area described in the section.

A suggested route for a walk is shown in red.

Stars point out the best sights or exhibits that no visitor should miss.

6 Star Sights
At least one page is dedicated to each major sight. Historic buildings are dissected to reveal their interiors, and parks are illustrated to show the main attractions.

Photographs illustrate the most interesting areas and the most impressive sights within an attraction.

Cut-outs show the sight in its surroundings and some parts of the interior.

INTRODUCING THE BALEARIC ISLANDS

DISCOVERING THE BALEARIC ISLANDS

Whether island hopping or exploring only one of the islands, the Balearics have so much to offer – from beaches to ancient ruins, caves to nightclubs. The itineraries mentioned below have been designed to include most of the major sights of Palma, Mallorca, Menorca and Ibiza. The final itinerary is a two-week tour concentrating on Mallorca. There are many frequent flights and ferries between the islands, but note that vehicles rented on one island cannot be taken to another island. Pick, combine and follow your favourite tours, or simply dip in and out and be inspired: if, for example, you only have five days in Mallorca, spend a day in Palma (see p12), followed by Days 5 to 8 of the two-week Mallorca itinerary (see pp14–5).

A harbour view of Dalt Vila, Eivissa
Ibiza's oldest remaining part, Dalt Vila, with its intriguing history and beautiful sights, is a UNESCO World Heritage Site and a must-visit for tourists.

0 kilometres 15
0 miles 15

3 days in Ibiza

- Explore **Eivissa town**, its handsome squares and cobbled streets enclosed within formidable-looking fortifications.

- No trip to Ibiza is complete without a visit to one of the island's heaving nightclubs, such as Pacha in **Eivissa**.

- Enjoy **Els Amunts**, the rolling mountains along the island's north coast.

◄ Detailed fresco painted by an Arab artist

4 days in Menorca

- Sample the small-town delights of both **Maó**, the island capital, and pretty **Ciutadella**, with its compact centre crowded with attractive stone mansions that nudge up towards the harbour.

- Among the resorts, aim for **Fornells**, the prettiest resort on the island, with a scattering of holiday villas sitting tight against a rocky slice of coast.

- Relax on an isolated cove beach, such as the beautiful **Cala Turqueta**.

- Head to the top of **Monte Toro**, Menorca's highest point, which has fabulous views.

Key

━━ 5 days in Mallorca
━━ Two weeks in Mallorca
━━ 4 days in Menorca
━━ 3 days in Ibiza

A view of Deià, Mallorca
The lovely mountain town of Deià was home to the well-known English novelist and poet Robert Graves.

5 days in Mallorca

- Spend time in **Palma**, the wonderful capital city of the Balearics, rich with historical attractions.

- Take the vintage train over the mountains to **Sóller**, once a fruit merchants' town.

- Explore the verdant gardens of the **Jardines d'Alfàbia** and the picturesque resort of **Port de Sóller**.

- Visit the **Santuari de Lluc**, home to the much-revered statue of the Virgin Mary.

- Investigate the various nooks and crannies of **Pollença**, a charming little town.

Two weeks in Mallorca

- Admire the magnificent scenery of Mallorca's northwest in the pretty mountain hamlets of **Deià, Banyalbufar, Estellencs** and **Valldemossa** which has a beautiful monastery.

- Relax and unwind at **Port de Pollença**, the archetypal family resort which has a great vibe, and sits alongside a lovely sandy beach.

- Explore the medieval hilltop town of **Artà** and the prehistoric site of **Ses Païsses**.

- Enjoy the easy charms of **Porto Cristo**, an agreeable port and resort with an attractive centre and a harbourside beach.

- Take the passenger boat to **Cabrera Island National Park**, renowned for its rare plant species and marine life.

For keys to symbols see back flap

2 days in Palma

- **Arriving** Son Sant Joan international airport is about 11km (7 miles) from Palma. Public buses run approximately every 15 minutes in Palma, and taxis are also available.

- **Moving on** Inter-island flights are frequent. A car is recommended for exploring the island.

Day 1
Morning Begin your visit to Palma at the **Cathedral – La Seu** – (see p54), a beautiful sandstone edifice, whose mighty buttressed walls soar high above the seafront. Explore the exquisite Gothic cathedral and then pop over to the **Palau d'Almudaina** (see p52), once a royal palace and now home to a small but superb collection of Renaissance tapestries. Admire the sculptures in the courtyard of the **Palau March** (see p58) and walk over to the Palau Episcopal. This palaca is home to the **Museu Diocesà** (see p59) which has a remarkable collection of medieval religious paintings.

Afternoon Stroll down the narrow lanes of the **Old Town** that are lined by ancient stone houses, and go for a walk along part of the old **city walls** (see p59), stretching out behind the seafront. Be sure to visit the old Arab baths, the **Banys Àrabs** (see p59) and **Santa Eulàlia** (see p58), the handsome church with an imposing interior. Round off the afternoon with

a tour of the **Basilica de Sant Francesc** (see p59), which boasts a splendid rose window and is littered with the tombs of the local aristocracy.

Day 2
Morning Start the day by strolling up the elegant **Passeig d'es Born** (see p53), once the city's main thoroughfare sheltered from the sun by ancient plane trees. Enjoy the charm of one of Palma's most interesting houses, **Casal Solleric** (see p53), and continue onto **Es Baluard Museu d'Art Modern i Contemporani** (see p58), a prestigious museum of modern art located in a massive Renaissance bastion. Thereafter, proceed to **Plaça Mercat** (see p53) to sample the freshest of food at Palma's biggest and best market. Visit the **Plaça Major** (see p58), a handsome open square. Don't forget to check out the modern art of the fascinating **Museu Fundació Juan March** (see p60).

Evening Take a tour to the **Castell de Bellver** (see p61), a medieval castle perched high on a hill overlooking Palma. Be sure to examine the collection of classical sculptures inside and enjoy the views out over the Bay of Palma. Keep aside a couple of hours for the intriguing **Fundació Pilar i Joan Miró** (see p62), where the famous artist lived and worked for several decades – at a safe distance from Franco, the dictator. Here, you should spend time in the Miró museum, with its prized collection of the artist's work, and even gaze into his former studio.

Part of the Renaissance city wall in Palma, dating back to the 1500s

3 days in Ibiza

- **Arriving** Ibiza Airport is approximately 7 km (4 miles) away from Eivissa and is well-connected by a public bus service.

- **Transport** Eivissa town is best explored on foot, but a car is essential for the rest of this itinerary.

Day 1: Eivissa Town
Spend at least a day in **Eivissa town** (see pp120–23), exploring the ancient buildings and narrow lanes and alleys of the old town, known as **Dalt Villa** (see p121). Highlights include the cathedral and the imposing city walls that zigzag around the city centre. Also, look out for the antique exhibits at the excellent **Museu Arqueològic** (see p122) and drop by the **Museu d'Art Contemporani d'Eivissa** (see p122), which boasts a collection of modern art. Round off the day with a visit to a nightclub – Eivissa has some of the best in Europe, including Pacha.

Day 2: West Coast
Head for Ibiza's lovely west coast, stopping just for the short hike up to the **Mirador des Savinar** (see p130) viewpoint and watchtower. Carry on to **Cala d'Hort** (see p130), where you can unwind on a shingly cove beach. Lounge

The Gothic cathedral of La Seu, towering over Palma, Mallorca about in **Cala Vedella** (see p130) nearby, an appealing mini-resort with a strip of golden sand arching round the back of a slender cove. Continue north along to **Cala Molí** (see p130), where a lovely sandy beach is framed by pine-dusted hills. Proceed further north, and enjoy the assorted water sports of **Cala Bassa** (see p131), a large beach resort teeming with life.

Day 3: North Coast
Escape the tourists by heading inland to **Santa Agnès de Corona** (see p127), a pretty little village set in the heart of the countryside. Hike out of the village to the chapel of **Santa Agnès** (see p127), an unusual grotto church of ancient provenance. Thereafter, proceed east along the main road with farmlands on one side and the peaks of the **Els Amunts** (see p132) mountain range on the other. Junipers, fan palms, carobs and strawberry trees dot the mountains. Keep an eye out for falcons, greenfinches, goldfinches and hoopoes.

> **To extend your trip...**
> Eivissa town is just a short ferry ride from the fourth inhabited Balearic island, **Formentera** (see p136–43), a small, flat island with several splendid beaches, the longest of which is **Platja Migjorn** (see p142).

Colourful sails and people enjoying the sunshine on Platja Migjorn, Formentera

The shores of Es Grau, a small fishing village with a wide beach

4 days in Menorca

- **Arriving** Menorca's airport is a short journey from the main town, Maó. Shuttle buses and taxis connect the airport to Maó.

- **Transport** A car is required to explore the island.

Day 1: Maó
Enjoy the cosy, small-town atmosphere of **Maó** (see p98) and admire its pretty harbourside setting – Maó has one of the finest harbours in the Mediterranean. Explore the old town, visiting the bustling **Mercat Plaça Sa Carme** (see p98) and the intriguing church of **Santa Maria** (see p99). With ample time in hand, visit **Museu de Menorca** (see p100), with its collection of prehistoric and Roman artifacts. Wander down the harbour around **Xoriguer Distillery** (see p100), which stands testimony to bygone days when the Menorcans supplied British sailors with gin.

Day 2: North Coast
Heading north from Maó, make a beeline for **Es Grau** (see p102), an intimate resort draped around a sandy bay. Take a boat ride to the craggy, offshore islet of **Illa d'en Colom** (see p102), where you can hike up to the lighthouse or laze on the beach. Continue north to **Fornells** (see p108), a beguiling village that strings along a rocky, sun-bleached coast. The bay here is ideal for windsurfing – there is almost always a breeze – or you can push on to the beautiful **Cap de Cavalleria** (see pp108–9), a rugged headland with empty beaches and an ancient British watchtower.

Day 3: Inland towns and villages
The attractive old centre of the town of **Alaior** (see p104–5) rolls over the top of a steep hill. Cheese is the big deal here – be sure to sample some. Take a detour to **Torralba d'en Salord** (see p105), an impressive prehistoric ruin. Proceed onto **Es Mercadal** (see p105), a quaint hamlet at the base of **Monte Toro** (see p105), the island's highest hill. Drive to the top to visit the monastery. The next stop is **Santa Galdana** (see p110), a resort that nestles in a steep wooded gully, which is conveniently located near several delightful beaches: **Cala Turqueta** (see p110) is the best.

Day 4: Ciutadella
Spend the day in **Ciutadella** (see pp112–15), the pearl of Menorca, where beautiful, honey-coloured stone mansions fan out from the **Plaça d'es Born** (see p112), the town's elegant main square. Explore the medieval **cathedral** (see p112), and investigate the assorted antiquities of the **Claustre de Convent de Sant Agustí** (see p113). Wander along the **harbour** (see p114–15), where fishing boats dock and restaurants line the quay. Finally, drop by the **Museu Municipal** (see p114), where an excellent collection of prehistoric finds is lodged within the safe confines of the old city wall.

Two weeks in Mallorca

- **Arriving** Mallorca's international airport is a short bus or taxi ride from Palma, capital of the island.

- **Transport** Palma is best explored on foot, but a car is essential for the rest of this itinerary. You should take the vintage train which runs across the island from Palma to Sóller (6–7 times daily; 1hr; *see p74*).

- **For a shorter trip** If you only have five days in Mallorca, select a day in Palma from the two-day itinerary on p12, take the vintage train from Palmer to Sóller and then follow days 5 to 8 of this itinerary.

Tourists enjoy the beach on Cala Tuent

Green waters of Estellencs, a charming town on the northwestern coast

Day 1: Palma
Pick from the Palma itineraries on p12.

Day 2: Port d'Andratx; Sant Elm; Parc Natural de Sa Dragonera
Travel via **Port d'Andratx**, enjoying the pine-covered hills, to **Sant Elm** (*see p65*), which has a small beach. From here take a boat trip to the island of **Sa Dragonera** (*see p65*), for its hiking trails, cove beaches and bird life.

Day 3: Estellencs; Banyalbufar; Port de Valldemossa; Valldemossa
Explore Mallorca's rugged **northwestern coast** (*see p66*), beginning with the charming

village of **Estellencs** (*see p66*). Push on to **Banyalbufar** (*see p67*), which is – if anything – even prettier, with its honey-coloured stone houses ringed by terraced olive groves. Take the minor road as it zigzags over the mountains to the dramatic cove of **Port de Valldemossa** (*see p70*), home to a wide, shingly beach. Finish the day with a visit to **Valldemossa** (*see p70*), a handsome old town whose famous monastery once sheltered the composer Chopin.

Day 4: Son Marroig; Deià; Cala Deià
Sense the history of Mallorca at **Son Marroig** (*see p72*), a manor house perched high above the ocean. Linger at **Deià** (*see p72*), a beautiful mountain village made famous by the English poet and writer Robert Graves (*see p73*), who lived here for several decades. Visit the intriguing museum devoted to him – **La Casa de Robert Graves** (*see p72*). Brave the steep, curving road to reach **Cala Deià** (*see p73*), a narrow cove battered by the surf and home to two excellent beachside restaurants.

Day 5: Sóller town; Jardines d'Alfabia; Port de Sóller
Savour the charms of **Sóller** (*see p73*), the prettiest town on Mallorca, where an exquisite collection of old stone houses flanks a cobweb of narrow cobbled lanes and alleys. Detour south to the **Jardines d'Alfabia** (*see p75*), a lush garden of water fountains and jasmine

trellises, waterlily ponds and bulrushes – all set behind an attractive manor house. Be sure to take the vintage train, which clanks down from Sóller to **Port de Sóller** (*see p74*), a family-friendly resort that arches around a beautiful horseshoe-shaped bay.

Day 6: Cala Tuent; Sa Calobra; Santuari de Lluc
Escape the tourist throng by driving over the mountains to **Cala Tuent** (*see p75*), where soaring peaks frame a shingle beach. Admire the even more dramatic coastal scenery at tiny **Sa Calobra** (*see p75*), a popular day-trippers' destination, which is famous for the impressive box canyon, where the River of the Twins crashes down to the sea-shore. Make a beeline for the **Santuari de Lluc** (*see p76*), a beautiful monastery set in a shallow valley amid the mountains and home to a revered statue of the Virgin Mary, known as La Morenta.

Day 7: Pollença; Port de Pollença; Cap de Formentor
Explore **Pollença** (*see pp78–9*), a lovely little town of fine old mansions and stone churches. Be sure to climb its **Via Crucis** (Way of the Cross), a long and wide stone stairway that leads up to a shrine with great views over land and sea. Take a stroll along the long sandy beach at **Port de Pollença** (*see p79*), a charming family-friendly resort that is especially popular with the British. Venture out to the

Cap de Formentor *(see p79)*, at the tip of a wild and mountainous peninsula.

Day 8: Alcúdia; Port d'Alcúdia; Parc Natural de S'Albufera
Be sure to visit **Alcúdia** *(see p79)*, an amenable little place with medieval walls and a clutch of Roman remains. The best time to visit is on market days – Tuesdays and Sundays. Relax on the beach at **Port d'Alcúdia** *(see p79)*, an immaculate arc of golden sand crowded with tourists, or take a boat trip around the bay. Introduce yourself to the island's wonderful birdlife at the **Parc Natural de S'Albufera** *(see p80)*, a reedy, marshy wetland backing onto Alcúdia bay.

Day 9: Interior towns: Muro; Sineu; Petra
Avoid the more commercialized parts of Mallorca by heading inland to the towns of the central plain. Begin with **Muro** *(see p80)*, a sleepy place with a handsome main square and church, the imposing Sant Joan Baptista. Proceeding south, you soon reach **Sineu** *(see pp80–81)*, a lively and particularly pretty little town where the kings of Mallorca once held court, and then **Petra** *(see p81)*, where the prime target is the birthplace of Junípero Serra, one of the first Europeans to explore modern-day California.

Day 10: Interior towns: Vilafranca de Bonany; Els Calderers; Randa; Llucmajor
Sample the atmosphere of rural Mallorca at **Vilafranca de Bonany** *(see p85)*, a quiet village where they sell the freshest of produce – especially peppers. See how the local landed gentry while away the hours at **Els Calderers** *(see p85)*, an elegant manor house surrounded by a working farm, and then go up to the top of **Puig de Randa** *(see pp90–91)* to visit the hilltop monastery and its beautiful shrine. Complete the day with a quick ramble around **Llucmajor** *(see p90)*, a quiet town with a particularly pleasant main square.

The medieval battlements of the Artà fortress

Day 11: Artà; Capdepera; Cala Rajada
Begin the day with an exploration of **Artà** *(see p82)*, a pretty hilltop town with a splendid set of medieval walls. Clamber up to the sanctuary at the top of the town for the magnificent views over land and sea. Stroll over to **Ses Païsses** *(see p82)*, one of the island's most atmospheric prehistoric sites. Push on to **Capdepera** *(see p82)*, the proud possessor of a medieval castle, and round off the day at **Cala Rajada** *(see p82)*, an agreeable resort and fishing port with several lovely sandy beaches.

Day 12: Coves d'Artà; Cala Millor; Safari–Zoo
Don't miss the **Coves d'Artà** *(see p82)*, one of the most impressive cave systems on the island with huge stalactites and stalagmites illuminated in a variety of striking colours. Push further down the coast to **Cala Millor** *(see p84)*, a large, sprawling resort with

a striking sandy beach and facilities for all sorts of water sports. Spend the rest of the day relaxing on the beach, before dining at one of the resort's many restaurants and rounding off the day by dancing in one of the clubs.

Day 13: Porto Cristo; Coves del Drac; Felanitx; Parc Natural Mondrago
Enjoy the charms of **Porto Cristo** *(see p84)*, an agreeable port and resort with an attractive centre and a harbourside beach. Stroll over to the **Coves del Drac** *(see p84)* – the Dragon's Caves – a subterranean maze of caverns, where you can take a boat ride on an underground lake to the sound of a string quartet. Pause at **Felanitx** *(see p86)* for a brief look around this historic town and continue onto the **Parc Natural Mondragó** *(see p86)*, a protected slice of coast offering peaceful country walks and a delightful pine-covered beach.

Day 14: Colonia de Sant Jordi; Cabrera island
Relax at **Colònia de Sant Jordi** *(see p87)*, the pick of the resorts dotting the south coast and a charming combination of an old seaport and a holiday destination. Laze on one of the resort's several beaches or head off to **Es Trenc** *(see p87)*, a long strip of sandy beach that extends as far as the eye can see. Catch the passenger boat to **Cabrera Island National Park** *(see pp88–9)*, a bare and rocky archipelago renowned for its wildlife, particularly its picnic-eating lizards.

Yachts in the coves of Parc Natural Mondragó

Putting the Balearic Islands on the Map

This little group of islands off the east coast of Spain is the Mediterranean's westernmost archipelago. An autonomous province, the Balearic Islands are 82 km (51 miles) from the Iberian Peninsula, a three-hour journey by ferry. The total area of the islands is slightly over 5,000 sq km (1,930 sq miles). Mallorca, the largest island, has an area of 3,640 sq km (1,405 sq miles). The smallest of the four main islands is Formentera.

Northern coast of Mallorca
The northern shore of the Balearic Island descends steeply via craggy cliffs. There are few beaches here, but hiking trails are highly recommended.

Barcelona

Söller

Ma-11

Ma-10

Sa Dragonera

Andratx

Palma

Ma-1

Palma Mallorca

Eivissa, Ibiza
The Old Town at the centre of Ibiza is particularly interesting when viewed from above. One can see the maze of narrow streets layered within the beautiful old city walls.

Valencia

Valencia, Dénia

Ibiza

Valencia

PM810

Sant Antoni de Portmany   C-733

Dénia   C-731   Santa Eulària des Riu

PM803   **Eivissa**

Ibiza ✈

Valencia, Dénia

La Savina

Sant Francesc   *Formentera*

PM820

Formentera
El Mirador's restaurant terrace provides a stunning view of the island.

Key

▬▬ Motorway/highway

▬▬ Major road

▬▬ Minor road

···· Ferry route

0 km   15

0 miles   15

Sa Foradada, Mallorca
The picturesque cape jutting out into the sea near the Son Marroig estate of the Archduke Ludwig Salvator shows the true beauty of the Balearic coast, which some associate only with golden beaches. This landscape is typical of the northern shores of the islands.

↖ Barcelona

↖ Barcelona

Cala en Porter
This Menorcan beach is reached either by road or via a steep set of steps. The water is shallow and there's plenty of sand, making it a popular spot for those travelling with children.

Location of the archipelago
A short hop from Spain, the Balearic Islands are one of the most popular European resorts. Flights from northern Europe take less than three hours. As a result, the islands attract many visitors all year round.

A PORTRAIT OF THE BALEARIC ISLANDS

The Balearic Islands are blessed by a hot Mediterranean sun that is tempered by cooling sea breezes. Holidaymakers crowd onto the beaches every summer, while the young make the most of the numerous clubs and bars. Away from the resorts, time seems to have moved at a gentler pace, and inland the islands are quiet and undeveloped.

An ideal staging post between Europe and Africa, these beautiful islands have had their fair share of invaders, including the Phoenicians and the Romans, who made the islands part of their Empire. In recent times, the islands have fallen to a full-scale invasion of tourists, which began in the 1960s.

The islands' nightlife, particularly on Ibiza and Mallorca, is legendary and attracts a young crowd. There is far more on offer than clubs however, and if chic cafés are more your thing, the Balearic Islands supply these too. Indeed, the islands have proved to be popular with the rich and famous, many of whom have homes on the hillsides, away from the prying lenses of the paparazzi.

Even before the influx of tourists, the islands' climate attracted celebrities. The composer Frédéric Chopin journeyed to Mallorca with his lover George Sand in the winter of 1838–9. Other artists, including the painter and sculptor Joan Miró and the English poet Robert Graves, liked it so much that they settled down here.

Menorca is quieter than Mallorca or Ibiza. It has low-key resorts, golden beaches and a rocky landscape that is rich in fascinating prehistoric remains.

Formentera, 4 km (2 miles) south of Ibiza, is the smallest of the Balearic Islands. Living in the shadow of its party island neighbour, it remains the hippy haven that Pink Floyd and Bob Dylan retreated to in the 1970s. Few tourists stay on the island and, despite the numerous summer day-trippers, Formentera remains a rural haven.

Cala Tarida on the western shores of Ibiza

◀ Charming old fishing neighbourhood of Sa Penya in Eivissa, Ibiza

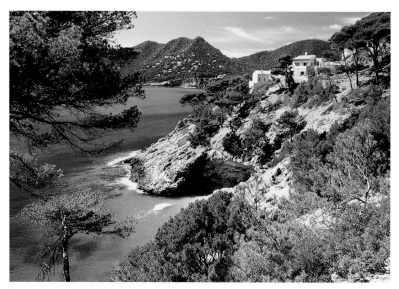

Rocky coast near Coves d'Artà in Mallorca

Tourist Paradise

It was in the early part of the 19th century that tourists first began to arrive on the Balearic Islands, and since that time the local economy has taken full advantage of the opportunities these new arrivals offered. Over 11 million visitors travel here every year to enjoy the islands' many attractions.

Mallorca, the largest island, is by far the most culturally rich, but the other islands are not short of attractions. Ibiza is famous as the clubbing capital of Europe; Menorca is an ideal resort for families, while those in search of peace and quiet head for the smaller island of Formentera.

You may even spot the occasional celebrity – Annie Lennox and Claudia

Portal of the main entrance to Palma's cathedral

Schiffer have homes on Mallorca, while Elle MacPherson and Noel Gallagher (to name but a few) have opted for life on Ibiza. The Balearic Islands are also very popular with politicians and royalty, including the Spanish royal family who have their summer residence in Palma.

The glitterati and other visitors are attracted to the Balearics by the cultural flavours of the islands. The archipelago has many fascinating historic sights ranging from Neolithic remains and castle ruins to stunning cathedrals and fine examples of British colonial architecture. Gourmets can delight in the famous Menorcan cheeses and Mallorcan wines, as well as sample the products of the local distilleries, including gin (inherited from the English) and the potent Ibizan herbal liqueurs. The famous *caldereta de llagosta* (Menorcan lobster stew) is not to be missed.

Natural Treasures

The greatest riches of the archipelago are its landscape and natural beauty. The local authorities, hoping to preserve these assets for future generations, have issued several legal decrees that are aimed at protecting the natural environment.

Currently, over 40 per cent of the archipelago is legally protected. There is a total of 82 areas of outstanding natural beauty, while the whole of Menorca is designated as a UNESCO Biosphere Reserve, with 18 designated sites that are currently assigned special protection. Mallorca's stunning Parc Natural de S'Albufera is a unique ornithological reserve and is one of southern Europe's most precious water marshes. Among Mallorca's parks and nature reserves are Cala Mondragó and Dragonera Island.

Cabrera Island National Park, to the south of Mallorca, also enjoys special protection. The number of boats permitted to land here is strictly limited. This has halted the mass influx of tourists, who come here to experience its unique natural beauty and swim in its crystal-clear waters. Here, the island's landscape is protected, as well as its surrounding waters.

National parks can be explored on foot or by bicycle, using special trails and signposts. There are also organized tours. The natural wonders of the islands can also be seen outside the parks. Some charming places are to be found, particularly in the valleys of the Serra de Tramuntana mountain range in Mallorca and in the secluded coves of the northwestern part of the island, as well as along most of the coastline of Menorca. The Pitiusan (Pine Trees) archipelago, comprising Ibiza,

Fishermen sorting their catch in Eivissa's harbour

Formentera and numerous neighbouring uninhabited rocky islands, forms a combined ecosystem visible from the air. A region of outstanding ecological value in Ibiza is the system of salt marshes, Ses Salines, which includes areas inhabited by thousands of birds. Since the Carthaginians discovered the islands these salt marshes have been used to supply salt extracted from seawater.

In Ses Illetes in Formentera, declared a World Heritage Site by UNESCO, the seabeds are carpeted with fields of *Posidonia oceanica*, a sea-grass species, which gives the water its crystal-clear appearance and makes it ideal for scuba diving.

People and Events

Although the impact of tourism has been far reaching, island customs and traditions have survived intact. This is particularly apparent in the rural areas. To see this side of island life, visit a local farmers' market in one of the small inland towns, or sit down with the locals in a village bar.

Solemn procession held during Corpus Christi

Entrance to El Palacio Hotel in Palma

The Arts

The islands have long been a draw for artists. Frédéric Chopin came to Valldemossa on Mallorca, though the weather was far from ideal (one of his Mallorcan compositions was the *Raindrops Prelude)*. The picturesque Mallorcan village of Deià was for many years the home of the English writer Robert Graves, whose guests included Pablo Picasso and the actors Alec Guinness and Peter Ustinov. The most famous artist associated with Mallorca, however, is Joan Miró, whose works can be seen in the Fundació Pilar i Joan Miró, on the outskirts of Palma.

Another important element of island life is the numerous national, local and religious holidays and fiestas *(see pp30–33)*. Normally these are days devoted to the patron saints of local parishes, but they can also be held at the end of harvest time or to celebrate an anniversary of an important public event.

A long calendar of fiestas begins in January with the Festa de Sant Antoni in Mallorca, where costumed revelers parade past bonfires. Perhaps the most colourful is the Festa de Sant Joan in Ciutadella, Menorca (23–24 June), with horseback processions along the narrow streets, firework displays and a jousting tournament.

Sports

The archipelago is famous for its water sports, particularly the many races held on the waters of the Badia de Palma. The most important of these are held under the patronage and with the participation of King Felipe VI. They are attended by leading members of the yachting world. The big events, including the King's Cup and Queen Sofia's Cup, are celebrated as public holidays.

Tennis is popular, too, and the islands hold a good number of clay courts –

The cosy writing studio of English novelist Robert Graves in his house in Deià, Mallorca

Felipe VI, the King of Spain

Pollença Bay. In the 1960s, Ibiza was "discovered" by hippies. Soon after, charter flights began operating to Mallorca. Mass tourism developed rapidly before the death of General Franco in 1975.

In 1983, the islands became an autonomous region of Spain. The authorities made Catalan and its local dialects (*Mallorquín* on Mallorca, *Menorquín* on Menorca and *Eivissenc* on Ibiza) the joint official language with Spanish and introduced strict control of the local economy.

Following a string of environmental protest marches in 1998 and 1999, an "eco-tax" was introduced in 2002. The tax, levied on visitors to the islands, was intended to tackle some of the environmental havoc that had been wreaked by unregulated tourism over the last 30 years. In its first year the tax's benefits included funding the demolishing of a number of unsightly hotels. The "eco-tax" was always controversial, however, and the government finally decided to scrap it in 2003, though its revival – and reimposition – is likely to happen soon. The commercial success of tourism in the Balearics seems assured, but a majority of the islanders – and their politicians – are keen to make the islands an upmarket destination and keep the seamier side of tourism at bay.

not surprising, perhaps, since the tennis star Rafael Nadal hails from Manacor, on Mallorca – but the true local passion is *fútbol* (football). Real Mallorca, based in Palma, is one of the leading Spanish sides and won the 1998 Spanish Cup. It is worth attending a match, not just as a sporting event but to enjoy the good-natured enthusiasm of the crowd.

Other sports associated with the islands include windsurfing, horse riding and golf. Excellent golfing conditions exist in the islands, even in winter.

Present-Day Balearics

Once removed from the mainstream of international life, the Balearic Islands have now found themselves drawn in, thanks to tourism. At first, it was the great and the good who were drawn here – or, at least, the great and the rich – and this high-society tourism reached its peak in the 1930s, when the poet Adam Diehl built the luxurious Hotel Formentor on

Kite-surfing off the coast of Mallorca on a sunny winter's day

Architecture of the Balearic Islands

The Balearic Islands boast a rich and diverse architectural heritage. The sights worth seeing range from prehistoric chamber tombs to magnificent aristocratic mansions and palaces. Palma has the most to see, notably the fine Gothic cathedral which was renovated by Antoni Gaudí, while Menorca has many remains from the Talayotic period. Ibiza's houses, influenced by the Arabs, have inspired some of the greatest architects of the 20th century including Le Corbusier and Walter Gropius.

Main entrance to a residence in Els Calderers in Mallorca

Country Houses

The typical village landscape is marked by low, often white-washed houses. Built of the local stone, many have aged to a yellow-brown colour, blending with their surroundings. Thick walls and few openings ensure that the interior stays cool even on the hottest days. A farmstead often also includes some modest outbuildings; the whole surrounded by a garden and fields.

Whitewashed stone walls

Small window in a recess

Narrow entrance door

More modest homes are often adjoined by farm buildings, with a small granary on top. Village houses are almost always single-storey dwellings.

Country Estates

At the centre of each country estate was a fine *hacienda* (or *possessió*). Their owners vied with each other by building ever more extravagant dwellings attesting to their wealth and importance. The interiors were furnished with magnificent furniture and paintings. The accommodation included formal apartments, private rooms and domestic quarters. Some are now let as holiday homes.

Great country houses, such as La Granja on Mallorca's southwest coast, belonged to wealthy landowning families and were run according to a feudal system.

Villas

This form of architecture appeared on Mallorca in the 19th century. Villas, serving as summer residences, were built in line with the fashion of the day. Their numbers rose with the increasing popularity of the island.

Modern villas are often owned by the rich and famous. They stand in beautiful, secluded spots on many of the islands.

Old villas, with their delightful architecture, can be seen in many large town centres and in seaside resorts on Mallorca.

Churches

Whitewashed churches are typical of Ibiza, although they can also be seen on Menorca and Formentera. Often they stand at the centre of the village or on a hillside at its outskirts. The entrance to the dark interior is usually preceded by a triple arcade.

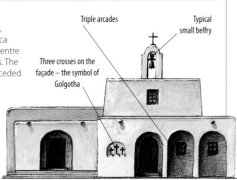

Triple arcades

Typical small belfry

Three crosses on the façade – the symbol of Golgotha

The belfry on a village church is usually a simple affair. It consists of a distinctive arcade rising above the façade, crowned with an iron cross and housing a bell.

A church is often adjoined by a single-storey parish building or a vestry. It may be surrounded by a low stone wall and feature an enclosed forecourt.

Watchtowers

The stone towers that can be seen along the coastline were built to protect the islands from attacks by pirates, mainly from North Africa, who raided the ports and inland towns. The towers stand in secluded, inaccessible spots, so that they could be easily defended. Most of the towers are deserted, and closed to visitors. A few are used as viewpoints.

Towers on Mallorca are slender. For extra protection, their entrances were high above the ground. Their walls feature narrow loopholes.

Martello towers are dotted all over Menorca. These round towers with thick walls and flat roofs were built by either the British or the Spanish.

Windmills of the Balearic Islands

Stone-built windmills are another typical feature of the Balearic landscape. Early mills were used to grind grain; later they were used to pump water. Most stone-built mills are no longer in use and are slowly falling into disrepair. Some have lost their sails, and they now resemble watchtowers. Others have been converted into restaurants, with the machinery and millstones serving as tourist attractions.

Windmills were built mostly on the plains among green fields, and were used to grind corn or to drive the pumps of deep-water wells. Some farmers still use wind power to pump water even today because they are cheaper to run than petrol-driven pumps.

Typical windmills were usually built near towns with food markets, such as Sineu. The miller would often live in the tower.

Landscape and Wildlife of the Balearic Islands

Thanks to the huge variety of habitats, from mountains and cliffs to sandy beaches and wide plains, the Balearics have a wide diversity of wildlife including some rare birds and reptiles. Mallorca's characteristic terrain is *garrigue*, an open scrubland, interspersed with small pockets of forest. At higher altitudes the scrub is replaced by *maquis* – a mix of mainly rosemary, broom and laurel. Menorca, in particular, is noted for its wild flowers and shrubs while large swathes of Ibiza are covered by forests of pine.

The craggy cliffs, sharp-edged and forbidding, appear inaccessible. Consisting of limestone, they are sparsely covered with vegetation.

Forests are rare on the islands. The largest woodland areas can be found in Mallorca. These are mainly pine forests, featuring Aleppo pine mixed with holm oak.

Olive groves are seen mainly in Mallorca, inland as well as near the coastline. Tree trunks and boughs are sometimes twisted into curious shapes.

The northern shores of the islands are mostly steep and craggy. Inland, the vegetation is dense and lush. There are few beaches and those that are accessible are rocky or pebbly. The northern shores have been less affected by tourism, and provide stunning views as well as excellent natural areas to explore.

Balearic Landscape

Of all the Balearic Islands, Mallorca's landscape is the most diverse. As well as its many secluded coves, it has magnificent green plains and the Serra de Tramuntana mountain range.

Cove beaches are one of the features that make the islands so attractive. Some are now resorts. Others can be difficult to reach, but their soft sands, gentle waves and clear water attract a steady flow of visitors.

High mountains are found only in the northern part of Mallorca. Puig Major – the highest peak in the Serra de Tramuntana – rises to a height of 1,445 m (4,740 ft).

Flora

There are some 1,500 species of flowering plant on the islands, of which 50 or so are native. Some of them grow only in Mallorca and the Cabrera archipelago. Most flower in spring and at this time the islands are a blaze of colour. For the rest of the year, the islands are green, but the sun-bleached foliage is no longer quite so lush.

Common broom is typical of Mediterranean flora. Its bright yellow flowers, which blossom in March, can be seen from afar.

Small foxglove, with its distinctive, thimble-like flower, is a highly ornamental plant. It is one of the plants native to the Balearic Islands. Few people realize that the species is also poisonous.

Holm oak is widespread throughout the islands. Its tough, evergreen leaves protect it against water loss.

Coves with sandy beaches are typical of the Balearic Islands' landscape.

Macchia, an evergreen shrub, grows on the rocky mountain slopes.

Fauna of the Balearic Islands

Fauna on the Balearic Islands includes a handful of native species, such as the rare Lilford's wall lizard. The islands are also home to some rare species of birds, including the black vulture, rock falcon and the Balearic shearwater. Several smaller mammals such as rabbits and hedgehogs are commonplace in the lowlands of the archipelago.

Rabbits have easily adapted to the wide variety of landscapes on the islands, particularly since they have no natural predators.

The Mallorcan midwife toad is an endangered species that inhabits the remoter areas of northern Mallorca.

The black vulture, with its wingspan of almost 3 m (10 ft), can be spotted flying around the mountains of Mallorca.

The Underwater World

Some four million years ago, the Balearic archipelago was joined to the continent. The sinking seabed caused the islands to become separated from the mainland by the Balearic Sea. The coastline is topographically varied, featuring sandy beaches with shallows stretching far out into the sea, and cliffs with distinct layers of rock, full of cracks, niches and caves. Facing them, rising up from the sea, are small rocky islands and solitary rocks created by sea abrasion. In the coastal and offshore waters there is a rich variety of marine life.

Cardinal fish live in small shoals. The tiny red fish can be seen mostly among sea grass or hiding near the entrances to underwater caves and grottoes.

Marine Species

The waters surrounding the archipelago are too cold for coral reefs. The only variety found here is the soft gorgonia. The sea grass meadows are home to a variety of animals, from lugworms to fish. The rocky seabed supports the richest variety of life. Here, you will find varieties of molluscs, starfish, lobster and fish – from the smallest goby to the giant grouper.

Ray fish eggs

Cuttle-fish shells

Sea grass

Shark eggs

The great pipefish hides among sea grass. It feeds on small marine animals, including crustaceans and fry, which it sucks in with its long snout. Pipefish eggs hatch inside the male's pouch.

Seahorse

Psi shark

The cuttlefish is a predator that uses its long tentacles to catch its prey. It hunts while swimming or lying buried in the sand, almost invisible to its victim. The cuttlefish can change its colour to blend in with the background. When threatened, it ejects an inky fluid that disorientates the attacker.

Pinna are huge, long-lived molluscs that dig into the sand with the sharp end of their shells.

Starfish inhabit the coastal regions of the Balearic Islands, up to a depth of 35 m (115 ft). They live mainly on the rocky bottom, and are conspicuous by their red colour.

The Lilford's wall lizard can be seen everywhere, even close to beaches, in dry, sunny places. There are 22 known subspecies, which are spread throughout the archipelago.

The Balearic shearwater, also known as the "Moresque shearwater", is a common sight. It gathers food by sitting on the water and catching crustaceans, squid and small fish. The shearwater is native to the Balearic Islands and nests in large colonies.

The Mediterranean monk seal was once a common sight in the archipelago but is now almost extinct.

Red clingfish have no scales and attach themselves to the surfaces of rocks with a sucker situated between their ventral fins.

The Haliotis clam prefers rocky bottoms close to the shore. This primitive snail is highly valued by gourmets.

Mediterranean scallop

Gorgonia

Link wrasse

Amarela

The species of moray found in the Mediterranean has no venom, but its bite can be dangerous. Hidden amid rocks, it springs surprise attacks, feeding on fish and crustaceans.

The slipper lobster is not as common as the cicada lobster, which is twice its size. Its body is covered with a hard shell and is armed with spikes, while its antennae have evolved into short, wide plates.

The Dusky grouper is, despite its fearsome size, a gentle fish. Because of this, and its sheer bulk, it presents an easy target for spear-fishing.

THE BALEARIC ISLANDS THROUGH THE YEAR

The inhabitants of the Balearic Islands are deeply attached to their traditions, a fact that is reflected in the many religious feast days, or fiestas, they celebrate. Fiestas are generally associated with the cult of saints, particularly the patron of the local parish or the island. Though mostly religious, fiestas are an opportunity for people to enjoy themselves, with parades, music and much dancing. The most spectacular of these is the Festa de Sant Joan, which has been celebrated in Ciutadella, Menorca, since medieval times. In the resorts, fiestas are less conspicuous, but elsewhere everybody joins in the fun. During the fiesta, normal life stops and only minimal bus services run. It is also difficult to find hotel accommodation, so book in advance. Tourist information offices can provide details of local fiestas.

Almond blossom in early spring in Mallorca

Spring

With the advent of spring, life in Spain moves out into the streets, and the café terraces fill with guests. This is a very beautiful time of year. Before the arrival of the summer heat, trees, flowers and wild herbs burst into flower. The famous Semana Santa (Holy Week) before Easter is a time of religious processions.

March

Semana Santa On Maundy Thursday in Palma, a procession leaves the church of La Sang at Plaça de Hospital, carrying a crucifix. On Good Friday, solemn processions are held in many towns, including Palma and Sineu in Mallorca and Maó on Menorca. The sombre ceremony of laying in the tomb *(Davallament)* is held at the church of Nostra Senyora del Àngels, in Pollença. In Monastir de Lluc the faithful conduct a penitential Way of the Cross.

April

Festa Sant Francesc *(2 Apr)*. The popular feast of St Francis is celebrated throughout the islands, in parishes of which the saint is the patron.
Princess Sofia Trophy *(One week, dates vary)*, Palma. One of the most important yachting regattas in the Balearics.
Festa Sant Jordi *(23 Apr)*. Feast day of the patron saint of many towns and villages, celebrated on all the islands.

May

Festa de Maig *(1st Sun in May)*, Santa Eulàlia, Ibiza. This springtime flower festival is one of the most colourful and beautiful fiestas in the Balearic Islands.
Festa de Nostra Senyora de la Victòria *(2nd Sun in May)*, Sóller and Port de Sóller, Mallorca. Mock battles pit Christian against Moor, and are staged to mark the raid by Turkish pirates, on 11 May 1561.
Eivissa Medieval *(2nd Sun in May)*, Eivissa, Ibiza. A festival to celebrate the declaration of Dalt Vila as a World Heritage Site in 1999, with dancing and concerts.
Festa de Primavera de Manacor *(27 May)*, Manacor. This spring festival is the most important festival in Manacor. It lasts until early June.

Princess Sofia Trophy yachting regatta

Average daily hours of sunshine

Hours of Sunshine
During July and August, there are nearly 11 hours of sunshine daily. Not surprisingly, these months coincide with the peak of the tourist season. Fewer sunny days occur in November, December and January. At this time of the year the islands are at their least attractive.

Summer

June marks the beginning of the peak tourist season in the Balearic Islands, which will last until September. It is ushered in by numerous cultural events, including concerts, festivals and folk group performances. The latter half of summer features various fiestas associated with gathering the harvest.

Holidaymakers on a Cala Millor beach, Mallorca

Festa de Nostra Senyora de la Victòria in Sóller

June

Corpus Christi, Pollença, Mallorca. The Dance of Eagles, performed in the main square of the town, is followed by a procession.
Sant Antoni de Juny *(13 Jun)*, Artà, Mallorca. A local feast featuring parades of people dressed as horses.
Sant Joan *(24 Jun)*, Ciutadella, Menorca. The climax of this popular festival is when the horses, ridden by islanders in fancy dress, rear up.
Romeria de Sant Marçal *(30 Jun)*, Sa Cabeneta, Mallorca. A fair where they sell *siurells*

(clay whistles). Similar fairs are also held in Campos, Sineu, Felanitx and Manacor.

July

Día de Virgen de Carmen *(15–16 Jul)*. The feast of the patron saint of sailors and fishermen is celebrated with parades and a blessing of the fishing boats.
Passejada díes Bou i Carro Triunfal *(27–28 Jul)*, Valldemossa, Mallorca. The feast of Catalina Thomàs. A bull is led through the streets of this small town, followed the next day by a procession of carts, with one girl playing the role of St Catalina.

August

Copa del Rey *(1st wk in Aug)*, Palma, Mallorca. International yachting regattas held under the patronage of King Juan Carlos.
Sant Ciriac *(8 Aug)*, Ibiza, Formentera. A feast held to commemorate the Spanish recapture of these islands.
Festa de Sant Lorenç *(2nd wk in Aug)*, Alaior, Menorca. Riding displays in the streets.

Assumption of the Virgin *(15 Aug)*. A festival celebrated throughout Spain.
Sant Bartomeu *(24 Aug)*. Horse races in Capdepera; devil dances in Montuïri.
Sant Agustín *(28 Aug)*. Felanitx, Mallorca. A joyful fiesta in honour of St Augustine, with festivities such as dancing and horse-riding shows.

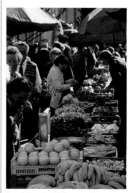

Busy fruit stalls at Pollença market in Mallorca

Average monthly rainfall

Rainfall
The lowest rainfall is in July; the highest between October and December. Storms are rare in the summer. Visitors should bear in mind that in the mountainous regions clouds may be thicker and rain more frequent than in the coastal areas.

Performing a traditional dance in Palma to celebrate the Diada de Mallorca

Autumn

After the summer scorchers, autumn days bring cool air and rain. With the passing of the peak holiday season, the resorts empty out. Harvest fiestas continue and the wine festivals come to the fore, particularly in Binissalem, Mallorca. The first juice extracted from the grape harvest is blessed and in some places wine is served free.

September

Processió de la Beata (1st Sun in Sep), Santa Margalida, Mallorca. A procession of colourful floats and people dressed in folk costumes honouring Sant Catalina – known as beata – the blessed one.
Diada de Mallorca (12 Sep). Commemorates the signing of the Majorcan Statute of Rights by King Jaume II in 1276, with lively concerts, conferences and fun sporting events at sea and in the mountains.

Festa des Vermar (last Sun in Sep), Binissalem, Mallorca. A grape-harvest festival with floats and open-air concerts.
Festa des Meló (first Sun in Sep), Vilafranca de Bonany, Mallorca. Watermelon Festival, marking the end of harvest.

October

Día de la Hispanidad (12 Oct). Spanish National Holiday

Es Vedrà on the coast of Ibiza, shrouded in clouds

celebrating the discovery of the "New World" by Christopher Columbus, in 1492.
La Beateta (16 Oct). Fancy-dress procession in Palma. Fairs in Alcúdia, Campos, Felanitx, Porreres and Llucmajor. Raft races in Porto Portals.
Festa de Les Verges (21 Oct), Palma. Festival where enormous quantities of buñelos de vientyo cakes are consumed and young people sing serenades in honour of Santa Ursula and the 11,000 virgins.
Festa d'Es Botifarró (3rd Sun in Oct), Sant Joan, Mallorca. This festival includes dancing and music to accompany the eating of large amounts of sausage (berenada de butifarra) and vegetable pies (coca amb trampó).

November

Todos los Santos (1 Nov). All Saints' Day and the following day – Día dels difunts (All Souls Day) – are a time when people visit the graves of relatives and friends.
Sant Carles (4 Nov), Ibiza. Patron saint's day, celebrated throughout the island.
Dijous Bo (3rd Thu in Nov), Inca, Mallorca. Important agricultural feast in Mallorca, featuring fairs and revelry.
Birthday of Junipero Serra (24 Nov). Celebrated throughout the archipelago as the birthday of this Franciscan monk who founded the cities of San Diego, Los Angeles and San Francisco (see p81).

Average monthly temperature

Temperature
Temperatures in the Balearic Islands rarely fall below zero. This happens only occasionally in December and early January. For this reason, many people enjoy out-of-season visits. Summer temperatures may soar to 40° C (104° F).

Winter

The Balearic winter is not particularly severe. Nights are cold, but days are often sunny and mild. Christmas is a time of special celebration throughout Spain, with families gathering to participate in religious festivities.

Working in the fields during early spring

December
Noche Buena *(24 Dec)*. Christmas Eve is celebrated within the family circle, and often includes midnight Mass. Numerous nativity plays and scenes are organized in Palma.
Santos Inocentes *(28 Dec)*. The Spanish equivalent of Britain's April Fool's day.
Festa de l'Estandard *(31 Dec)*, Palma, Mallorca. Feast commemorating the town's conquest by Jaume I, in 1229.

January
Revetlla i Beneïdes de Sant Antoni Abat *(16–17 Jan)*, Mallorca. Fiesta with bonfires, parades and the blessing of animals. People wander between the bonfires, dressed in costumes, dancing and consuming large quantities of eel and vegetable pies.
Processo dels Tres Tocs *(17 Jan)*, Ciutadella, Menorca. The Procession of the Three Strikes marks the victory of Alfonso III over the Muslims, in 1287.
Festa de Sant Sebastià *(20 Jan)*, Pollença, Mallorca. Procession carrying a banner with the image of the saint and with two dancers, called *cavallets*, mounting wooden horses.

February
Carnival Parades *(Feb/Mar)*. Fancy-dress balls marking the end of Carnival, before Lent. The most spectacular

Carnival in Palma, Mallorca

fiesta, called *Sa Rua* (the Cavalcade), takes place in Palma and its surrounding resorts.

Public Holidays

Año Nuevo New Year's Day (1 Jan)

Día de Reyes Epiphany (6 Jan)

Jueves Santo Maundy Thursday (Mar/Apr)

Viernes Santo Good Friday (Mar/Apr)

Día de Pascua Easter (Mar/Apr)

Fiesta de Trabajo Labour Day (1 May)

Corpus Christi (early Jun)

Asunción Assumption of the Virgin (15 Aug)

Día de la Hispanidad National Day (12 Oct)

Todos los Santos All Saints' Day (1 Nov)

Día de la Constitución Constitution Day (6 Dec)

Inmaculada Concepción Immaculate Conception (8 Dec)

Navidad Christmas Day (25 Dec)

Fishing from a traditional Balearic boat in Autumn

THE HISTORY OF THE BALEARIC ISLANDS

The Balearic Islands were often a target for conquest and this turbulent history has left behind numerous reminders. Consecutive waves of raiders continually destroyed the heritage of their predecessors and it was not until the conquest of the islands by Jaume I, in 1229, that a period of relative stability began. But even the centuries that followed this defeat were not a period of calm.

Earliest Inhabitants

The first people to live in the Balearic Islands probably arrived from the Iberian Peninsula. Archaeological findings indicate that human occupation was well established in Mallorca by 2800 BC and in Menorca by 2300 BC. Archaeological remains include flint tools, primitive pottery and artifacts made of horn, giving evidence that these early settlers were shepherds and hunters. As well as herding sheep, the earliest inhabitants of the Balearic Islands hunted the local species of mountain goat *(Myotragus balearicus)*, which is now extinct. Most archaeological finds were discovered in caves, which were used for shelter and also for ritual burials. The best-preserved complex of caves, developed and extended by the Talayotic settlers who came to the islands in 1300 BC, are the Cales Coves discovered near Cala en Porter, in Menorca.

The Beaker ware found in Deià, in Mallorca, represents a style known throughout Western Europe. Beaker People are so named because of their custom of placing pottery beakers in graves. The representatives of this culture were capable of producing excellent bronze tools and utensils. They appeared in the islands around 2300 BC.

Talayotic Period

The mysterious structures made of giant stones found on the islands date from around 1300 BC. The most typical of the time, which also gave the period its name, is the *talayot* derived from the Arabic word *atalaya,* meaning "observation tower". These structures appear in greatest numbers in Menorca, with somewhat fewer in Mallorca. None has been found in Ibiza. Other common sights are *taulas* and *navetas (see p103).* In southern Europe similar structures can be found only in Sardinia *(nuraghi).*

These early inhabitants of the islands represented a relatively advanced civilization. Some of them lived in fortified settlements, such as Capocorb Vell, Mallorca, where over 30 stone houses and four massive *talayots* have been found.

2300 BC Beaker culture flourishes in the Iberian Peninsula

2800 BC Human occupation well established on the Balearic Islands

1300 BC Beginning of the Talayotic civilization; development of Cales Coves

1500 BC Bronze Age starts in the Balearics

| 6000 BC | 4000 BC | 3000 BC | 2000 BC |

Around 5000 BC Probable arrival of man can be dated from finds around Sóller and Valldemossa

Arrowhead dating from the Talayotic era

◄ A painting of Maó harbour, Menorca, in the early 19th century

Temple at Torralba d'en Salord, a Talayotic settlement in Menorca

Phoenicians, Greeks and Carthaginians

The Phoenicians arrived in the islands in the early part of the 1st millennium BC. They founded a trading settlement, Sanisera, on the northern coast of Menorca. Two hundred years later, the islands attracted the attention of the Greeks, who were exploring the western regions of the Mediterranean. The Greeks did not settle in the Balearics, as they lacked the metal ores that would have made the islands suitable for colonization. They were also discouraged by the hostile reception from the local inhabitants. But the archipelago owes its name to the Greeks. It derives from the Greek word *ballein* (to throw from a sling). The islanders were famed as outstanding slingshots and, more than once, made life a misery for various raiders.

The Carthaginians also took an interest in trade in the western region of the Mediterranean. Carthaginian sailors started to explore the Balearic Islands in the early 7th century BC. In 654, they took Ibiza, where they founded the fortified capital of Eivissa (the famous Carthaginian general, Hannibal, is thought to have been born on Ibiza). After conquering the entire archipelago, they founded new towns, including Jamna (Ciutadella) and Maghen (Maó) in Menorca.

The Balearic Islands played a strategic role during the Punic Wars. Following their defeat at Zama in 202 BC, the Carthiginians were crushed. Soon afterwards, they left Mallorca and Menorca but remained in Ibiza for a further 70 years.

Roman Empire and Byzantium

The Romans conquered Ibiza in 146 BC. Meanwhile, the inhabitants of Mallorca and Menorca, taking advantage of the political upheavals, turned to piracy. This lasted until 123 BC, when the Roman Consul Quintus Metellus occupied the islands. He was awarded the honorary title of *Balearico* for his deeds. Roman rule lasted for over 500 years and the islands were renamed: Balearis Major (Mallorca), Balearis Minor (Menorca) and Ebusus (Ibiza). The *Pax*

Ruins of the Christian basilica in Son Bou, Menorca

800 BC Twilight of the Talayotic civilization. Greeks visit the islands

654 BC Carthaginians conquer Ibiza

202 BC Carthaginians defeated at Zama

1000 BC | **700 BC** | **400 BC** | **100 BC**

Around 1000 BC Phoenician merchants arrive on the islands

Figurine of the goddess Tanit, 2nd century BC

146 BC Romans conquer Ibiza

Romana brought prosperity: Roman settlers planted vineyards, built roads and founded Palmeria and Pollentia, a settlement near Alcúdia in Mallorca. They also founded Portus Magonis (Maó) in Menorca, which subsequently became the island's capital and extended the Phoenician port, Sanisera, making it one of the biggest harbours of the empire.

A mosaic from the Calvià library, Mallorca, showing the conquest of Mallorca by the Arabs in 904

By the 3rd century AD, the expansion of Christianity had begun on the islands. Roman rule was already in decline when, in 425, the Vandals invaded and destroyed both the Roman and Christian cultural heritages.

Subsequently, the Byzantine army led by Belisarius expelled the Vandal tribes from the Balearic Islands. For over 100 years the islands remained within the sphere of influence of the Byzantine Empire. This ensured their stability until the declining empire came under attack – first from pirates, then from the Vikings and, finally, from the Arabs.

The Moors

The conquest of Menorca and Mallorca by the Emir of Cordoba at the beginning of the 10th century marks the start of Moorish influence over the islands, which lasted for more than three centuries. During this period the Muslims transformed the Balearic Islands, introducing new irrigation techniques, planting crops like rice and cotton and, on terraced hillsides, oranges, limes and olives. In 1114, Muslim rule was interrupted when an army of 70,000 Italian and Catalan soldiers attacked Ibiza and Mallorca. Supported by the pope, the Christian troops slaughtered most of the Muslims and set sail, filling their ships with spoils. The Moors quickly re-established themselves, however, and flourished once again under the rule of the Almoravids, a Berber dynasty from North Africa. Reminders of Moorish presence on the islands include the agricultural terraces, architecture and designs for embroidery and ceramics.

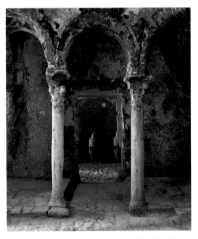

Arab Bath in Palma, one of few surviving relics of Muslim culture on the islands

Sacking of Pollentia by Vandals

798 Raid by Moorish pirates

1085 Islands gain the status of caliphate ruled by the Almoravids

707 First raids by the Arabs

AD 200   **500**   **800**   **1100**

426 Vandal invasion

859 Vikings raid the islands

1114 Mallorca invaded, unsuccessfully, by Christian army – "Small Crusade"

533 Beginning of Byzantine rule over the archipelago

902 Mallorca becomes a member of the Cordoba Caliphate

Jaume I

In September 1229, on the beach near Santa Ponça, Mallorca, the Catalan King Jaume I, later known as "El Conqueridor", landed with his army, which consisted of 16,000 soldiers and 1,500 cavalry. The pretext for the attack was the seizure of several Catalan vessels by the Emir of Mallorca. In the ensuing battle, Jaume I captured the capital and conquered the entire island. In 1232, he returned to Mallorca with a handful of soldiers. From there he sent delegates to Menorca, who were to negotiate a surrender. Meanwhile, Jaume I built a camp on the mountain slopes near

Cross in Santa Ponça, marking Jaume I's conquest

Capdepera. In the evening, he ordered numerous bonfires to be lit, to look as though a large army was preparing to attack. The ruse worked and the Moors surrendered Menorca to the king, who left them to rule the island as his vassals.

In 1230, Jaume I had issued the *Carta de Població* (People's Charter), which encouraged Catalans to settle on the conquered islands, granting them exemption from taxes and guaranteeing equality before the law to all its citizens. Special privileges were granted to Jews, in an effort to stimulate trade. After the king's death, his successors fought for the inheritance, which was finally won by Alfonso III.

Alfonso and his Successors

Despite being nicknamed "The Liberal", Alfonso III massacred the rebels of Palma and the remaining fortresses after he had conquered them, a bloody deed that led to his excommunication from the Catholic Church. Worse was to follow. In 1287, Alfonso III's army attacked and conquered Menorca. The Muslim defenders were sold into slavery or slaughtered. Medina Menurqua was renamed Ciutadella and its mosques turned into churches or destroyed. Following the death of Alfonso III in 1291 at the age of 25, Jaume II took control of Mallorca and Menorca. Jaume II, who had been crowned king of Mallorca and

Miniature with the image of Jaume I

1229 Mallorca captured by the army of Jaume I, who is hailed as "El Conqueridor"

1230 Declaration of *Carta de Població* (People's Charter) by Jaume I

1285 Palma conquered by Alfonso III

1200　　**1250**　　**1300**　　**1350**

1203 The Almohads assume rule over the archipelago

1233 Ramon Llull, philosopher and theologian, father of the Catalan language, is born in Palma

Statue of Alfonso III by the cathedral in Maó, Menorca

Menorca in 1276 before being deposed by Alfonso III, was an altogether more enlightened ruler. He and his successors presided over a "Golden Age" that saw great advances, including the building of the Castell de Bellver and Palau de l'Almudaina, the establishment of a weekly market in Palma and the reintroduction of gold and silver coinage to stimulate trade. The next ruler of the archipelago was Jaume II's son, Sancho, who built a strong fleet to defend the islands against pirates. After his death, in 1324, control passed into the hands of his nephew, Jaume III, whose two-decade reign also marked a period of great prosperity. The "Golden Age" came to an abrupt end in 1344 when an Aragonese conquest, led by Pedro IV, landed on Mallorca and took it in only a week. The islands of Menorca and Ibiza soon suffered the same fate.

Decline and Fall

Now part of the kingdom of Aragón, the Balearic Islands found themselves to be outside major politics. The economy soon suffered as a result of high taxes and in 1391 Mallorca was the scene of an uprising by the poorest parts of the

Painting of Saint George slaying the dragon, by Francesca Comesa

community. In Menorca, the rivalry between Ciutadella and Maó ended in armed conflict. The economic position of the Balearic Islands was worsened further by the discovery and colonization of the Americas at the end of the 15th century, which shifted the hub of European trade to the shores of the Atlantic Ocean. This downturn led, in 1521, to a bloody revolt by peasants and craftsmen in Mallorca, which ended in the slaughter of many of the nobility and their supporters.

Throughout the 16th and 17th centuries, there were frequent pirate attacks. Many of the islands' fortifications date from this period including Eivissa's surviving defences and Maó's Fort San Felipe.

Painting of the port in Palma de Mallorca, now at the city's Museu Diocesà

Gothic rosette from a museum in Palma, Mallorca

1521 Armed insurrection of peasants and craftsmen

1531–1558 Devastating raids by Turkish pirates

1400　　　　1450　　　　1500　　　　1550

1391 Insurrection of the poor in Mallorca

1479 Unification of Aragón and Castile

Barbarossa, the conqueror of Maó in 1535

Junipero Serra setting up a mission in California

Under British and French Rule

During the 17th century, Menorca became the subject of Anglo-French rivalry. In 1708 the British occupied Maó's harbour, and subsequently the whole of Menorca. In 1756, the island was captured by the French, although they soon returned it to the British, in 1763. The government of the island changed hands several more times until, finally, in 1802, Menorca was handed over to Spain. The town of Sant Lluís, founded by the French, stands as a reminder of French rule.

The British colonial legacy on Menorca includes the building of the garrison town of Georgetown (now known as Es Castell) and major improvements to the roads. The choice of Maó as Menorca's capital is thanks to the British governor, Richard Kane. Reminders of Georgian architecture, including the sash windows in Hannover Street in Maó, can still be seen today.

The 19th Century

The 19th century proved very difficult for the islands. The inhabitants were plagued by periods of famine and epidemics, Spanish was declared the official language, and many inhabitants of the Balearics decided to emigrate. During the 19th century the islands acquired scheduled links with Barcelona and Valencia and the situation began to improve. In 1838, Chopin visited Mallorca and in 1867 Archduke Ludwig Salvator (*see p72*) settled here. At the same time, the development of agriculture, particularly almond-growing in Mallorca, and footwear production in Menorca, led to a rise in the standard of living. Catalan culture was also becoming popular and *Modernista* buildings, including designs by Antoni Gaudí, began to appear in Palma and other town centres.

Franco's Dictatorship

During the Spanish Civil War (1936–9), which originated in Morocco, the Balearic Islands were divided. Mallorca became an important base for the Fascists, while Menorca and

The *Modernista* exterior of La Caixa Grand Hotel in Palma, Mallorca

1652 Islands devastated by horrific plague

1713 Junipero Serra born in the small town of Petra, in Mallorca

1756 Menorca conquered by the French

| 1600 | 1660 | 1720 | 1780 |

Baroque stone tablet from 1672

1708 Menorca conquered by the British

1763 British regain Menorca

1802 Menorca passes into the hands of the Spanish

Monument at Monte Toro for those killed in Morocco in 1925

Ibiza declared themselves for the Republicans. In retaliation, Italian planes bombed Ibiza. Menorca was the last stronghold of the Republicans. Following a peace deal, negotiated with the help of the British, 450 refugees left Menorca aboard HMS *Devonshire*, and the island was left under the control of Franco. Formentera, which had backed the Republicans, became the site of a concentration camp established by the Fascists, where some 1,400 people were imprisoned. Throughout the entire 40 years of Franco's dictatorship, the Catalan language and culture were suppressed, as elsewhere on the mainland.

Modern Times

After Franco's death in 1975, a process of decentralization began. In 1983, the inhabitants of the islands succeeded in creating the Comunidad Autónoma de las Islas Baleares, and the islands became an autonomous region. This led to the introduction of Catalan in schools and offices and greater control of the local economy. Most of the money earned by the islands now remains here and is reinvested locally.

Initially, the most important factor driving the local economy was tourism. Where the hippies led, others followed. In 1966 Mallorca received one million tourists. By 2012, this number had grown to more than nine million and the islands, so poor until fairly recently, now boast perhaps the highest income per capita in the whole of Spain. This economic achievement has come at a price. Large numbers of foreigners, mainly German and British, have settled here, pushing up the cost of real estate, while the construction of a number of poor-quality resorts has left a blot on the islands' otherwise idyllic landscape. Factors such as these gave rise to a growing environmental movement and the introduction of an "eco-tax" *(see p23),* designed to sustain the islands' tourism. The tax was scrapped in 2003, but there are moves to re-impose it. The islanders appreciate their good fortune, but they want the islands to be a high-end destination, with strong environmental controls.

Beach near the marina of Port de Sóller, Mallorca

Archduke Ludwig Salvator

1926 Argentinian poet Adan Diehl opens the Hotel Formentor

2007 Attempts to limit helter-skelter tourist development gather strength

1975 Death of General Francisco Franco

2015 Podemos, an anti-corruption party, makes gains in regional elections

| 1840 | 1900 | 1960 | 2020 |

1867 Mallorca visited by Habsburg Archduke Ludwig Salvator, subsequent promoter of the island

1936–1939 Spanish Civil War

1950 The first charter plane, from Germany, lands in Mallorca

1983 Creation of the Autonomous Community of the Balearic Islands

Tourists in a hotel bar

THE BALEARIC ISLANDS AREA BY AREA

The Balearic Islands at a Glance

The hot climate, cooling sea breezes, lively resorts and excellent beaches make the Balearic Islands an ideal holiday destination. Those who want to rave choose Ibiza, with its frenetic clubs and all-night entertainment. Those who prefer a more sedate holiday can find peace and quiet on all the islands, where charming little towns and miles of empty trails are perfect for walking, riding and cycling. Mallorca's caves and grottoes can provide interesting exploration while Menorca's prehistoric structures offer a fascinating glimpse into life on the islands many thousands of years ago.

Palma is the capital of Mallorca and of the Balearic Islands. Full of historic sights and throbbing with life, it is the archipelago's finest city.

Cala Bassa's Blue Flag beach is typical of Ibiza's beaches. Small, with fine, golden sand, it is hidden in a sheltered cove.

IBIZA
(See pp116–135)

Santa Eulària des Riu

Eivissa

Santa Eulària des Riu is one of the loveliest resort towns in Ibiza. It has good restaurants and bars, plenty of shopping and a beautiful beach.

FORMENTERA
(See pp136–143)

Sant Francesc

Sól

Palma

Platja Migjorn is a narrow sandy beach, stretching over 5 km (3 miles) along the southern coast of Formentera. It is always possible to find an isolated spot.

0 kilometres   20

0 miles   20

◀ Palma's harbour at night, Mallorca

Cap de Cavalleria is the northernmost point of the Balearic Islands and one of Menorca's wildest regions. The road to the lighthouse on the headland runs through an undulating area. The steep cliffs here provide a nesting ground for a number of seabirds including, the sea eagle and kite.

Ciutadella

MENORCA
(See pp94–115)

Maó

Alcúdia

Artà

MALLORCA
(See pp46–93)

Manacor

Llucmajor

Colònia de Sant Jordi

Poblat de Pescadors, Binibeca Vell, Menorca, with its distinctive development of white houses, was purpose-built for holidaymakers to resemble a Mediterranean fishing village.

Aqualand El Arenal, in S'Arenal near Palma, is one of several water parks in Mallorca. With pools, water flumes and plenty of space, it provides a fun day out for the children.

Cap de Formentor is Mallorca's northernmost peninsula. It makes a good destination for a day-long excursion during which you can take in the clifftop views or swim in one of the coves below. At the very tip of the peninsula is a lighthouse, which also serves as a viewing point.

MALLORCA

Mallorca's landscape is incredibly diverse for such a small island – ranging from the fertile lowlands of the central region, to the high peaks of the Serra de Tramuntana. Its warm climate, fine beaches and historic capital, Palma, make it one of Europe's most popular holiday destinations. Venture away from the resorts and you also find picturesque inland villages, thick forests and peaceful coves.

With an area covering 3,640 sq km (1,405 sq miles), and a population of around 846,000, of which nearly half live in Palma, Mallorca is the largest island of the Balearic archipelago. Consisting mainly of limestone, the terrain has a large number of cave systems, particularly in the wild central region of the Serra de Tramuntana and on the east coast. Some of these, such as the Coves d'Artà, can be visited as part of a guided tour. Elsewhere on the island, there is much to enjoy, from stunning nature reserves and charming fishing villages to picturesque ruins and impressive country estates.

The climate on the island is typically Mediterranean, with dry summers and up to 65cm (26 in) of rainfall during the autumn–winter season. Cold winters are rare. The island has unique flora and fauna, with a wide variety of birds. Native species of flowers and flowering shrubs are also in evidence, though the cultivation of fields, vineyards and olive groves has partly displaced the natural vegetation.

The island has been settled since ancient times, and traces of Roman and Arab civilizations can still be seen. Once an independent kingdom, Mallorca became part of Aragón and Catalunya in the 14th century, and was later incorporated into Spain. Since 1983, the Balearic Islands have been an autonomous region of Spain.

Much of the island is virtually untouched by tourism. Mallorca offers wonderful beaches and nightlife for visitors who want a lively holiday, and rural retreats, peaceful coves and historic ruins for those seeking a quiet break.

Palma's imposing Gothic cathedral, La Seu, built on the site of the former mosque

◄ Torrent de Pareis, a major attraction of the Tramuntana mountain range

Exploring Mallorca

Most visitors to Mallorca come in search of sun and make the most of the nightclubs, discos, waterparks and the plentiful supply of clean beaches. Many also enjoy the historic towns and villages, particularly the winding streets of the island's capital, Palma, which has lots to see and a wide range of shops and restaurants. Visitors looking for the best beaches go to the Badia de Palma region or to the northeastern shores of the island.

Locator Map

Historic tram in the main square in Sóller

Sights at a Glance

1. Palma pp50–61
2. Badia de Palma
3. Cala Major
4. Calvià
5. Andratx
6. Sa Dragonera
8. La Reserva Puig de Galatzó
9. La Granja pp68–9
10. Valldemossa
11. Son Marroig
12. Deià
13. Sóller
15. Jardines de Alfàbia
16. Sa Calobra
17. Santuari de Lluc pp76–7
18. Inca
19. Pollença
20. Cap de Formentor
21. Alcúdia
22. Parc Natural de S'Albufera
23. Muro
24. Sineu
25. Petra
26. Artà
27. Capdepera
28. Cala Rajada
29. Cala Millor
30. Porto Cristo
31. Manacor
32. Vilafranca de Bonany
33. Felanitx
34. Santanyí
35. Parc Natural Mondragó
36. Ses Salines
37. Colònia de Sant Jordi
38. Cabrera Island National Park pp88–9
39. Llucmajor
40. Capocorb Vell
41. Puig de Randa
42. Algaida
43. S'Arenal

Tours

7. Northwestern Coast of Mallorca pp66–7
14. Train from Palma to Port Sóller

For hotels and restaurants in this region see pp148–50 and pp155–9

Getting There

Mallorca has air links with Menorca and Ibiza, as well as with many Spanish towns and cities. However, most visitors arrive by international flights. Mallorca's airport is 11 km (7 miles) east of Palma. It is also possible to get here by ferry, from one of the Spanish mainland ports. The high-speed ferry linking Valencia, Ibiza and Palma reduces the journey time considerably. When travelling around Mallorca, you can use its efficient bus service or the one or two railway lines connecting Palma with Sóller and also with Inca, Sa Pobla and Manacor. However, the best way to explore the island is by car.

CAP DE FORMENTOR 20

Cala Sant Vicenç
Los Encinares
Ma-2210
Hotel de Formentor

Port de Pollença

POLLENÇA 19
Ma-2220
Cap des Pinar

Ma-10
Mortitxet
Ma-2200

ALCÚDIA 21
SANTUARI DE LLUC
Ma-13A
Port d'Alcúdia

Crestatx

Campanet
Ses Fotges

Selva
Sa Pobla

PARC NATURAL DE S'ALBUFERA 22

Ma-13
Can Picafort

Cap de Ferrutx

Ermita de Santa Magdalena
MURO 23
Ma-3410
Colònia de Sant Pere
Betlem
Ermita de Betlem

Cala Mezquida

INCA 18
Ma-12

Llubí
Santa Margalida
Ma-12
ARTÀ 26
CALA RAJADA 28

ual

Maria de la Salut
MA-3240
Ma-3340
Ma-3330
CAPDEPERA 27
Coves d'Artà

Sencelles
SINEU 24
Ariany
Ma-15
Canyamal
Ma-4040

Lloret de Vista Alegre
PETRA 25
Calicant
Son Servera
Port Nou

-3130
Sant Joan
Sant Llorenç des Cardassar
CALA MILLOR 29

Montuïri
VILAFRANCA DE BONANY 32
Son Carrió

LGAIDA
Ma-15
MANACOR 31
Cala Moreia

10
PUIG DE RANDA 41
Albocàsser
Ma-4020

Porreres
Ma-14
PORTO CRISTO 30

LUCMAJOR
Ma-5020
Son Macià
Coves del Drac
Cala Romàntica

Es Monjos
FELANITX 33
Cales de Mallorca

Ma-19
Ma-5100
Santuari de Sant Salvador

Campos
Castell de Santueri
Portocolom

Ma-6030
Ma-19
Ma-14
Cas Concos
Calonge

Ma-6040
SANTANYÍ
Ma-19
Cala d'Or

Sa Ràpita
Portopetro

atja Es Trenc
SES SALINES 36
34
PARC NATURAL MONDRAGÓ 35
Cala Figuera

ÒNIA DE NT JORDI 37

des Ses Roquetes

Cap de Ses Salines

Key

— Motorway
— Major road
— Minor road
— Scenic route
— Railway

CABRERA ISLAND NATIONAL PARK 38

Beach in Palmanova on the Badia de Palma

For keys to symbols see back flap

● Street-by-Street: Palma

In 1983, Palma became the capital of the newly created Autonomous Community of the Balearic Islands and transformed itself from a provincial town into a metropolis. Today, it has more than 400,000 inhabitants and captivates all visitors as it once captivated Jaume I, who, after conquering it in 1229, described it as the "loveliest town that I have ever seen". It is pleasant to stroll along the clean, attractive streets past renovated historic buildings. The town and harbour are full of life, while bars and restaurants, busy with locals and tourists, remain open late into the night.

Caixa Forum Palma
Built in 1902, this is the most beautiful 20th-century building in Palma. Formerly the Grand Hotel, it now houses a cultural centre.

★ Palau de l'Almudaina
This former royal residence was the home of Jaume II and was built after 1309, on the site of an Arab fortress.

La Llotja
The elevation of this small Gothic building, which once housed the stock exchange, is decorated with magnificent sculptures.

Key

— Suggested route

PLAÇA REI JOAN CARLES

CARRER UNIO

PASSEIG DES BORN

AVINGUDA D'ANTONI MAURA

Parc de la Mar

★ Cathedral
The Gothic cathedral, standing near the shore and towering over the town, is built of golden sandstone excavated in Santanyí.

0 metres   100
0 yards   100

For hotels and restaurants in this region see pp148–150 and pp155–9

★ Basílica de Sant Francesc
This magnificent church took almost 100 years to build. Its façade is decorated with a rose window and a Baroque portal.

Plaça Major

PL. MAJOR

Plaça del Marquès de Palmer

CARRER SANT CRIST

CARRER JAUME II

CARRER MOREY

SANT PERE NOLASC

SANT ALONSO

MIRADOR

CARRER DALT MURADA

City walls

Bishop's Palace

Museu de Mallorca
This excellent art collection includes this 1920 work by painter Bruno Beran.

Banys Àrabs
The main room of these 10th-century Arab baths is covered with a dome resting on 12 columns. This is one of the few architectural reminders of a Moorish presence on the islands.

Horsedrawn cabs in Palau de l'Almudaina

Exploring Palma

Palma is rich in historic sights. Christian kings, Arab rulers and Jewish merchants have all left their mark on the Balearic capital and it is a genuine pleasure to stroll through its narrow streets and quiet courtyards.

Cathedral (La Seu)

Plaça Seu. **Tel** 902 022 445.
After the capture of Palma by Jaume I, the town's main mosque was used as its cathedral. Work on the present building *(see pp54–5)*, known in Catalan as La Seu, began in 1230, immediately after the fall of Palma. The main work lasted for almost 400 years and resulted in a monumental Gothic church.

It has three entrances, each framed with a portal. The most beautiful of these is the 14th-century Portal del Mirador, overlooking the Bay of Palma to the south. It is topped with a pediment depicting the Last Supper. Built above the Gothic Portal de l'Almoina is a fortified belfry. The main Portal Major (Great Door), facing the Almudaina palace, has a Neo-Gothic finish and is the least successful of the three.

The splendid interior features 14 slender octagonal pillars supporting the vault. The 44-m (145-ft) central nave is one of the highest in Europe.

The eastern rose window, measuring over 12 m (40 ft) in diameter, is made of 1,200 pieces of stained glass.

The cathedral features stalls made of walnut, an interesting stone pulpit and 14 chapels, including Nostra Senyora de la Corona, with statues of allegorical angels.

In the oldest part of the cathedral, hidden behind the altar, is the Trinity Chapel, containing the tombs of Jaume II and Jaume III (not open to visitors). In the early 20th century, Antoni Gaudí removed the Baroque altar and put in its place an alabaster table, with an illuminated canopy symbolizing the crown of thorns.

Palau de l'Almudaina

Carrer de Palau Real. **Open** 10am–6pm Tue–Sun (to 8pm Apr–Sep). **Tel** 971 214 134.
Almudaina means "citadel" in Arabic. This royal residence of Jaume II was built after 1309, using the walls of an Arab fortress. The Gothic palace includes Moorish-style arches and carved wooden ceilings.

It is the official residence of the Spanish monarch. The museum here includes the Santa Ana chapel, with a fine vaulted and embossed ceiling, and a side chapel dedicated to St Praxedis.

Parc de la Mar

The Parc de la Mar was established in the 1960s in the area between the southern section of the city walls and Ronda Litoral. Its designers, Josep Lluís Sert and Joan Miró *(see p62)*, built the park on several levels and its landscape includes a man-made lake in which you can see a reflection of the cathedral. Nearby **Ses Voltes** is an exhibition space, used for art exhibitions and concerts.

La Llotja

Plaça Llotja.
This late Gothic building (a former stock exchange) was erected between 1426 and 1456 from plans by Guillem Sagrera – the designer of La Seu's Portal del Mirador. The vault rests on slender spiral pillars, the walls are pierced by tall windows. The entrance is framed by a portal, is adorned with a pediment featuring a statue of the Guardian Angel. La Llotja's interior is open only for special exhibitions.

A section of the giant mural by Joan Miró, Parc de la Mar

For hotels and restaurants in this region see pp148–150 and pp155–9

🏛 Consolat de Mar
Passeig de Sagrera.

This Renaissance-Baroque building, erected in 1614–26, is the official residence of the governor of the Balearic Islands.

The façade features a magnificent covered arcade and the interior has a fine coffered ceiling (1664–9). The Consolat building joins with La Llotja via **Porta Vella del Moll** – a former harbour gate, brought here in the late 19th century.

🏛 Passeig d'es Born
This is one of Palma's most beautiful corners. In Arab times it featured a moat that guarded access to the walls. Now this wide avenue, which gets its name from the 17th-century jousting tournaments held here, is Palma's main promenade and it forms the axis of the entire city.

At the southern end is **Plaça de la Reina**. The entrance on this side is guarded by stone sphinxes. At the north end is **Plaça del Rei Joan Carles I**, with a stone obelisk resting on bronze turtles standing at its centre. The avenue's most noteworthy house is the **Casal Solleric** residence (No. 27). It was built in 1763 as the home of a merchant who traded in cattle and olive oil and has a beautiful Baroque courtyard. Now a cultural centre, it also has a gallery, café and bookshop.

East frontage of the beautiful Passeig d'es Born

🏛 Avinguda Unió and Plaça Weyler
This lively area is full of shops and there are also numerous cafés in the squares and streets leading off Avinguda Unió.

In **Plaça Mercat** two identical buildings stand side by side. These fine examples of *Modernista* architecture were built by banker Josep Casasayas in 1908.

The real gem of the district's architecture, however, is the **Caixa Forum Palma** in Plaça Weyler. The former Grand Hotel was given its present name after the Fundació La Caixa savings bank financed its restoration. It was reopened in 1993 by King Juan Carlos and Queen Sofia. Built in 1903, this prime example of Catalan architecture is the work of Lluís Domènech i Montaner. As an outstanding masterpiece of the *Modernista* style, it has been included on the UNESCO World Heritage list and houses, (among other things), a restaurant and exhibition rooms, including a permanent collection of paintings by the important *Modernista* artist Hermengildo Anglada-Camarasa.

Almost opposite Fundació La Caixa is the **Forn d'es Teatre** (theatre bakery). This is a small, eye-catching patisserie where you can buy deliciously flaky spiral pastries *(ensaimadas)*. Adjacent to the bakery is the **Teatre Principal** (1860). This is the most important ballet, opera and theatre venue in town.

Entrance to Forn d'es Teatre

Train and Bus stations 300 m (350 yards)

Son Sant Joan Airport 9 km (6 miles)

0 metres 200
0 yards 200

Cathedral – La Seu

Mallorca's cathedral, La Seu, is the most precious architectural treasure of the Balearic Islands and is regarded as one of Spain's most outstanding Gothic structures. Begun by Jaume II on the site of the city's main mosque seven years after the conquest of 1299, the work took some 300 years. In the first half of the 15th century, the building works were supervised by the prominent Mallorcan sculptor and architect Guillem Sagrera. Partly destroyed during the 1851 earthquake, the cathedral was subsequently repaired by Juan Bautista Peyronnet. In the early 20th century, its interior was modernized by Antoni Gaudí. An integral part of the cathedral is its museum, which stores precious works of religious art.

Belfry
The mighty belfry was built in 1389. The biggest of its nine bells is called *Eloi*.

Mallorca Cathedral
Towering over the harbour in Palma, the cathedral looks most beautiful when viewed from the sea, or at night, when it is illuminated.

KEY

① **Portal Major** (1601)

② **19th-century pinnacle**

③ **Entrance to the Cathedral Museum**

④ **Flying buttress**

⑤ **The great organs**, built in 1795, stand within a Neo-Gothic enclosure; they were restored in 1993 by Gabriel Blancafort.

⑥ **Stalls made from the dismantled corro**

⑦ **The Capella Reial** (presbytery) was remodelled by Gaudí during 1904–14.

⑧ **Chapel of the Holy Sacrament (Barceló Chapel)** was designed by contemporary painter Miquel Barceló (b.1957) and boasts a large ceramic mural and stained-glass windows.

⑨ **Portal del Mirador** (1420)

Cathedral Museum
One of the masterpieces on display in the Old Chapter House, now housing the museum, is the reliquary containing wood from the Holy Cross, encrusted with jewels.

★ **Giant Rose Window**
The largest of the seven rose windows, measuring 12 m (40 ft) in diameter, is filled with 1,200 pieces of stained glass.

VISITORS' CHECKLIST

Practical Information
Plaça Almoïna s/n. **Tel** 902 022 445.
Open 10am–3:15pm Mon–Fri
(Apr, May, Oct: to 5:15pm; Jun–
Sep: 6:15pm), 10am–2:15pm Sat.
Closed public hols. ▨ ✝ 9am
daily; 7pm Sat; 9am, 10:30am,
noon, 1pm, 7pm Sun & pub hols.
♿ Ⓦ catedraldemallorca.org

Trinity Chapel
The chapel, built in 1329, contains the tombs of the Mallorcan kings Jaume II and Jaume III.

★ **Baldachin** (1912)
Antoni Gaudí's ceremonial canopy with lights and a multicoloured crucifix is suspended above the main altar.

Central Nave
Nineteen metres (62 ft) wide and 44 m (145 ft) high, the central nave, with its vault supported by 14 pillars, is one of the world's biggest.

Museu de Mallorca

The best museum in the Balearic Islands can be found close to La Seu, in Palau Ayamans, a residence built around 1630. The palace was erected on the foundations of an Arab house, dating from the 12th to 13th century, which is still visible in the underground rooms of the museum. Opened in 1968, the museum houses a superb collection of works of art associated with Mallorcan history. The collection comprises several thousand exhibits and includes prehistoric artifacts found during archaeological excavations, stone fragments of fallen buildings, priceless Moorish ceramics and jewellery, and medieval and Baroque paintings.

★ **Lar Augustal**
From Son Corro Sanctuary in Costixt, this 1st-century-AD bronze statue of a Roman domestic deity was an object of daily worship.

Paris i Helena (c.1665)
Italian painting is represented by this Baroque work by Mattia Preti, whose extensive legacy can also be seen in Rome and Malta.

★ **Almohad Treasure**
Items of Arab jewellery are among the museum's most precious exhibits. They are kept in the treasury room, behind bulletproof glass.

Key

- ☐ Vaults
- ☐ Ground floor
- ☐ 1st floor
- ☐ 3rd floor

Gallery Guide

The museum's collection is arranged on four floors, in chronological order. The oldest relics, including archaeological finds, are kept in the underground vault. The most recent art, including 19th- and 20th-century paintings, is exhibited on the top floor. The second floor is occupied by offices.

Urna Turó
Dating between the 3rd century BC and 1st century AD, this vase from Turó de Ses Abelles in Calvià imitates the ceramics of the Iberian peninsula.

Entrance

VISITORS' CHECKLIST

Practical Information
Carrer de sa Portella 5, 07001.
Tel 971 177 838.
Open 10am–6pm Mon–Fri,
11am–2pm Sat. **Closed** Sun
and public holidays. 📧
W museudemallorca.caib.es

Transport
🚌 San Marco.

Cabeza de Mercurio
The *Head of Mercurio* is one
of a group of 17th-century
stone sculptures by artists
Jaume and Rafel Blanquer.
It is one of the few remain-
ing examples of secular
Baroque sculpture.

Modernista Panel
This 20th-century, decorative glazed *Modernista* panel came
from the Mallorcan ceramic factory, La Roqueta.

Altarpiece of St Bernardo (1325)
Painted on a wooden panel by an unknown
artist, this Gothic altarpiece is the first known
monumental depiction of St Bernardo.

★ Statuette of a Warrior
The 4th-century-BC bronze figure
is of a divine warrior from Son Favar
and forms part of a series known as
Mars Balearicus.

Plaça del Marquès de Palmer

This square lies at the end of Carrer Colom – a shopping street running from Plaça Cort, the site of the Ajuntament (Town Hall). It features a five-storey *Modernista* apartment building, Can Rei (20th century). Equally interesting is the nearby building, L'Aguila.

Plaça Major

This pedestrianized 19th-century square has a number of souvenir shops and lively cafés. Many of the square's restaurants have outdoor tables under its arcades.

The centre of the square is given over to stalls that sell a wide variety of handicrafts. There's also a stage that is frequently used by musicians and jugglers who entertain crowds.

The porticoed square was laid out in 1823 following the demolition of the headquarters of the Inquisition. The new square became the main food market until the 1950s. A large underground shopping centre and car park have since been added.

Santa Eulàlia

Plaça Santa Eulàlia. **Open** 8am–12:30pm & 5:20–8:30pm Mon–Fri 8am–12:30pm Sat (Sunday Mass).

The vast Gothic church standing at the end of Carrer Morey was built on the site of a mosque in the 13th century on the orders of Jaume II. It was completed in just 25 years. Renovations in the

Oriel window of Can Rei, Plaça del Marquès de Palmer

19th century involved adding the belfry and remodelling the central nave. The aisle chapels feature magnificent original Gothic paintings, and there is a splendid Baroque altarpiece.

The most precious relic in the church is the crucifix kept in Capella de Sant Crist. Jaume I is supposed to have carried this when he conquered Mallorca in 1229.

Another dramatic event is associated with this church. In 1435, it was the site of a mass baptism of Jews, who converted to Christianity in order to escape being burned at the stake.

Es Baluard Museu d'Art Modern i Contemporani

Plaça Porta de Santa Catalina. **Open** 10am–8pm Tue–Sat (to 3pm Sun) **Closed** 1 Jan & 25 Dec.

Es Baluard is housed in a modern building of concrete and glass, completely and beautifully integrated in the Sant Pere bastion (*baluard* in Catalan) that was part of the Renaissance wall surrounding the city of Palma. It has a wide-ranging collection of works by prominent artists who have converged on these islands from the beginning of the 20th century. The works of Catalans Santiago Rusiñol, Joaquín Mir and Joaquín Sorolla are displayed, while Joan Miró and Pablo Picasso have exclusive rooms dedicated to their works. Contemporary artists are led by the well-known Mallorcan Miquel Barceló, who also painted one of the chapels of the Palma Cathedral and the dome at the UN headquarters in Geneva.

Palau March

Palau Reial 18, 07001. **Open** Nov–Mar: 10am–6:30pm (to 2pm Sat).

An exhibition space, an auditorium and a library, Palau March was built in the 1940s as the family residence of financier Juan March Ordinas. Today, it houses an excellent collection of modern and contemporary sculpture, as well as more than 2,000 pieces of 18th-century Neapolitan nativity crib figures. Spectacular but controversial murals by Josep M Sert adorn the dome ceiling over the main staircase and the music room.

Casa Olesa

Carrer Morey 25.

Built in the mid-16th century, this Renaissance residence is one of Palma's most beautiful. The house is private but you can admire its courtyard through the wrought-iron gate.

Plaça Mayor, the main town square, with live entertainment

For hotels and restaurants in this region see pp148–150 and pp155–9

Monastery courtyard of Basilíca de Sant Francesc

🔼 Basilíca de Sant Francesc

Plaça Sant Francesc. **Open** 9:30am–12:30pm & 3:10–6pm Mon–Sat, 9am–12:30pm Sun. 🐾

The building of the Gothic church and Franciscan monastery started in 1281 and lasted 100 years. During the Middle Ages, this was Palma's most fashionable church and to be buried here was a major status symbol. Aristocratic families competed with each other by building ever more ostentatious side chapels in which to place their dead.

The church was remodelled in the 17th century after being damaged by lightning. Its severe façade, with giant rose window, was embellished around 1680 with a Baroque doorway, decorated with stone statues and the Triumphant Virgin Mary in the tympanum. Next to the Madonna is the carved figure of the famous medieval mystic Ramón Llull *(see p91)*, who is buried in the church.

The dark interior (its Gothic windows have been partially bricked up) contains many fine works of art, which are mainly Baroque in style. Particularly eye-catching (if you can see in the dimness) are the vast altarpiece, dating from 1739, and the organ. The delightful Gothic cloisters, planted with orange and lemon trees, offer light relief.

Standing in front of the basilica is a statue of Junípero Serra *(see p81)*, a Franciscan monk and native of Mallorca, who was sent to California in 1768 and founded Los Angeles and San Francisco.

🔲 Banys Àrabs

Carrer Can Serra 7. **Tel** 637 046 534. **Open** 9am–7:30pm daily (to 6pm Dec–Mar). 🐾

The brick 10th-century *hammam* (bathhouse) is one of the few architectural reminders of a Moorish presence on the islands. A small horseshoe-arched chamber, with a dome supported by irregular columns and what would once have been underfloor heating, it has survived in its original form. There's not a lot to see, but the pleasant garden has tables where you can sit and rest.

🔲 Palau Episcopal and Museu Diocesà

Carrer Mirador 5. **Open** 10am–2pm Mon–Sat. **Closed** Sun. 🐾

Just behind the cathedral, the Palau Episcopal (Bishop's Palace) is mostly 17th century, though work began in 1238, initiated by Bishop Ramon de Torell. The palace, which is built around a large courtyard, adjoins the city walls. Its façade was completed in 1616.

Several rooms of the palace have been given over to the charming **Museu Diocesà** (Diocese Museum). The museum displays items from various churches in Mallorca, including a wonderful selection of medieval religious paintings. Particularly noteworthy are: a picture of St George slaying the dragon in front of Palma's city gate, painted in 1468–70 by Pere Nisart; Bishop Galiana's panel depicting the life of St Paul (who is portrayed holding a sword) and the Gothic pulpit in a Mudéjar (Spanish-Moorish) style. There is also the jasper sarcophagus of Jaume II, which stood in the cathedral until 1904.

Sundial from Palau Episcopal

🔼 City Walls

The Renaissance city walls were built on the site of earlier medieval walls. This restored section once included a gallery running along the top, from where the city's defenders could fire at besieging enemies. Progress in artillery design meant that the fortifications became lower and thicker. Work on remodelling the walls began in the mid-16th century, but the bastions were only completed in the early 19th century. Today, Palma's city walls feature a walkway that provides a wide view over Badia de Palma, the cathedral and the Old Town.

Restored city walls in Palma's old town

Painting by Pérez Villata in the Museu Fundación Juan March

Further Afield

If you want to relax away from the hubbub of the crowded streets in Palma's Old Town, take a trip to the outskirts of the city. A stroll along the **harbourfront**, or a trip to **Castell de Bellver**, with its lovely view of the city, is always a treat.

Carrer Sant Miquel

A narrow street that runs north from Plaça Major to Plaça Conquista, Carrer Sant Miquel is closed to traffic and is one of Palma's main shopping streets. Here, you can buy almost anything, though souvenir shops are a rarity. Here, too, you will find the Museu Fundación Juan March and, a little further on, the church of Sant Miquel. Nearby, in Plaça Olivar, stands the large iron structure of the market hall that was built in the early 20th century.

Museu Fundación Juan March

Carrer Sant Miquel 11. **Tel** 971 713 515. **Open** 10am–6:30pm Mon–Fri, 10:30am–2pm Sat.

The museum occupies a Renaissance building that was remodelled in the early 20th century by Guillem Reynes i Font in the *Modernista* style. Purchased in 1916 by Juan March, the building was the first headquarters of Banca March.

The museum's exhibition occupies the first and second floors and features works by contemporary Spanish artists including Pablo Picasso, Joan Miró and Salvador Dali.

Most of the 50 or so exhibited works are paintings and sculptures by less well-known artists, who nevertheless played an important role in the shaping of Spanish modern art. The museum, which also stages temporary exhibitions, is part of Fundación Juan March, a major cultural foundation.

Rose window on the façade of Sant Miquel

Sant Miquel

Carrer de Sant Miquel 21. **Tel** 971 715 455. **Open** 9am–1:30pm & 4–8pm Mon–Sat, 10am–1pm & 4–8pm Sun.

This 16th-century church is one of the most popular in town. It was built on the site of a mosque in which the first victory Mass was said after the conquest of Mallorca by Jaume I. The Baroque altarpiece with a picture of St Michael is the work of the Spanish religious painter Francesc Herrera.

La Rambla

Palma's biggest flower market can be found in this shadowy avenue, lined with plane trees. Towards the lower section of the boulevard are two statues of Roman emperors, erected by the Francoists in honour of Mussolini. At La Rambla's northern end stands the vast building of **La Misericordia**, remodelled in the mid-19th century in a Neo-Classical style. It houses, among other things, a conservatoire. Next to it is a botanical garden.

Plaça d'Espanya

This sprawling square, containing an equestrian statue of Jaume I, is Palma's main transport hub. The two railway stations run services to Sóller, Binissalem and Inca. Just off the square is the large and modern long-distance bus station; local city buses stop on the square itself.

Nuevo Pueblo Español

Poble Espanyol, s/n. **Tel** 971 737 070. **Open** 10am–6pm Mon–Fri (Nov–Mar: 9am–5pm).

"Miniature Spain" is located a short way west of Palma's Old Town. It was built in the 1960s on the orders of the Spanish dictator General Franco. Twenty or so mini versions of outstanding examples of Spanish architecture include Granada's Alhambra Palace, El Greco's house in Toledo and Barcelona's Palau de la Generalitat. There's also a craft workshop, restaurants, a bar and a souvenir shop.

Copy of Alhambra in Nuevo Pueblo Español

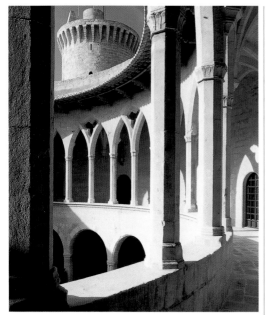
Arcades surrounding Castell de Bellver's courtyard

Opposite the entrance to Nuevo Pueblo Español stands the monumental **Palau de Congressos**. The congress centre features, among other things, the Roman Theatre and the Imperial Hall.

🏛 Castell de Bellver
C/Camilo José Cela s/n. **Tel** 971 735 065. 🚌 to Plaça Gomila. **Open** Apr–Sep: 10am–7pm Tue–Sat, 10am–3pm Sun; Oct–Mar: 10am–6pm Tue–Sat, 10am–3pm Sun. 🎫 (entrance to the castle is free on Sun). 🅿

About 2 km (1 mile) west of Palma's cathedral, on a pine-clad hill high above the harbour, stands one of Europe's most beautiful Gothic castles. Though it has, alas, been over-restored, the Castell de Bellver affords spectacular views of the city and bay. Built as a summer residence for Jaume II by Pere Selvà in the early 14th century when Mallorca was an independent kingdom, it was later turned into a prison and remained as such until 1915.

The castle, circular in shape, has an inner courtyard that is surrounded by two-tier arcades. Three cylindrical towers are partly sunk into the wall.

The freestanding Torre de Homenaje is joined to the main building by an arch and was designed to be the final stronghold. The castle's flat roof was built to collect rainwater into an underground cistern.

The entire complex is surrounded by a moat and ground fortifications.

A part of the castle has been turned into a museum. It has an exhibition of archaeological finds and Roman sculpture collected in the 18th century by Antonio Despuig – a historian and cardinal who left his collection to the city.

🏛 Museu Krekovic
Carrer de Ciutat de Querétaro 3. **Tel** 971 219 606. **Open** 9:30am–1pm & 3–6pm Mon–Fri, 10:30am–1pm Sat. **Closed** Aug.

The museum of the Croatian painter Kristian Krekovic (1901–85) opened in 1981. It includes not only works by the artist but also paintings and handicrafts from Spain and Latin America.

⛴ Harbourfront
Palma's harbour, overlooked by the cathedral, bustles with life, as magnificent yachts come and go. Here, at the wharf, you can see fishermen at work. The nearby **Reial Club Nautic** has an excellent restaurant that often plays host to Spanish royalty.

Further on, opposite the **Auditorio** in Passeig Marítim, is a jetty for pleasure boats from where you can take a trip around the harbour. Beyond **Club del Mar**, to the south, is the ferry terminal providing regular services to the other islands of the archipelago and mainland Spain. Nearby, is a naval base. You can see most of the harbour on foot. Alternatively, hire a bicycle or horse-drawn cab. Routes end at the 15th-century **Torre Paraires** or by the lighthouse in **Potro Pi.**

Environs
Five km (3 miles) to the north lies the district of **Establiments**. Its historic sights include an old windmill that now houses a restaurant. Music lovers may be interested to know that it was here, in villa "Son Vent", on the outskirts of town, that Frédéric Chopin and George Sand stopped while on their way to Valldemossa.

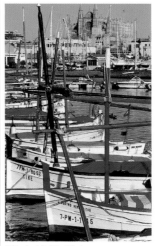
Fishing boats in Palma's harbour

Rough waters of the Badia de Palma

❷ Badia de Palma

The Bay of Palma is bounded by Cap de Cala Figuera to the west and Cap Enderrocat to the east. During the tourist boom, in the 1960s–1970s, the bay became surrounded by miles of high-rise hotels and hemmed in by hundreds of restaurants, bars, nightclubs and shops. Today, the eastern part of this beautiful bay is popular with German visitors, while the British tend to congregate to the west.

Platja de Palma, stretching from S'Arenal to C'an Pastilla, is one of the best beaches on the islands if you can ignore the sprawl fringing the shore. The western side is more varied, featuring pine-clad hills, sloping down to the water's edge. The beaches are smaller here, situated in picturesque coves. Along the coast are the popular resorts of Bendinat, Portals Nous, Palma Nova and Magaluf.

Joan Miró (1893–1983)

One of the best-known artists of the 20th century, Miró was a Catalan through and through. Initially influenced by Fauvism, and later by Dadaism and Surrealism, he developed his own style, marked by lyricism and lively colouring. After arriving in Mallorca he became interested in graphics, ceramics and sculpture, scoring significant successes in every art form. His works can be seen in his studio on the outskirts of Palma, where he lived and worked from 1956. He died in Palma in 1983.

Joan Miró, one of modern art's most influential figures

❸ Cala Major

🛈 Carretera Andrax 33, Illetes.

This resort area west of Palma is known for its **Fundació Pilar i Joan Miró**. Miró lived and worked on the island for 40 years. After his death in 1983, the artist's wife converted the house and former studio into an art centre. This edifice, nick-named the "Alabaster Fortress", is the work of Rafael Moneo, a leading Spanish architect. The new building houses a permanent exhibition of Miró's paintings, drawings and sculptures, as well as a library, auditorium and shop where you can buy items decorated with the artist's colourful designs. The Foundation owns some 140 paintings, 300 graphics, 35 sculptures and over 1,500 drawings by Miró. Standing nearby is the **Marivent Palace**, a

A sculpture by Miró

carefully guarded holiday residence of the Spanish royal family. Cala Major's main street is lined with *Modernista* villas, which remain from the days when this was a smart resort, visited by the rich and powerful. The **Nixe Palace Hotel** is a throwback to those days.

🏛 **Fundació Pilar i Joan Miró**
C/ Joan de Saridakis 29. **Tel** 971 701 420. **Open** 10am–7pm Tue–Sat (to 6pm in winter); 10am–3pm Sun. 🚫 (free from 3pm on Sat).

Environs
Some 8 km (5 miles) west of Palma stands the 13th-century **Castell de Bendinat**. Remodelled in the 18th century, the castle is sur-rounded by pine woods and its imposing walls and towers are decorated with a Baroque frieze. Today, the castle houses a confer-ence centre and is not open to the public.

Five kilometres (3 miles) northwest of Palma are the **Coves de Genova**. Discovered in 1906, the caves have some fine formations of stalactites and stalagmites.

Palmanova is famous for its picturesque, though crowded, beaches and lively nightlife. Nearby **Magaluf** is a busy resort with a variety of high-rise hotels and numerous restaurants and English-style pubs where you can order a full English breakfast or fish and chips.

🏞 **Coves de Genova**
Carrer de Barranc 45. **Tel** 971 402 387. **Open** 11am–1:30pm & 4–6pm Tue–Sun (timings vary in winter). 🚫

Beaches Around Palma

Some of the best beaches on Mallorca are located within a short distance of the capital, Palma, and these are readily reached by bus. East of the city are the longer, sandier beaches that culminate in the golden strand at S'Arenal, famous for the beautiful bodies that sun themselves here. To the west are the smaller beaches – sometimes sand, sometimes pebble and sometimes a mixture. These beaches are very pretty, especially those in rocky, forested coves, with Ses Illetes being arguably the pick of the bunch.

⑥ S'Arenal
S'Arenal, at the eastern end of Platja de Palma, is the most popular resort along this part of the coast. Its main attraction, apart from the beach, is Aqualand El Arenal fun park, with its pools and rides.

① Palmanova
A good base for family holidays. Nearby buildings are hidden among dense greenery, and the Serra de Tramuntana hills can be seen in the distance.

③ Cala Major
This small bay is lined with houses and hotels. The golden beach is hardly secluded, but it is one of the nicest in this area.

④ Palma
Inhabitants of the capital head to C'an Pere Antoni beach or to other beaches along the Badia de Palma.

⑤ Platja de Palma
At the height of the holiday season, this 5-km- (3-mile-) long beach becomes exceptionally crowded. Behind the row of cafés and bars next to the beach are hotels, apartments and clubs.

② Ses Illetes
This small beach, barely 120 m (390 ft) long, is off the beaten track. Despite that, and the lack of facilities, it remains popular.

Key

- ▬ Motorway/highway
- ▬ Major road
- ▬ Scenic route
- ▬ Other road

Map labels: MA-1130, MA-1040, MA-13, Ma-11, Ma-13A, MA-3013, Pont d'Inca, Son Ferriol, Ma-20, MA-19, MA-1, Costa d'en Blanes, Ma-19, MA-6010, Sant Francesc, Ma-19

0 km 3
0 miles 3

❹ Calvià

🚐 ℹ️ Passeig de la Mar 13, Palmanova, 971 682 365. 🎭 Sant Jaume (25 Jun). 🏛️ Mon.
🔲 visitcalvia.com

This quiet little town in the foothills of the Serra de Tramuntana mountains is the administrative centre of Calvià Province, which includes the resorts from Ses Illetes to Santa Ponça.

Standing on a hill in the centre of Calvià is the church of **Sant Joan Baptista**; its forecourt provides a fine view over the surrounding farms and olive groves. The original church was built here in 1245; the present structure dates from the late 19th century. The ceramic tiles lining the walls of the neighbouring public library provide a crash course in the town's history.

Few tourists make it to Calvià, where life proceeds quietly. The bars and restaurants here serve authentic Mallorcan cuisine.

Environs
Santa Ponça is a small port, situated 7 km (4 miles) southwest of Calvià. Nearby are golf courses, good beaches and opulent residences. It was here that Jaume I landed in 1229, freeing Mallorca from Arab domination. The event is marked by the Creu de la Conquesta.

Neo-Gothic Sant Joan Baptista, Calvià

Typical Mallorcan fishing boats in Port d'Andratx

❺ Andratx

🚐 ℹ️ Av de la Cúria 1, 971 628 019.
🎭 Sant Pere (29 Jun), La Virgen del Carmen (16 Aug). 🏛️ Wed.

Andratx has ancient origins and was known as Andrachium by the Romans. It lies in a valley of olive and almond groves, at the foot of the Puig de Galatzó (1,028 m/ 3,400 ft). The local architecture is typical of the inland settlements that used to defend the island against raids by pirates. Old ochre-colour houses with colourful shutters blend well with the narrow cobblestone streets. The main historic sight is the fortified church of **Santa María**, towering over the town. It was built in the 13th century and remodelled in the early 18th century. The main tourist attraction, however, is the local market, which is held on Wednesday mornings. A visit to the CCA Andraxt, an exhibition space devoted to contemporary art, is a must.

Church tympanum in Andratx

Environs
Some 5 km (3 miles) southwest of Andratx is **Port d'Andratx**. The sheltered bay provides a mooring ground for upmarket yachts. As recently as the 1960s, this was just a small fishing village, which later transformed itself into a swanky resort with luxurious residences built within the woodland setting on the slopes of the La Mola cape, and affording beautiful views of the harbour. The coastal boulevard offers the best place for viewing the magnificent sunsets.

About 5 km (3 miles) east of Port d'Andratx, in **Camp de Mar**, is a sandy beach and lovely bathing spot with large hotels situated close to the sea. Neighbouring **Peguera** has many inexpensive hotels. Its pleasant and safe beaches are particularly favoured by families with small children and by older visitors. **Cap Andritxol**, between Peguera and Camp de Mar, is a small peninsula with an observation tower at its tip dating back to 1580. It is an excellent destination for walks and offers hikers the chance to see some rare animals and many species of native flora. **Cala Fornells**, a short way from Peguera, is a small, picturesque village and beautiful cove. Surrounded by pine trees, it has great views of the bay. It is also a good place for swimming.

A particularly scenic road runs northwards, from Andratx to Estellencs. The **Mirador de Ricardo Roca viewpoint** and Es Grau restaurant provide good stopping points for a rest en route *(see pp66–7)*.

The delightful hillside village of **S'Arracó** lies 3 km (2 miles) west of Andratx, on the road leading to Sant Elm. The local church has a marble statue of Nostra Senyora de Sa Trapa, brought to the Trappist monastery near Sant Elm in the 18th century.

❻ Sa Dragonera

A narrow rocky island, Sa Dragonera lies at an angle to the coast, about 1km (half a mile) from Sant Elm. It has been a nature reserve since 1988 and is home to a wide variety of birdlife and wild flowers.

According to legend, the island is visited nightly by dragons. However, its name has more to do with its shape than its popularity with mythical beasts.

This wild island is just 4 km (2 miles) long and 700 m (765 yards) wide. A rocky path runs between its two headlands, both marked by lighthouses. The only inhabitants of the island are wild goats and birds – the island supports cormorants, Cory's shearwater and many birds of prey including the largest colony anywhere of Eleonora's falcon.

Sa Dragonera can be reached by a ferry from Sant Elm (Feb–Oct), which disembarks to allow you several hours to wander and explore the island. There are also cruises around the island, and these leave from both Sant Elm and Port d'Andratx.

Environs
Sant Elm (San Telmo) is a quiet resort with a good sandy beach, a wide selection of cafés and restaurants and beautiful scenery. About 4 km (2 miles) northeast of Sant Elm, and accessible along a steep footpath, is an abandoned monastery. **Sa Trapa** has a mill displaying some preserved agricultural equipment. A commemorative stone stands

Hiking trail in La Reserva Puig de Galatzó

as a warning against getting too close to the edge of the precipice, which affords a fantastic view over the island of Sa Dragonera.

❼ Northwestern Coast of Mallorca

See pp66–7.

❽ La Reserva Puig de Galatzó

18 km (11 miles) north of Palma, 4 km (2 miles) west of Puigpunyent. **Tel** 971 616 622. **Open** Apr–Oct: 10am–6pm daily; Nov–Mar: Fri–Sun only. 🚌 🌐 **lareserva mallorca.com**

This private nature reserve is situated on the eastern slope of the mighty Puig de Galatzó peak, in the southern region of the Serra de Tramuntana. Here, in an area of 250 sq km (100 sq miles), you can sample some of the splendours of nature, as the area features springs and streams, dozens of scenic waterfalls and caves,

Sign of La Reserva Puig de Galatzó

as well as a variety of interesting rock formations.

Specially designated pathways lead through the park. Notice boards explain the local flora, the origins of its unusually shaped rocks and the habits of local birds. There is much else of interest, too, including bears, a falcon show, a 1,000-year-old olive tree, *carboneros* (huts belonging to charcoal burners) and the Cova des Moro – Moor's Cave. Real adventures, such as rock climbing, abseiling and archery, are also on offer.

Environs
Set amid lemon groves, 2 km (1 mile) northeast, is the quiet little farming village of **Puigpunyent**, which has a 17th-century church.

Galilea, situated a little way south of La Reserva, is a favourite haunt for artists from all over Europe. It affords a magnificent view of the southwestern coast of Mallorca. The founder of the local church of the Immaculate Conception was Captain Antonio Barceló, a man with a fierce reputation who, in the 18th century, defended Mallorca against pirates. In nearby El Capdella the same captain Barceló founded the church of Virgen del Carmen.

Sa Dragonera, Dragon Island, viewed from Sant Elm

❼ Northwestern Coast of Mallorca

The northern slopes of the Serra de Tramuntana provide some magnificent views and a wonderful sense of isolation. Banyalbufar and Valldemossa have a number of interesting historic sights, but it is the scenery of the rugged coastline, which manages to be both imposing and beautiful, that is most impressive. The route is dramatic, traversing tunnels and gorges, but it is not difficult, except for the approach to Port d'es Canonge and Port de Valldemossa. It can be covered in a single day. If you are fit, you could even cycle.

④ **Mirador de Ses Ànimes**
The former defence tower, standing on a steep rock, now serves as a viewpoint. The entrance to the tower is narrow, but the panoramic views are very rewarding.

③ **Estellencs**
A small town with old stone houses, an interesting, mostly 18th-century, church and a handful of souvenir shops. The route follows the main street.

② **Mirador de Ricardo Roca**
This viewpoint is situated on the terrace of the Es Grau restaurant. It affords a spectacular view of the northwestern coastline.

① **Andratx**
A charming little town with attractive houses and cobbled streets. The market is held on Wednesday and is a time when the usually empty streets teem with life.

Serra de Tramuntana

Ma-10

MA-1032

MA-1031

Calvià

0 kilometres 2
0 miles 2

Ma-1
Ma-1A
Palma

⑤ Banyalbufar
Founded by the Arabs, this small town is surrounded by terraced fields descending to the sea. Until the late 19th century, the district was famous for its vineyards.

⑦ La Granja
Once a country estate, La Granja now houses one of the island's most interesting museums. It stages shows of regional dance, crafts and local winetastings.

Tips for Drivers

Length: 50 km (31 miles).
Stopping-off points: Most places along the route have a bar or restaurant; the restaurant at Mirador de Ricardo Roca is superb. Accommodation can be found in Andratx and Valldemossa.
Further information:
Valldemossa, Av da Palma 7.
Tel 971 612 106.

⑥ Port d'es Canonge
The road to this small fishing port and beach is narrow and winding, but the beauty of the spot makes it worth the trek. Fishermen's huts and a restaurant are by the beach, as well as lots of modern villas.

⑧ Esporles
At the centre of this friendly town, far from the tourist haunts, is the shady Passeig del Rei, lined with numerous cafés and restaurants. The nearby church was built in the early 16th century.

⑨ Port de Valldemossa
A small, shingly beach and a good fish restaurant are the main reasons to follow the winding road from Valldemossa to this pretty hamlet. It offers peace and idyllic scenery, and is visited by only a handful of holidaymakers.

⑩ Valldemossa
Frédéric Chopin wintered here in 1838. It is worth taking a stroll through the town's narrow alleys, after visiting the monastery and the royal palace.

Key

▆ Suggested route
═ Other road
▆ Scenic route

For keys to symbols *see back flap*

❾ La Granja

This country house *(finca)* lies in a wooded valley, near Esporles. From the 13th to the 15th centuries it belonged to an order of Cistercian monks, and after this to the Fortuny family. The estate has survived almost unchanged since the 19th century and is now a museum of folklore, full of antique furniture, ceramics and other artifacts. Mouthwatering hams hang in the antique kitchen, peacocks stroll around the beautiful garden, and the local restaurant serves delicious Mallorcan cuisine. In the mornings it is quieter, and you can still see displays of horse dressage and local crafts.

Dye-house
This formed part of the domestic quarters, most of which were situated in basements and cellars.

Park
The estate, situated in a valley, is surrounded by a park to the south and west. Its landscaping includes streams and waterfalls; the house is almost completely hidden by a dense growth of trees.

Library
Situated next to the Renaissance bedroom, the library also served as the master's study.

Courtyard
The house is arranged around a courtyard. Don't miss the old carriage that is parked in an open garage. The courtyard has a wide entrance gate to the east.

KEY

① **Restaurant**

② **Gate to the park**

③ **Main entrance**, where the shop and café are located.

★ **Salon**
The formal rooms are situated on the north side. Next to the salon are the games room and a small theatre. From here, French windows open onto the garden.

VISITORS' CHECKLIST

Practical Information
2 km (1 mile) west from Esporles.
Tel 971 610 032.
Open 10am–7pm daily (summer), 10am–6pm (winter).
Art & craft exhibition and horse dressage shows: Feb–Oct Wed & Fri 4pm.
W lagranja.net

★ **Garden**
At the centre of the garden is a small fountain; the escarpment hides a grotto.

Corridor
Windows overlook the courtyard. On its east side is a row of smaller rooms, where you can see, among other things, an exhibition of toys.

Exhibitions
Visitors can see an equestrian show with professionals training horses (Wednesday and Friday afternoons from February to October), as well as local artisans working in traditional crafts such as shoemaking, basketwork and embroidery.

Enchanting little alleys of Valldemossa

❿ Valldemossa

🏔 1,750. 🚌 ℹ Av. Palma 7, 971 612 019. 🚌 Sun. 🎭 Santa Catalina Thomàs (28 Jul), Sant Bartomeu (24 Aug), Chopin Festival (Aug). 🌐 **valldemossa.es**

The historical records of Valldemossa go back to the 14th century, when the asthmatic King Sancho built this palace in the mountains to make the most of the more rarefied air. In 1399, the palace was handed over to the Carthusian monks, who remodelled it as a monastery. The **Real Cartuja** y Palacio del Rey Sancho (Royal Carthusian Monastery of Jesus of Nazareth) was abandoned in 1835, when the monks were dispossessed.

The composer Frédéric Chopin rented a former monk's cell here in 1838 with his lover George Sand, the feminist French writer, and the monastery is now the town's main tourist attraction. In front of the entrance, in Plaça de la Cartuja de Valldemossa, is a monument to Chopin.

The monastery includes a chapel with a ceiling decorated with late Baroque paintings by Miguel Bayeu, a relative of Goya's. Behind the chapel are rows of shady arcades. The prior's cell, despite its name, consists of several spacious rooms with access to a private garden offering a magnificent view of the valley below. The rooms house an exhibition of religious artifacts of considerable interest.

The adjacent cells contain mementos of Chopin and George Sand. The 17th-century monastery pharmacy contains a variety of ceramic and glass jars with wonderfully detailed descriptions of their contents (look out for the jar containing "powdered beasts' claws").

The monastery also houses the excellent **Museu Municipal d'Art**, which includes a small collection of works by distinguished Spanish artists including Antoni Tàpies, Joan Miró and Juli Ramis – a *Modernista* painter and native of Mallorca. There is also a cycle of illustrations by Pablo Picasso, *Burial of Count Orgaz*, inspired by the famous El Greco painting.

On leaving the cloisters, you can proceed to the **Palau del Rei Sanç** – the Palace of King Sancho. This is the oldest fortified part of the monastery. The main point of interest is the wooden drawbridge connecting the two chambers over the palace's

original entrance. Once used as a political prison, the palace now serves as a venue for displays of folk dancing and recitals of Chopin's music.

Valldemossa itself is charming and always bustling. Most visitors are keen to see the places associated with Chopin, but a stroll along the town's narrow cobbled alleys is definitely worthwhile.

The modest house at Carrer Rectoria 5 is where the saintly nun Catalina Thomàs was born to a peasant family. The house has been converted into a richly decorated chapel, with the statue of the saint standing in front, holding a jug with flowing water. Nearby is the 15th-century church of Sant Bartomeu, now, unfortunately, partly destroyed.

🏛 **Real Cartuja y Palacio del Rey Sancho**
Plaça de Cartuja de Valldemossa. **Tel** 971 612 986. **Closed** Sun (Nov–Mar). 🚫 ♿ 🌐 **cartuja devalldemossa.com**

Environs
Port de Valldemossa lies some 6 km (4 miles) north of Valldemossa. This is a small fishing village scenically poised on the shores of a wide bay and surrounded by rugged cliffs. It is reached by a narrow, hairpin road. The local beach, although small and pebbly, is enchanting and occupies a beautiful location. The demanding journey is rewarded by a renowned restaurant specializing in seafood.

Tile with the image of the Saint, on one of Valldemossa's houses

Santa Catalina Thomas (1531–74)

Catalina Thomàs is the only Mallorcan saint. At the age of 23, she joined an Augustinian order. Known for her humility, she declined the position of Mother Superior, saying that she did not wish to govern but to serve God. She is buried in the chapel of Santa María Magdalena convent in Palma, where she spent many years of her life. She was canonized in 1930.

Frédéric Chopin and George Sand

The acclaimed Polish composer Chopin spent four months in Valldemossa's 14th-century monastery *(see opposite)* during the winter of 1838–9. Chopin was accompanied by Aurora Dupin, better known as the French novelist George Sand, and her children. Their arrival here was partly to escape the prying eyes of Parisian society and partly on account of the composer's health. Chopin suffered from tuberculosis, though the weather was so bad during his stay that it made him worse. The short visit to the town by this unusual couple, described by Sand in *A Winter in Mallorca*, has contributed to the popularity of Valldemossa, despite the fact that Sand labelled the locals as "savages".

The garden in front of cell No. 2, in which Chopin's scores and George Sand's manuscripts are held, has a fine terrace. There is some dispute over which cell Chopin occupied, although it is generally believed to be No.4.

Portrait of George Sand
A French writer and journalist, Sand was a highly unconventional figure. She was way ahead of her time – she wore trousers, smoked cigars and lived with men she was not married to.

Portrait of Frédéric Chopin, by Italian painter Luigi Calamatta, in the form of a photomontage over an original partiture composed by the musician, displayed in the Royal Carthusian Monastery.

The Pleyal Piano is the composer's oldest piano, conserved in cell No. 4, where he finished his Preludes. Chopin's major partitures are on show in the museum.

GEORGE SAND

UN INVIERNO EN MALLORCA

El inmortal músico Frédéric Chopin y la escritora George Sand residieron en Valldemossa · Mallorca el invierno de 1838/9. La apasionada pluma de George Sand nos describe su experiencia e intensa de su experiencia.

MALLORCA

A Winter in Mallorca
George Sand's description of her visit to Mallorca with Chopin has enjoyed lasting popularity.

Rotunda in the garden of Son Marroig

⓫ Son Marroig

3 km (2 miles) northeast of Deià.
Open 9:30am–6:30pm Mon–Sat
(to 5:30pm in summer).
W sonmarroig.com

This late medieval mansion, perched high above the seashore, was remodelled in the 19th century to become the residence of the Habsburg Archduke Ludwig Salvator. The Austrian aristocrat was fabulously rich and came to Mallorca hoping to escape from the strict morality of the Viennese court. He fell in love with the island, settled here and gave himself over to exploring and promoting the Balearic Islands.

The house is now a museum, dedicated to his life and work and including some of his pen drawings and manuscripts. It is surrounded by a terrace and graced by a rotunda of white marble. From here, the Archduke enjoyed fine views over the wooded shore to the narrow promontory of **Sa Foradada**, where he used to moor his yacht *Nixe*. It takes less than an hour's walk to get there.

Environs

A short way southwest of Son Marroig is the **Monestír de Miramar**. The house was built in 1276 for Ramon Llull but was acquired by Ludwig Salvator in 1827. The Archduke entertained Princess Sisi here during her visit to Mallorca.

Monestír de Miramar

Open 9am–5:45pm daily (to 4:45pm in winter).

⓬ Deià

700. Sant Joan Baptista
(24 Jun). **W** deia.info

This lovely mountain town lies at the spot where the mighty Puig d'es Teix meets the sea. Deià is mostly associated with the English novelist and poet Robert Graves. Graves settled here in 1929 and for the next 56 years lived and worked at his home, **Ca N'Alluny**, making the place popular with other artists, including Picasso and the writer Anaïs Nin.

Perched high above the town is the modest church of **Sant Joan Baptista** (1754–60). The adjacent building houses the **parish museum**, with a collection of religious objects. Deià also has an interesting **Museu Arqueológic**, founded by the American archaeologist William Waldren, displaying the prehistory of Mallorca.

Hotel La Residencia, in the grounds of a former estate, has attracted such famous guests as Princess Diana and Sir Bob Geldof.

Ludwig Salvator

The Habsburg Archduke Ludwig Salvator was born in 1847. He first visited Mallorca at the age of 19 and became captivated by the island. He settled here semi-permanently, learned the local dialect and created a scandal by marrying a local carpenter's daughter. He was tireless in exploring and promoting Mallorca, producing a seven-volume work devoted to the island's history, archaeology, folklore and topography. It is largely thanks to him that a 10-km (6-mile-) long stretch of the coast that he owned has never been developed. In 1910, he was awarded honorary citizenship of Mallorca. He died in 1915.

Ca N'Alluny: La Casa de Robert Graves

Carretera Deià–Sóller s/n.
Tel 971 636 185. **Open** Apr–Oct: 10am–5pm Mon–Fri, 10am–3pm Sat; Nov–Mar: 9am–4pm Mon–Fri, 9am–2pm Sat. **W** lacasa derobertgraves.com

Hotel La Residencia viewed from the church hill

Modernista building of Banco de Sóller, one of Sóller's landmarks

🏛 Museu Arqueológic

Es Clot Deià. **Tel** 699 957 902.
Open Apr–Sep: 5–7pm Sat,
11am–1pm Sun.

Environs

A winding road leads to **Cala Deià**, a pretty cove with a shingle beach and clear water.

⓭ Sóller

🚌 🚊 *i* Plaça Espanya 1. **Tel** 971 638 008. 🚊 Sat. 🎉 Festes de Moros i Cristians (2nd Sun in May).

Situated in a valley, Sóller is sheltered by the Serra de Alfàbia mountain massif and is located just a handful of kilometres from the ocean. Its name reputedly derives from the Arabic word *suliar*, meaning "golden bowl" – the valley is famous for its many orange groves.

Arabs, who settled here in the late 8th century, built canals and irrigation ditches and the town grew rich thanks to its plentiful supply of oranges and the vineyards and olive groves, planted on the slopes of the Serra de Tramuntana. In exchange for its oranges and wine, it imported goods from France and links between the town and France remain strong.

Plaça Constitució is a lively square and the centre of Sóller. Mature trees, fountains and lively cafés give the place its unique atmosphere. Notable buildings include the *Modernista* castle-like **Banco de Sóller**, which is the work of Joan Rubió i Bellver, a disciple of Antoni Gaudí, and the

Robert Graves (1895–1985)

Robert Graves was an English novelist, poet and classical scholar. Severely wounded on the Somme during World War I, his frank autobiography, *Goodbye to All That*, earned him enough money to move to Mallorca, where he set up home, accompanied by his muse and mistress, the poet Laura Riding. Here, he wrote two tremendously successful historic novels: *I, Claudius* and *Claudius the God*, which made him world-famous. The outbreak of the Spanish Civil War interrupted his stay but he returned to the island in 1946. He died in 1985 and is buried in the local church of Sant Joan Baptista beneath a simple gravestone. His house is now a museum.

Robert Graves' tombstone in Deià's cemetery

Neo-Gothic church of **Sant Bartomeu**, also designed by Rubió. Particularly eye-catching is the vast rose window on the church façade, carved in stone, and the Baroque sculptures contrasting with the dark interior.

Museu Balear de Ciències Naturals (Balearic Museum of Natural Science), on the outskirts of Sóller, was opened in 1992 in a late 19th-century mansion house. Its exhibits include a collection of Mallorcan fossils and rocks and specimens of the local flora.

The adjacent **Jardí Botànic** contains plants native to the Balearic Islands. The town's **vintage electric train**, nicknamed the "Red Arrow", which runs between Palma and Sóller, provides a superb ride through the mountains. From

Fountain in Plaça Constitució in Sóller

the Sóller terminus you can hop aboard a **vintage tram**, which takes you on to Port de Sóller (*see p74*). Sóller train station is a singularly attractive building, and the main station hall exhibits a pair of large photos of two of its most famous visitors – Miró and Picasso.

Environs

Port de Sóller, situated 5 km (3 miles) from Sóller, is a pleasant although crowded resort with many seafood restaurants next to the harbour and by the beach. Here, you can enjoy a boat trip along the coast, or go for a hike to the nearby lighthouse.

🏛 Museu Balear de Ciències Naturals and Jardí Botànic

Ctra Palma–Port de Sóller. **Tel** 971 634 064. **Open** 10am–6pm Tue–Sat (Nov–Feb: to 2pm).

Punta Grosa lighthouse, near Port de Sóller

⑭ Train from Palma to Port de Sóller

The most enjoyable way to travel from Palma to Sóller is aboard the "Red Arrow", an electric narrow-gauge railway line, which opened in 1912. After passing through farmland, the 27-km (17-mile) route winds its way through the steep peaks and valleys of the Serra de Tramuntana. The line is justifiably regarded as one of the most attractive in Europe, and the narrow-gauge rolling stock and musty carriages only add to the experience.

④ **Sóller**
After a one-hour ride the train reaches Sóller. From here a vintage tram running through the busy town centre takes you to Port de Sóller.

③ **Mirador Pujol d'en Banja**
Two special tourist trains, leaving Palma daily at 10:50am and noon, stop briefly at this viewpoint to provide a splendid view of Sóller, the surrounding mountains and the coastline.

② **Bunyola**
This is the last stop before passing through the dizzying Serra de Tramuntana mountains. This typical Mallorcan town, towered over by its church, enjoys an idyllic location in a beautiful verdant valley.

⑤ **Port de Sóller**
The journey from Sóller to Port de Sóller takes 15 minutes. The tram route runs along the beach and ends at the harbour. Trams run much more frequently than the train.

Key
- ▬ Suggested route
- ▪ ▪ Route through the tunnel
- ▭ Motorway
- ▭ Scenic route
- ═ Other road

① **Palma**
A trip aboard this vintage electric train is a real delight. The line was originally built to transport fruit to Palma from Sóller at a time when the journey by road took an entire day.

Tips for Passengers
Length: 27 km (17 miles).
Stopping-off points: Sóller has many cafés and restaurants.
Information: Eusebio Estada 1, Palma (971 752 051); Plaça d'Espanya, Sóller (971 630 130); or contact 🆆 trendesoller.com

⑮ Jardines de Alfabia

14 km (9 miles) north of Palma. 🚌 **Tel** 971 613 123. **Open** Mar: 9:30am–5:30pm Mon–Fri, 9:30am–1pm Sat; Apr–Oct: 9:30am–6:30pm daily. **Closed** Nov–Feb.
🅿 Ⓦ jardinesdealfabia.com

Most visitors come to see the magnificent Moorish gardens of this old manor house, set amid lemon groves. Footpaths shaded by pergolas crisscross streams and take you past murmuring fountains, ivy-clad walls and beds of splendid roses. The house is approached via a long stately avenue of plane trees.

Following the conquest of the island by Jaume I, the estate was given to the Moorish governor Benhabet. Benhabet had been the governor of Pollença but supported the king by provisioning the Catalan army during the invasion. For this help, Jaume I gave Benhabet this land and he set about planning an estate in the Moorish style. After his death the castle became the residence of the Mallorcan nobility. The origin of the estate's name goes back to the days of Arab rule, when it was called *Al-Fabi* ("Jug of olives").

The house itself, with its courtyard surrounded by domestic buildings and shaded by a giant plane tree, is actually modest though attractive. Most notable is the 14th-century oak throne made for Jaume IV. The gatehouse features a lovely Mudéjar (Spanish-Moorish) style vault, with an inscription praising Allah.

Sun shining through a pergola in Jardines de Alfabia

Beach at the end of Torrent de Pareis canyon, near Sa Calobra

⑯ Sa Calobra

30 km (19 miles) NE of Fornalutx.

This tiny hamlet occupies a beautiful cove surrounded by high cliffs. A busy tourist centre, its main attraction is the **Torrent de Pareis** (River of the Twins) canyon, which is reached by a coastal walkway, leading partly through a tunnel.

It is also possible to reach this impressive canyon from **Escorca**, a hamlet on the way from Sóller to Pollença. This route is extremely difficult, however, and requires rock-climbing skills, ropes and wetsuits. It takes about six hours to cover it. During the winter and spring or after heavy rainfall, it is virtually impassable, as the bottom of the canyon, known as the "Great Canyon of Mallorca", fills with torrential waters. Once upon a time Sa Calobra was accessible only by boat. Now there is a twisting road leading to it, which in view of its break-neck descents and bends has been nicknamed *Nus de la Corbata* ("Knotted Neck-tie"). Two kilometres (1 mile) before Sa Calobra, you can take a left turn to the popular resort of **Cala Tuent**. Set against the northern slopes of Puig Major, the quiet village has a modest gravel and sand beach. The Es Vergeret restaurant has a large selection of fish dishes and its terrace affords a fine view of the rocky coast.

Serra de Tramuntana

The northern coast of Mallorca is dominated by the Serra de Tramuntana (Mountains of the North Wind), which run from Sa Dragonera in the west to Formentor in the east. The highest peak of this 90-km (55-mile) stretch is Puig Major (1,445 m/4,740 ft), though part of this is used by the military and closed to visitors. The steep slopes are covered with sweet-smelling wild rosemary and are home to goats, sheep and rare birds. The best way to enjoy this area is on foot, and a number of maps are easily available that list walking routes through all or part of the mountain range. Alternatively, you can explore the mountains by car, although great care should be taken on the narrow and twisting roads and frequent hairpin bends that descend through steep cliffs to the sea.

Steep mountain slopes west of Santuari de Lluc

For hotels and restaurants in this region see pp148–50 and pp155–9

⑰ Santuari de Lluc

The monestir at Lluc is the spiritual centre of Mallorca and has been a place of pilgrimage for over 800 years. The main point of interest is the little statue of the Virgin *(La Moreneta de Lluc)*, which, so the story goes, was found in a cave by an Arab shepherd boy who had converted to Christianity. The image was initially moved to the church but it kept returning to the same spot. A chapel was built to house this miraculous object and this has since been decorated with precious stones. Thousands of pilgrims now arrive here every year to pay homage.

Statue of Joaquim Rosselló i Ferra`
Father Rosselló, who arrived in Lluc in 1891, was the founder of the Sacred Heart Missionary Congregation and the spiritual reviver of the sanctuary.

Statue of Bishop Campins
A patron of the sanctuary, Bishop Pere-Joan Campins commissioned Antoni Gaudí and Guillem Reynés to renovate the basilica and build its Way of the Cross.

KEY

① **Church** The original Renaissance-Baroque church was built during 1622–84 and was designed by Jaume Blanquer. Much of the complex dates from the 18th and 19th centuries.

② **Dormitories**

★ **Museu de Lluc**
Opened in 1952, the museum houses local handicraft, such as *siurells* (whistles) and majolica, as well as works of art, paintings, coins and archaeological finds.

School Grounds
The buildings behind the church belong to the Els Blauets, a school choir founded in 1531. The name derives from the choir's blue cassocks.

La Dormició de la Verge
The first of the seven steles carved by Miquell Cosquell and Pere Merçol (1399), once standing along the road between Caimari and the sanctuary, now stands in Plaza dels Pelegrins.

★ Els Porxets
The 16th-century building was extended in the early 18th century. It consists of pilgrim quarters on the first floor and stables on the ground floor.

★ La Moreneta de Lluc
The tiny statue of *La Moreneta* ("the little dark One") is just 62 cm (24 in) high. It stands in a niche inside the chapel, built between 1707 and 1724, at the back of the main altar.

Plaza dels Pelegrins
The drive leading to the monastery is surrounded by greenery and lined with bars, cafés and souvenir shops. It provides a magnificent view of the Serra de Tramuntana.

⑱ Inca

🏛 29,000. 🚉 🚌 🛇 Thu. 🎭 Dijous
Bo (3rd Thu in Nov). **w** incaturistica.es

Inca, on the train journey from
Palma, is the third largest town
on the island. A modern industrial place, visitors come here
nevertheless, attracted by
the cheap leather goods in
Avinguda General Luque and
Gran Via de Colon. Thursday,
market day, is Inca's busiest
time. The stalls lining the streets
and squares stretch over several
districts of town. Here you can
buy almost anything – souvenirs,
household goods, flowers and
food. Inca is also known for its
traditional Mallorcan cuisine,
including *caracoles* (snails) and
for its wine cellars converted
into restaurants *(cellers)*.

Environs
About 2 km (1 mile) past the
town, heading towards Alcúdia,
is a right turn in the road that
leads to the top of **Puig d'Inca**
(296 m/970 ft), with a small
sanctuary, **Ermita de Santa
Magdalena**. For nearly 800
years on the first Sunday after
Easter crowds of pilgrims have
congregated here. There is a
good view from the top over
the surrounding fields and
mountains. Near the road
to Alcúdia are the **Coves de
Campanet**, a complex of small
but beautiful caves surrounded
by tropical gardens. The neighbouring small town of **Sa Pobla**
holds one of the best Sunday
markets on the island.

🕳 Coves de Campanet
Autopista Palma–Alcúdia, exit 37, 39
km (24 miles). **Tel** 971 516 130. **Open**
from 10am daily. 🅿 📷 ♿

Steps of the Via Crucis, leading to El Calvari, in Pollença

⑲ Pollença

🏛 17,000. 🚌 **ℹ** Claustro de Santo
Domingo, C/Guillem Cifre, 971 535
077. 🛇 Sun. 🎭 Sant Antoni (17 Jan),
Los Moros y los Cristianos (2 Aug).

Founded by the Romans in
the foothills of the Serra de
Tramuntana, Pollença has
retained much of its old-world
charm with narrow, twisting
streets, some good restaurants
and a lively Sunday market.
The remains left by the town's
founders include **Pont Romà**,
a bridge spanning the banks
of the Torrente de Sant Jordi
river, at the north end of town.

After 1229, the Knights Templar
began the building of the parish
church of **Nostra Senyora dels
Angels**. Remodelled in the 17th
century, the church façade has
a fine rose window, while its
dark interior is decorated with
paintings and a vast altar that
is several storeys high.

The pride of the town is the
beautiful **Via Crucis** (Way of the
Cross). It leads to the **El Calvari**
chapel standing on top of the
hills and housing a Gothic
statue of Christ. Climbing the
seemingly endless set of steps
(365 in all), you pass the Stations
of the Cross. The chapel may
also be reached by walking
along the streets. The statue of
Christ is carried down to the
parish church in a moving
torchlight procession every
Good Friday, during the
Davallament (the Crucifixion).

The former **Convent de
Sant Domingo** (Dominican
monastery) now houses the
Museu de Pollença, with its
collection of Gothic sacred art,
archaeological finds and a small
collection of modern paintings.

Colourful stall with souvenirs at Inca's Thursday market

For hotels and restaurants in this region see pp148–50 and pp155–9

To soak up Pollença's sleepy atmosphere, head for **Plaça Major**, where the locals gather in the cafés and bars.

Environs

The family-friendly resort of **Port de Pollença**, situated 6 km (4 miles) to the east beside a pleasant bay, has a long, sandy beach. Just southeast of Pollença a steep narrow road, then a footpath, climbs 330 m (1,000 ft) to **Puig de Maria**, where a 17th-century hermitage has a rustic restaurant and bar, and simple rooms to let with wonderful views.

🏛 **Museu de Pollença**
Convent de Santo Domingo. **Tel** 971 531 166. **Open** 10am–1pm Tue–Sat (Jun–Sep: also 5:30–8:30pm). 🖼

➋⓪ Cap de Formentor

6 km (4 miles) from Port de Pollença.

The Formentor Peninsula, at the northern end of the Serrà de Tramuntana, is a 20-km (12-mile) long headland of steep cliffs, that is in some places 400 m (1,300 ft) high. A short footpath from the road leads to the **Mirador des Colomer** from which you can enjoy spectacular views of the sea and the **El Colomer** rock. Staying on the serpentine path, there is also a beautiful view of the 16th-century watch tower, **Talaia d'Albercutx**. Further on, the road passes through the Mont Fumat tunnel and runs among rocky hills, covered with vegetation, up to the **lighthouse** rising to 260 m (850 ft). The rugged cliffs provide nesting sites for thrushes and rock doves, also falcons, swallows and martins.

A spur from the main road leads to the beach of **Platja de Formentor**, which is served by bus from Port de Pollença and gets very crowded in summer. The road ends at one of the oldest, most luxurious resorts on the island – the Hotel Formentor. Opened in 1929, it is noted for its opulence and fashionable clientele (*see p149*).

Interior of the Gothic church of Sant Jaume in Alcúdia

➋➊ Alcúdia

🏠 19,000. 🚌 ℹ C/Major 17, 971 897 113. 🚍 Tue–Sun. 🎆 Romeria de la Victòria (2 Jul). 🌐 alcudia mallorca.com

The delightful town of Alcúdia, surrounded by 14th-century walls, lies at the base of the peninsula separating Pollença Bay from Alcúdia Bay. Originally, this was a Phoenician settlement. Having conquered the island, the Romans built a town here, called Pollentia, which from the 2nd century was the capital of the island. In 456, it was destroyed by the Vandals. Around the year 800, Moors built their fortress here, naming it *Al-Kudia* (On the Hill). After the Reconquest, Alcúdia prospered as a trading centre well into the 19th century. The beautifully restored old town

Town hall window in Alcúdia

is entered through the handsome **Porta de Moll** gate. The Gothic church of **Sant Jaume** at the centre is 13th-century. The most interesting sight is the **Museu Monogràfic**, which displays objects from Roman and Phoenician times.

On the outskirts of town, along the road to Port d'Alcúdia, is the **Oratori de Santa Anna**. Built in the early 13th century, it is one of the oldest Mallorcan sanctuaries. Nearby are the remains of a first-century BC **Roman theatre** – this is the smallest Roman theatre to have survived in Spain.

Environs

Port d'Alcúdia, 2 km (1 mile) south of the town, is the most popular tourist destination on Mallorca's northeast shores. It has a lovely sandy beach, a marina and a harbour as well as hotels, restaurants and clubs. The road to Es Mal Pas brings you to **Cap des Pinar** where, in 1599, Philip II erected a watchtower, Torre Major. A branch road leads to the **Ermita de la Victòria**. It has a revered 15th-century wooden statue of Victoria, Alcúdia's patron saint.

🏛 **Museu Monogràfic**
Carrer de Sant Jaume 30. **Tel** 971 547 004. **Open** July–Sep: 9:30am–8:30pm Tue–Fri (10am–3:30pm Oct–Jun), 10am–2pm Sat & Sun. 🖼

Lighthouse on Cap de Formentor

The marshes of Parc Natural de S'Albufera, crisscrossed with canals

㉒ Parc Natural de S'Albufera

Tel 971 892 250. **Open** 9am–6pm daily (to 5pm Oct–Mar); Reception Centre (Sa Roca): 9am–4pm daily.

The wetland south of Port d'Alcúdia, occupying the shores of Lake Grande up to C'an Picafort, was once a swamp. Most of it was drained in the 1860s, but a portion remains, which in 1985 become the Parc Natural de S'Albufera. The marshes can be explored on foot, following the marked trails. A major conservation project, this is an excellent place for observing over 200 species of birds, including grey and purple herons, summer osprey and Eleonora's falcon. The park reception is in **Sa Roca** where you can obtain a free map and a list of some of the park's birds.

㉓ Muro

13 km (8 miles) east of Inca.
🚌 7,000. 🚌 🅿 Sun. 🎪 Revelta de Sant Antoni Abat (16–17 Jan).
🌐 ajmuro.net

The agricultural town of Muro is a pleasant, sleepy place, situated at the centre of the plain, surrounded by cultivated fields. It is full of old mansions built by rich landowners, which give the town its unique charm. Each year on January 16 and 17, Muro is the scene of the *Revelta i Beneides de Sant Antoni*

Baroque cartouche from the Museu Etnològic de Muro

Abat – a big fiesta on the eve of St Antoni's day. The town's inhabitants and visitors gather around bonfires, drinking wine and eating sausages and *espinagades* – delicious pies made with eels caught in the S'Albufera marshes.

The town is dominated by the church of **Sant Joan Baptista**, remodelled around 1530. This large structure, built in the Catalan-Gothic style, features colourful stained-glass windows and a beautiful rose window on the façade. The interior includes Baroque furnishings and a vast main altarpiece. Adjacent to the church is a huge, seven-storey belfry that once served as a watchtower. The view from the top can be stunning and encompasses all of the surrounding area.

The **Convent des Mínims** and the church of **Santa Ana** are in Plaça de José Antonio Primo de Rivera, once the venue for bullfights. Nearby is the **Museu Etnològic de Muro**, which is situated in an old mansion house. Here, you can see a collection of local furniture, folk costumes, agricultural tools and a series of workshops including a blacksmith's and a cobbler's. The museum also has a collection of *siurells* – whistles.

Environs

Some 11 km (7 miles) east of Muro, on Badia d'Alcúdia, adjacent to the Parc Natural

de S'Albufera, is the sandy beach of **Platja de Muro** with its stone-pines growing amid the dunes. About 3 km (2 miles) north is **Sa Pobla**, which has a lovely 17th-century Baroque church. The town's main square, Plaça Constitució, hosts a busy Sunday market, selling mainly agricultural produce. **Santa Margalida**, situated 5 km (3 miles) southeast, has a history reaching back to Roman times. The views of the mountains and plain are outstanding from here.

🏛 **Museu Etnològic de Muro**
Carrer Major 15. **Tel** 971 860 647.
Open 10am–3pm Mon–Sat; 10am–2pm Sun, also 5–8pm Thu.
Closed Aug.

Multistorey altarpiece in Muro's Sant Joan Baptista

㉔ Sineu

30 km (19 miles) northeast of Palma.
🚌 3,600. 🚌 🅿 Wed. 🎪 Fira Maig (24 Apr).

Sineu is one of the most interesting agricultural towns of the central Es Pla plain and has a rich history. Attracted by its strategic position, at the very heart of the island, Jaume II built his **palace** here. King Sancho came here to benefit from the fresh air, his choice confirming the importance of the town. Later, Jaume III slept here the night before the battle of Llucmajor, in which he was killed fighting the army of Pedro of Aragón. Today, the former palace is occupied by an order of nuns that is known as the *monges del palau* (sisters of the palace).

Adjacent to the former royal residence stands the biggest parish church on the island, **Santa Maria de Sineu**. This Gothic structure was built in 1248 and remodelled in the 16th century. The church has an important collection of Medieval ceramics that can be viewed in the adjacent rectory on Wednesdays. In front of the church, in Plaça de Sant Marcos, stands a statue of a winged lion – the symbol of St Mark the Apostle, the patron saint of the town.

In the neighbouring Sa Plaça square are two excellent restaurants serving traditional Mallorcan cuisine: the Celler Ca'n Font and the Celler Es Grop.

At one time, the Inca–Artà railway line passed through the town. Now, the former station building, dating from 1879, houses a restaurant. Wednesday's market is one of the biggest agricultural fairs in Mallorca and sells local produce and livestock.

Environs

About 4 km (2 miles) north, near the road to Llubia, are the ruins of a Talayotic structure.

Monumental church in Petra, towering over the neighbourhood

㉕ Petra

50 km (31 miles) east of Palma.
🚗 2,900. 🚌 🚏 Wed. ♨ Santa Pràxedes (21 Jul), Festa de Bunyols (30 Oct). 🌐 **visitpetramallorca.com**

Stained-glass window in Santa Maria de Sineu

This small town is the birthplace of Junipero Serra. Aged 54, the Franciscan monk travelled to America and Mexico, and after a series of arduous journeys on foot, founded missions in California. The old houses lining the labyrinth of narrow alleys have changed little since Serra's time here. The town makes the most of its famous son and all places associated with Junipero Serra are well marked. These include **Casa Natal Fray Junipero Serra**, a humble building in Carrer Barracar Alt, where Serra was born. Next to this is a small but interesting **museum**, opened in 1955. The exhibition is devoted to his life and work and includes wooden models of the nine American missions established by Serra, as well as a range of memorabilia. At the end of the street in which the Serra family house stands, on the outskirts of town, is the 17th-century monastery of **Sant Bernat**, which has a statue of Serra standing in front of it. The Majolica panels down a side street next to the monastery are a gift from grateful Californians and pay tribute to the famous monk's many achievements.

Environs

Some 7 km (4 miles) west lies the small town of **Sant Joan**. Its 13th-century parish church, remodelled in the 15th and 18th centuries, acquired its present form in the 1930s. If there is time, head for the Santuari de la Mare de Déu de la Consolació, standing on the outskirts of town. Built during the Reconquest period and restored in 1966, it is now a place of pilgrimage.

Ariany, 4 km (2 miles) to the north, is a small agricultural town. Famous during the days of Jaume I, it became the region's capital in 1982. Its houses are dwarfed by the high tower of the Neo-Romanesque church.

🏛 **Museu y Casa Natal Fray Junipero Serra**
C/Barracar Alt 6–8. **Tel** 971 561 149.
Open by appointment only.

Junipero Serra

Junipero Serra was born in Petra in 1713 and played an important role in the history of the Spanish colonization of North America. In 1749, he left on a mission to Mexico, and later travelled to California, where he established nine missions and sought to convert the native Indians to Christianity. Some of Serra's missions prospered after his death and became the cities of San Diego, Santa Barbara, Los Angeles and San Francisco. He died in 1784 and was beatified in 1988.

Statue of Junipero Serra in Palma

The medieval Castell de Capdepera

❷❻ Artà

🚍 🚌 Wed. 🎭 San Antonio (12–13 Jun), Sa Fira (2nd Sun in Sep).

This hilltop town was built on the site of an Arab stronghold; its name is derived from the Arabic word *jertan* (garden). Much of its medieval walls and fortifications have survived to this day.

The town's most interesting structure is the hilltop **Santuari de Sant Salvador**. It can be reached from the mid-13th-century parish church of **Transfiguració del Senyor** via steps (actually a Way of the Cross) shaded by a line of cypresses.

Madonna in Santuari de Sant Salvador, Artà

The chapel and its surrounding walls were built during 1825–32. It contains a revered 17th-century statue of the Virgin with Child. The courtyard affords a lovely view of the town's rooftops.

Environs
Ses Païsses, a short way to the south, is a 3,000-year-old Bronze Age settlement. The remains include fragments of the defensive walls and a huge watchtower. Some of the stone blocks weigh about eight tons. The archaeological findings from this site can be seen in Artà's regional museum. The **Ermita de Betlem**, about 7 km (4 miles) to the north, is built on a hill. Established in 1805, the tiny church has a number of primitive frescoes.

❷❼ Capdepera

🚍 🚌 Wed. 🎭 Fiesta Nostra Senyora d'Esperança (18 Dec).

Towering above the town is the **Castell de Capdepera,** which was built in the 14th century to defend the coast against pirates. At the highest point of the castle stands the Gothic church of **Nostra Senyora d'Esperança**. The outside stairs lead to a flat roof from which there is a nice view of the town's terracotta roofscape.

Environs
The **Coves d'Artà**, regarded as one of Mallorca's wonders, are situated some 6 km (4 miles) to the south. Two thousand Arabs were found hiding here by Jaume I during the Reconquest. In the 19th century, the caves were studied by a French geologist and became popular with tourists. Jules Verne is said to have written *Journey to the Centre of the Earth* after visiting.

🏰 **Castell de Capdepera**
Tel 971 556 479. **Open** 9am–8pm daily (mid-Oct– mid-Mar: to 5pm). 🎭

🕳 **Coves d'Artà**
Canyamel, Capdepera. **Tel** 971 841 293. **Open** Apr– Jun & Oct: 10am–6pm; Jul– Sep: 10am–7pm; Nov–Mar: 10am–5pm. **Closed** 1 Jan, 25 Dec. 🎭 🎥 only.
🌐 cuevasdearta.com

❷❽ Cala Rajada

ℹ️ Via Mallorca 36, 971 819 467.

A seaside resort and bay, Cala Rajada is famous for its beautiful beaches shaded by a stone-pine forest. The rocky coast surrounding it is regarded as one of the most attractive in this part of Mallorca. Until recently this was just a small fishing village – only the old jetty, which is now used by pleasure boats and sailing yachts, remains.

Above the Cala Gat bay stands **Sa Torre Cega**, a stately home named after its owner, Juan March, a banker, tobacco merchant and patron of the arts. Both this palace and its lovely gardens, which have about 40 sculptures by various Spanish artists, are open to visitors (by prior appointment).

Environs
From Cala Rajada, it is worth taking a 2-km (1-mile) walk to **Cap de Capdepera**, the easternmost headland of Mallorca. The nearby **Platja de Canyamel** is a small, quiet resort with lovely sandy beaches. There is also a local golf course, and the former watchtower Torre de Canyamel houses a restaurant specializing in tasty Mallorcan cuisine.

🏛 **Sa Torre Cega**
C/Joan March 2. **Tel** 689 027 353. 🕐 **Closed** Mon–Tue & Dec–Jan.

Fishing boat leaving Cala Rajada's harbour

Mallorca's Caves

A handful of the nearly 200 limestone caves found in Mallorca are open to the public as part of guided tours. Many were known by the locals for hundreds of years and they once provided shelter for the early settlers, or served as hiding places from marauding pirates, dens for smugglers or religious sanctuaries. In the 19th century Archduke Ludwig Salvator began to take an interest in them and recruited a French geologist, Edouard Martel, to study them. In 1896 Martel rediscovered the Coves d'Artà. He was amazed by their size (some are the size of a cathedral) and the large number of stalactites and stalagmites.

Underground lakes that can be found in many caves are an additional attraction to visitors. Caves with lakes have excellent acoustics and visitors are usually entertained with short concerts performed by musicians seated in boats.

Dripstones can assume the most fantastic forms. To emphasize their beauty, they are often illuminated by coloured lights.

Los Encinares
Pollença
Ma-10
Cova
de Sant Martí
Alcúdia
Sóller
Cova de
Sant Antoni
Coves de
Campanet
Ma-12
Artà
Ma-11
S'Avenc
de Son Pou
Coves d'Artà
Ma-10
Coves de
Génova
Ma-13
Coves
d'es Hams
Andratx
Palma
Manacor
Ma-15
Cova de la
Mare de Déu
Coves
des Pirata
Coves
del Drac
Ma-17
Ma-14
Cova
del Pilar
Santanyí

0 km   10
0 miles   10

Excursion routes in the caves are arranged so that everybody can see the chambers easily. There are steps and walkways provided in some places.

Entrances to the caves are hidden in the rock faces. Some of them are overgrown by dense macchia; others are situated up high, like the Coves d'Artà, where steps have been built to provide easy access for tourists.

Sandy beach of Cala Millor, one of Mallorca's most popular spots

❷❾ Cala Millor

📠 ℹ️ Passeig Maritim, 971 585 864.

Cala Millor is one of the most popular resorts on the east coast of Mallorca. The first hotels began to appear here as early as the 1930s, but the real tourist invasion did not start until the 1980s. Similar to neighbouring Cala Bona and Sa Coma, Cala Millor has many beautiful beaches; the main one is 1.8 km (1 mile) long and is quite magnificent. As you would expect, the resort has plenty of bars, restaurants and clubs.

Environs
Some 4 km (2 miles) northwest of Cala Millor is **Son Servera**. Not the prettiest of Mallorcan agricultural towns, its prime feature is the church, which was begun in 1905 by Joan Rubió, a disciple of Antoni Gaudí, and which remains unfinished to this day.

❸⓪ Porto Cristo

📠 ℹ️ Pl de l'Aljub s/n, 971 849 126.
🌐 visitmanacor.com

The ancient fishing port of Porto Cristo is situated at the end of a long bay, where the El Rivet flows into the sea. Today it is a pleasant family resort, but as early as the 13th century this was a seaport for the inland town of Manacor. As the best sheltered harbour on the eastern coast of Mallorca it was also an important naval base, and the lighthouse dates back to 1851. During the Spanish Civil War, Republicans landed here with the intention of taking over the island from General Franco's forces. Despite initial successes, the attack was repelled.

Accessible from the esplanade that takes you along the bay are the spectacular White Caves, which were inhabited by fishermen until the end of the 19th century.

Porto Cristo is one of the few places on the eastern coast of Mallorca where you can find last-minute hotel accommodation during the high season. Among its attractions is the sandy beach.

Environs
Some 2 km (1 mile) south of Porto Cristo are the **Coves del Drac**. The "Dragon's Caves" are considered one of Mallorca's natural treasures. Although they have been known for centuries, they remained unexplored until 1896. The caves feature an attractive array of dripstones, as well as the island's largest underground lake, 177 m (580 ft) long, 40 m (131 ft) wide and more than 30 m (98 ft) deep. A ride by boat under the stalactite vault is an unforgettable experience. Visits feature a 10-minute concert by a string quartet.

The **Coves d'es Hams**, 2 km (1 mile) to the east, derive their name from the hook-shaped stalactites (*hams*) found here. Boatloads of floating musicians on the underground lake produce an unusual musical ambience.

🎵 **Coves del Drac**
Tel 971 820 753. **Open** Apr–Oct: 10am–5pm daily; Nov–Mar: 10:45am–noon & 2–3:30pm daily. 🔗
🌐 cuevasdeldrach.com

🎵 **Coves dels Hams**
Tel 971 820 988. **Open** daily. Apr–Jun & 1–15 Nov: 10am–4:30pm, Jul–Oct: to 5pm, 16 Nov–Mar: to 4pm. 🔗
🔗 🌐 cuevas-hams.com

Yachting harbour at the end of Porto Cristo bay

For hotels and restaurants in this region see pp148–50 and pp155–9

㉛ Manacor

50,000. Pl Ramon Llull s/n, 971 847 241. **visitmanacor.com**

Manacor is Mallorca's second-largest town and boasts a centuries-long tradition of handicraft. It produces furniture and ceramics, including the famous Mallorcan black porcelain, but it is most famous for its simulated pearls. The town is also known for the local speciality – *sobrasada de cerdo negro* – spicy sausage, and sweets called *sospiros* (sighs).

Places worth visiting in Manacor include the church of **Nostra Senyora dels Dolors** in Plaça del Rector Rubi, built in the late 19th century on the site of a former mosque. Its lofty clock tower, resembling a minaret, is a town landmark. The most notable features of the church's interior are the vast wooden door and a figure of the crucified Christ, dressed in white robes, with long flowing hair.

Numerous shops in town sell simulated pearls, which have been produced here since 1890. In order to see them being made visit **Perlas Majorica**, a shop offering free demonstrations. Here, glass beads are covered with consecutive layers of a compound made of fish scale mixed with resin, dried, polished to a high shine and set in silver or gold.

Environs

Sant Llorenç des Cardassar is 9 km (6 miles) to the northeast. The local church has two figures of the Madonna. The first is a wooden statue dating from

Opulent interior of the Gothic church in Manacor

Music room in the stately home of Els Calderers

the 12th or 13th century. The second, carved in stone, was made in the 15th century, probably in France.

Perlas Majorica

Argenters (at the entrance of Manacor from Palma). **Tel** 971 550 900. **Open** 9:30am–6pm daily (Nov–Feb: to 5pm, Jun & Sep: to 7:30pm, Jul–Aug: to 8:30pm). **Closed** Sun, Dec & Jan.

Colourful fruit and vegetable stall in Vilafranca de Bonany

㉜ Vilafranca de Bonany

3,000. Wed. Festa de Meló (Sep).

The agricultural town of Vilafranca de Bonany lies on the road to Manacor. It is known for its colourful market stalls set along the highway. These sell peppers, sun-dried tomatoes and garlic, as well as fruit and vegetables grown in the local gardens. Also on offer are tiny doughnuts called *bunyelos*. The only historic building in town is the **Santa Barbara church** (1731–8).

Environs

About 2 km (1 mile) northeast, on top of Puig de Bonany (317 m/1,040 ft), is the **Ermita de Bonany** sanctuary. The monastery's stone cross was erected for Junipero Serra, who left from here in 1749 on a mission to California (*see p81*). The sanctuary is 17th century and was built as an act of thanksgiving for a good harvest – *bon any* or "good year". The modern church dates from 1925 and is entered via an imposing gate, decorated on top with ceramic tiles featuring portraits of St Paul and St Anthony. From the church forecourt you can see a splendid panorama of the central plain, Es Pla.

One kilometre (half a mile) northwest of Vilafranca de Bonany is **Els Calderers** – a landed estate established in the 17th century by the Veri family. The stately home is surrounded by fields and farm buildings. Today, parts of the estate are open to the public; these include the private chapel, the granary and the large kitchen. The rooms contain original furniture and are decorated with paintings, family photographs and *objets d'art*, all of which maintain the atmosphere of the former residence. The fire burning in the fireplace and the open piano give visitors the impression that the owners have only just stepped out.

Els Calderers

Tel 971 526 069. **Open** 10am–5:30pm daily. **elscalderers.com**

❸❸ Felanitx

🏙 18,000. 🚌 Sun. 🎭 Fiesta San Joan Pelós (24 Jun).

From a distance, the busy little town of Felanitx looks as though it is surrounded by a wall with many turrets. As you approach, it becomes apparent that these are windmills built on the outskirts of town. Felanitx is the birthplace of the outstanding medieval architect Guillem Sagrera (1380–1456) and the highly original 20th-century painter Miquel Barceló.

This small agricultural town has a fine **13th-century church**. Sant Miquel's magnificent Renaissance-Baroque façade, approached by steep stairs, hides a building erected in 1248. It is also worth visiting Felanitx to taste the locally produced *sobrasada de porc negre* – spicy pork sausage – and to buy some of the ceramics made here.

Environs

About 5 km (3 miles) south-east, on top of the 400-m-(1,312-ft-) high hill, are the ruins of Castell de Santueri, an Arab castle remodelled in the 14th century by the kings of Aragón. The view from the ruins is a magnificent panorama of the surrounding area. The Santuari de Sant Salvador stands 4 km (2 miles) east of Felanitx, on top of Puig de Sant Salvador, the highest mountain of the Serres de Llevant. Founded in the 14th century, and remodelled in the 18th

Huge façade of Felanitx's main church

Giant cactus in the Botanicactus garden, near Santanyí

century, the sanctuary is an important place of pilgrimage and there is a well-signed footpath between the castle and the sanctuary. The view includes the south-eastern coast of Mallorca.

❸❹ Santanyí

🏙 13,000.

This old town is full of stone houses built from the local honey-coloured sandstone. The same sandstone was used in the building of the cathedral in Palma and Castell Bellver.

One of the old town gates, **Sa Porta**, in Plaça Port is a reminder of medieval times when the town was an important fortress defending southeastern Mallorca, and surrounded by several walls. Towering over the town is the vast church of **Sant Andreu**. The interior of this 18th-century church features a huge Rococo organ brought here from a Dominican monastery in Palma.

Environs

North of town, on top of the Puig Gros hill stands a 16th-century chapel with a beautiful picture of the Madonna. The **Santuari de Consolació** is accessed via stone steps, which have been climbed for centuries by footsore and weary pilgrims. Some 5 km (3 miles) east of Santanyí is **Cala Figuera**, with an unspoiled fishing harbour set in a bay that resembles a fjord.

The adjacent and equally picturesque **Cala Santanyí** bay is situated at the end of a rocky canyon with steep banks, over-grown with trees. Here, rising from the sea, is the **Es Pontas rock**. Six kilometres (4 miles) east is the **Botanicactus**, a garden which has nearly 400 species of cacti.

Rocky coastline in the Parc Natural Mondragó

❸❺ Parc Natural Mondragó

8 km (5 miles) east of Santanyí. **Tel** 971 181 022. 🅿 by reservation (971 642 067). 🆆 balearsnatura.com

This relatively small, unspoiled area has wonderful footpaths and pretty country lanes and is an ideal destination for walking trips. The routes are marked and are generally easy-going. The coastline itself is rugged, but it is still possible to find small, sandy coves, the best of which are Mondragó, S'Amarador and Caló des Burgit. In the pine forest, which covers some of the park, there are small ponds and dunes.

❸ Ses Salines

ℹ️ Gabriel Roca, 971 656 073.

Ses Salines is a modest little town that is sometimes overlooked by visitors. It owes its origin, economy and name to the nearby saltworks. The **Salines de Llevant** are large salt lakes and marshes. This area is inhabited by numerous species of birds such as the spotted crane, marsh harrier, kestrel, warbler and hoopoe. During the migration season the marshes are visited by flocks of plover, avocet, tattler, godwit and osprey. There are many paths through the marshes, making them an excellent area for walking and cycling trips, particularly for birdwatchers, though the mosquitoes can be bothersome.

Environs
Cap de Ses Salines is 3 km (2 miles) south of Ses Salines. This is the southernmost promontory of Mallorca. The view from the lighthouse is magnificent and encompasses the entire south coast of the island.

Banys de Sant Joan de sa Font Santa lies 4 km (2 miles) northeast of Ses Salines. The local hot springs, with water temperatures rising as high as 38°C (100°F), have been known since the 15th century, when they were used to treat a variety of conditions, including leprosy. The local chapel dates from this period. The present bathhouse was built in 1845. Today, the waters are still believed to be beneficial and are used to treat rheumatism and a variety of respiratory ailments.

Campos, probably founded by the Romans, is situated 12 km (7 miles) from Ses Salines.

Sprawling across the flatlands, the town's central streets are lined with old houses. The Neo-Classical church of Sant Julià (1858–73) features a painting, *Sant Crist de la Paciència*, by the 17th-century Spanish master Bartolomé Esteban Murillo; the Gothic retable is the work of Gabriel Mògera. The church has a small parish museum. The former Torre de Can Cos, which once guarded the town against pirate attacks, became incorporated into the present town hall in 1649. Markets are held here every Thursday and Saturday.

Some 10 km (6 miles) to the north of Ses Salines is **Ermita de Sant Blas**, which has a restored 13th-century chapel.

Lighthouse at the Cap de Ses Salines headland

❼ Colònia de Sant Jordi

52 km (32 miles) east of Palma. ℹ️ Gabriel Roca, Ses Salines, 971 656 073.

The town of Colònia de Sant Jordi lies on the southern end of the island. It has a handful of modest hotels, a few restaurants, a pretty beach and an interesting harbour. Many people come here with the

Sa Ràpita beach, a favourite with windsurfers

sole purpose of catching a boat to nearby Cabrera Island (*see pp88–9*), which, according to Pliny, was the birthplace of the famous Carthaginian leader, Hannibal. The pleasure boats to Cabrera Island sail daily from May until mid-October.

The town's other main attraction is the nearby salt lake, **Salines de S'Avall**, from which huge quantities of salt are still extracted – the main source of the town's wealth.

Environs
One of Mallorca's most beautiful beaches is located 7 km (4 miles) to the north, in **Es Trenc**. This small but constantly developing resort is very popular with visitors to the southern coast of Mallorca. The 4-km (2-mile) stretch of beach can easily accommodate the large numbers of holidaymakers, and is not generally too busy.

Sa Ràpita is a small place near S'Estanyol de Migjorn. The local beach provides good conditions for windsurfing. In summer, the marina is also a popular place. The only historic remains are of the defence tower, which once guarded the coast against pirates. Equally beautiful beaches can be found to the south of Colònia de Sant Jordi. When they get too busy, try **Platja des ses Roquetes**.

🚢 **Excursions to Cabrera**
C/Explanada del Port. **Tel** 971 649 034.
w excursionsacabrera.es

Beach and harbour in Sa Ràpita, near Colònia de Sant Jordi

❸ Cabrera Island National Park

Cabrera ("goat island") lies just 18 km (11 miles) from mainland Mallorca. A rocky, bare place and virtually uninhabited, it nevertheless has a rich history. It served as a prison camp during the Napoleonic Wars and was used as a base by Barbary pirates. Since 1991, Cabrera Island, together with an archipelago of 157 sq km (60 sq miles), has been designated a national park. This protection extends not only to rare species of plants, but also includes the surrounding marine life.

Es Castell
The 14th-century castle is one of the few reminders of the island's past. A small museum close to the jetty includes a history of the island.

Cala Santa Maria
In the course of a few hours, you can see the shore areas surrounding the bay. Exploring the interior requires permission from the park staff.

Asteriscus aquaticus
Though this plant is found on all the islands of the archipelago, Cabrera is home to some rare native plant species.

Cap de N'Ensiola
At the island's southwest tip is a lighthouse that can be reached via a winding road. Permission for this must be obtained from the park's office in Palma.

Es Po
Caserio Cabrera
Can Felj

KEY

① **A memorial** was built for the French soldiers abandoned on Cabrera by the Spanish during the Napoleonic Wars. Of the 9,000 prisoners, only 4,000 survived.

0 kilometres 1
0 miles 1

Eleonora's Falcon
This rare species is
strictly protected.
In 1974, there
were only nine
nesting pairs;
now there are
about 30.

Na Pobre

Illa Plana

Illa Conejera

On Foradada
The northernmost rocky island of the
archipelago has a lone lighthouse and
a lighthouse keeper's cottage.

Illa Cabrera

Illa Redona

Sa Cova Blava
The 20-m- (66-ft-) high "Blue Grotto"
owes its name to the colour of
light that is reflected from the
water, which illuminates the
cave's walls. The grotto can be
seen as part of a boat trip.

L'Olla
In an effort to protect
the landscape and
surrounding waters,
this area is closed to
the public.

Cas Garriuer

Key

= Road

••• Footpath

For keys to symbols *see back flap*

Sunday market in Llucmajor

⑳ Llucmajor

🏘 37,000. 🚌 🛒 Wed, Fri & Sun.
🌐 visitllucmajor.com

Formerly the main town of the southern region, Llucmajor has long been associated with Mallorca's shoemaking industry and had a thriving market in medieval times. It was just outside Llucmajor's walls, in 1349, that Pedro IV of Aragón killed the last king of independent Mallorca, Jaume III. The monument standing at the end of Passeig de Jaume III commemorates the event.

The **town hall**, built in 1882, is in the main square. Nearby is the 18th-century church of **San Miquel**, built over a 14th-century church. The most prized historic building in town is the Franciscan **Església Conventual de Sant Bonaventura**. This 17th-century church contains many precious historic objects, including an impressive altarpiece (1597) painted by Gaspar Oms.

⑳ Capocorb Vell

📞 Tel 971 180 155.
Open 10am–5pm Fri–Wed. 🚗
🌐 talaiotscapocorbvell.com

Mallorca has fewer prehistoric remains than Menorca, but this Talayotic settlement on a rocky plateau on the southern coast of the island

is well worth visiting. The settlement was probably established around 1000 BC. Originally, it consisted of five *talayots* (stone structures resembling towers, covered with a wooden roof) and 28 smaller dwellings. It is worth taking a closer look at the remains of the Cyclopean walls, reaching 4 m (13 ft) in places, which would have served as protection for this ancient village. Not much is known about the inhabitants of the settlement, and the function of some of the rooms is unclear. The narrow underground chamber, for instance, is too small to be used for living quarters and may have served as a ritual site. A free leaflet, in English, provides more information on these fascinating remains and is available at the site entrance.

The megaliths scattered through this quiet area, amid fields and fruit trees, were declared a cultural heritage site as early as 1931. Apart from a restaurant and a small bar, there are few other traces of modern civilization here.

Environs
Some 5 km (3 miles) southeast of Capocorb Vell lies **Cala Pi**. This is a small cove with an enticing sand beach. Several

Ruins of the prehistoric settlement in Capocorb Vell

luxurious villas have sprung up around here, well hidden behind pine trees. During the high season, many yachts drop anchor here. The area is dominated by a watchtower (1659), which provides views of the entire Badia de Palma. About 7 km (4 miles) to the south is **Cap Blanc**, which has a lighthouse. From here there is also a splendid view over the coast towards Cabrera Island. A large section of the peninsula is used for military purposes, and it is therefore important not to stray from the route that leads to the lighthouse.

Tree-shaded courtyard of the church at Puig de Randa

⑳ Puig de Randa

8 km (5 miles) northeast of Llucmajor.
ℹ Santuari de Nostra Senyora de Cura: 971 660 994.

In the middle of the fertile plains of Es Pla rises the distinctive Puig de Randa hill (549 m/1,800 ft), which provides stunning views over the whole of the island. Nobleman-turned-monk Ramon Llull founded a hermitage on top of this hill in the 13th century, and it was here that he trained Catholic missionaries bound for Africa and Asia. Although nothing remains of the original building, Llull's legacy has ensured that the site is an important place for Catholics.

The monastery (the oldest part of which dates from 1668) is a popular destination for pilgrimages, particularly those associated with the blessing of the crops –

3/30/2023

LEFORT YVONNE

Item Number: 31901062976990

Hold Shelf Slip

Benedición de los Frutos –
on the 4th Sunday after Easter.

Tucked under a steep cliff
face, **Santuari de Nostra
Senyora de Gràcia** is the first
of the religious buildings you
come to. The interior of the
chapel is decorated with
beautiful majolica tiles. A
little further up the hill is
the16th-century **Santuari
de Sant Honorat**. This hermitage houses a courtyard that
is filled with ancient trees.
The passage to the church is
decorated with tiles depicting
the sanctuary's history.

On the summit is the
**Santuari de Nostra Senyora
de Cura**, which is on the site
where Llull once lived. The
gate in the wall surrounding
the monastery is 17th-century
and opens onto a court-
yard built of typical golden
Mallorcan sandstone. The
monastery, much of which
is fairly modern, houses a
library and a study centre.
The stained-glass windows
of the church depict the
most important moments
of Llull's life.

🕙 Algaida

🚌 🚭 Fri. 🎨 Sant Honorat (16 Jan),
Sant Jaume (25 Jul).

Most people pass through
the outskirts of this small town
on their way to Puig de Randa.
If you like churches, however,
it is worth stopping here in
order to visit the Gothic church
of **Sant Pere i Sant Pau**, with
its ornamental gargoyles.

Ceramic sign of Ca'n Gordiola, advertised
outside a Palma shop

One of several water slides in Aqualand El Arenal

Environs
The odd-looking castle
on the road from Palma to
Manacor dates from the 1960s
and houses **Ca'n Gordiola**, a
glassworks, museum and
shop. Here, you can see skilled
glass-blowers producing the
pale blue and green glass that
has been produced on the
island for hundreds of years.
On the first floor is a museum
exhibiting items collected by
several generations of the
Gordiola family.

Some 9 km (6 miles) to the
east is **Montuïri**. The town,
built on a hill, is famous for its
agricultural produce. Nineteen
of the original 24 windmills
still stand as testimony to
the town's former glory. Just
outside Montuïri, on the road
that leads to Pina, is one of the
best- preserved Mallorcan
Talayotic remains – **Son Fornés**.
This prehistoric settlement has
two *talayots* and includes nine
dwellings, which were used
up until Roman times.

🕒 S'Arenal

📧 **ℹ** C/Terral 23. **Tel** 971 669 162.
🚭 Thu.

A little to the east of Palma,
S'Arenal offers several kilometres
of sandy beaches. A tree-lined
boulevard runs along the
shore, with bars, restaurants,
nightclubs and shops. A series
of stainless-steel beach bars
stretches along the coast. These
balnearios are numbered: No. 1
is near the harbour, No. 15 is
by the Ca'n Pastilla marina (a
miniature "tourist train" travels
to the marina). In peak season,
the resort's narrow alleys
throb with life, day and night.
S'Arenal's harbour provides
mooring places for yachts.
On the outskirts of town is
Aqualand El Arenal, a children's
paradise of pools, water slides
and playgrounds.

🎢 **Aqualand El Arenal**
S'Arenal. **Tel** 971 440 000. **Open** May &
Jun & Sep 10am–5pm daily; Jul & Aug:
10am–6pm daily. 🅿 🌐 **aqualand.es**

Ramon Llull

This prominent Mallorcan was born in Palma to a
noble family around 1232. During his youth he
lived life to excess. Quite why he changed his
ways is not known, though legends abound.
One story has it that he abandoned court life
after seeing a vision of the crucified Christ.
At the age of 30 he became a monk and
devoted the rest of his days to the Catholic
faith. He became a religious scholar, founded
a missionary school and wrote over 260 works
of theology, philosophy, physics, chemistry
and warfare. During the final 30 years of his
life, he travelled around Europe, Asia and
Africa. He is believed to have been stoned
to death in Algeria in 1315.

Statue of Ramon
Llull in Palma

Mallorca's Beaches

Mallorca has scores of beaches. The best are around Badia de Palma (*see p63*) and to the north and north-east of the island. These are great for swimming and sunbathing and are very popular during the peak season. Some of the island's best beaches have been incorporated into larger resorts and include restaurants, fun parks, water sports and beachside bars. It is still possible to find more secluded beaches and coves, however, though these tend to have fewer facilities and may be difficult to reach.

Cala Tuent
A wide and arching shingle and pebble beach in a dramatic location, with the mountains crowding in on all sides.

Cala Deià
At the end of a delightful, lightly forested gulch, this narrow pebbly beach, in a hoop-shaped cove, boasts crystal-clear waters and a great beach bar and restaurant.

Andratx

Sóller

Ma-11

Ma-10

Ma-13

Palma

Sant Elm
One of the most appealing resorts on the island, pocket-sized Sant Elm enjoys a superb setting on Mallorca's western coast, and it boasts a sweet and compact sandy beach.

Key

▬ Major road

Port de Pollença
Curving round the bay, this sandy beach shelves gently into the ocean, making it ideal for children. Be sure to bring a bucket and spade for sand-castle building.

Port d'Alcúdia
Northern Mallorca's busiest resort also holds its finest beach, a long and immaculately maintained stretch of golden sand.

0 km   10

0 miles   10

Es Trenc
Mallorcans love this beach – a long and wide sandy strand where foreign tourists rarely venture – with the baking salt pans shimmering behind.

MENORCA

Menorca is the second largest of the Balearic Islands and has low-key, family-friendly resorts and nearly as many beaches as Mallorca and Ibiza combined. Situated furthest from the mainland, it is one of the quieter islands and has escaped most of the side-effects of package holidays. Its small towns and villages appear to be havens of tranquillity, even at the peak of the season.

Travelling across Menorca, the variations in landscape are perhaps less obvious than those of Mallorca. The changes are more gradual, as red-soil and sandstone farmlands become pine-clad ravines, and small, sheltered coves alternate with steep, rocky shores.

Most of the Balearic Islands' megalithic monuments from the Talayotic period are found on this island, including a good number of the cone-shaped towers *(talayots)* which give the period its name. As with the other islands, Menorca has had its share of visiting conquerors, including the Greeks, the Romans and, during medieval times, the Arabs, who defended the island until 1287. During the 18th century, the island was ruled by the English and French in turn, before becoming a Republican stronghold during the Spanish Civil War.

The two oldest and largest towns in Menorca are Maó and Ciutadella; both are full of historic buildings. The island's capital, Maó (often referred to by its Spanish name of Mahón), is the best natural harbour in this part of the Mediterranean. Ciutadella, Menorca's former capital, is situated on the northwestern end of the island and also has a natural harbour. When travelling around Menorca you can appreciate the charm of the island's unhurried lifestyle. Its inhabitants are attached to their traditions and customs – for instance, unlike the rest of Spain, they prefer local gin to wine. Fiesta celebrations are particularly lively.

Traditional folk dancers in Maó accompanied by live music

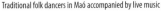
Brilliant blue waters at Cala Macarella, Menorca

Exploring Menorca

Menorca is sometimes referred to by the locals, jokingly, as "the bit between Maó and Ciutadella". The island mainly attracts those looking for peace and relaxation, such as older visitors and families with young children, who wish to avoid the late-night clubs and bars found elsewhere in the Balearic Islands. The island, proclaimed a biosphere reserve by UNESCO, is also a favourite with nature lovers. It has more than 70 beaches – the south has stretches of white sand, while the north has several inlets. In Fornells you can savour *caldereta de llagosta* – a delicious lobster stew for which the island is famous. Those who enjoy historic monuments can also find much of interest. The vast numbers of Talayotic structures, and the palaces and churches of Ciutadella and Maó, are all worth visiting. One way to explore the island is on horseback.

Locator Map

Lighthouse at Cap d'Artrutx

Getting There

The best way to travel to Menorca is by air. During the high season there are flights from many European countries and other regions of Spain. The most reliable way to travel out of season is via Palma or Barcelona. The airport is near Maó and has good transport links with major towns on the island. You can also travel to Menorca by ferry from Palma or Barcelona. The main road on the island connects Maó with Ciutadella. Minor roads branch from it, running towards the northern and southern coasts. There are no problems reaching large towns and resorts, but some small, attractive places maybe difficult to get to. It is best to travel around the island by hire car, as some of the smaller towns and villages have no bus service.

Sights at a Glance

1. *Maó pp98–101*
2. Es Grau
3. Es Castell
4. Sant Lluís
5. Binibeca Vell
6. Cales Coves
7. Cala en Porter
8. Alaior
9. Es Mercadal
10. Fornells
11. Cap de Cavalleria
12. Es Migjorn Gran
13. Ferreries
14. Santa Galdana
16. *Ciutadella pp112–15*

Tours

15. Western Coast of Menorca

Key

— Major road

≡ Minor road

— Scenic route

Beach and boats at anchor in Cala Binibeca

a des
orros

11 CAP DE CAVALLERIA

Punta de
Na Guillemassa

Cala
Tirant

10 FORNELLS

a
nda

Ses Salines

Son Parc

S'Arenal
d'en Castell

Port d'Addaia

Me15

Me7

Me9

Cap de Favàritx

ES MERCADAL

9

Me1

Monte Toro

Parc
Natural
S'Albufera

Illa d'En
Colom

Me18

M16

ES MIGJORN
GRAN

S'Albufera

2 ES GRAU

ALAIOR **8**

Me7

Torralba
d'en Salord

Serra Morena

Sa Mesquida

t Tomàs

Talatí de Dalt

Me1

Es Murtar

on Bou

Torre d'en
Galmés

Sant Antoni

Sant Antoni

MAÓ **1**

Cala Llonga

3 ES CASTELL

CALA EN PORTER **7**

Me12

Sant Climent

Trepucó

La Mola

6 CALES COVES

Els Canutells

4 SANT LLUÍS

Me8

S'Algar

Cala
Binisafúller

Cala d'Alcaufar

5 BINIBECA
VELL

Cala
Binibeca

Punta Prima

Illa de l'Aire

0 kilometres   3

0 miles   3

Taula and *talayot* in Trepucó,
Menorca's most famous
megalithic settlement

For keys to symbols *see back flap*

❶ Maó

In some respects, Maó (or Mahón in Spanish) is like a small, provincial town. A pretty place, it has a population of almost 30,000 and lies on the steep, southern shore of an inlet that is one of the best natural harbours in the world. The remains of the old city walls, several beautiful churches, colourful Spanish mansions and Georgian town houses make it a fascinating place to explore. At the same time, it is the island's capital and is a city of culture – its Teatre Principal was the first opera house in Spain when it opened in 1829.

Exploring Maó

When exploring Maó, it is best to start from Plaça d'Espanya. Here, and around the neighbouring squares, are the town's main historic buildings. The whole district is dominated by the vast Baroque church of **Santa Maria**. For most people, however, the real pleasure is in strolling along the narrow alleys of old Maó and soaking up its unique atmosphere. Some of Maó's streets have restricted car access, turning them into virtual pedestrian precincts. Stopping for a rest in one of the numerous cafés is an experience to savour.

Plaça Espanya, with the Baroque church of Santa Maria in the background

🏛 Església del Carme

Plaça Carme.

This imposing Baroque church began life as a Carmelite convent in 1751. In 1835, the convent was confiscated by the State, and the building was substantially restored in 1941 after being damaged during the Spanish Civil War. The cavernous interior of the former church, one of the biggest in Maó, is preserved in Neo-Classical style, but despite its proportions it gives an impression of emptiness.

The complex, mostly closed to visitors, occupies the vast quarter between Plaça Carme and Plaça de la Miranda. The square behind the monastery offers a beautiful view over the harbour.

🏛 Mercat Sa Plaça Carme

Plaça Carme. **Open** 9am–9pm Mon–Sat.

Maó's famous town market (Mercat) takes place in the deconsecrated cloisters adjoining the Església del Carme. The cool cloister has been turned into a picturesque fruit and vegetable market, where *queso Mahón*, one of Spain's most delicious cheeses, is much in evidence. Here, you can also buy meat and other food products, as well as souvenirs. The rows of market stalls set under the figures of the saints and other religious symbols provide a strange contrast.

🏛 Centre d'Art i d'Història Hernández Sanz

C/ Anuncivay 2. **Tel** 971 356 523.
Open 10am–1:30pm & 6–8pm Mon & Wed–Sat, 10am–1:30pm Sun.

This museum is something of a hotch-potch. The ground floor displays the mansion to fine advantage, especially its Italianate murals; a further section traces the evolution of Maó as a port through a collection of vintage maps. The most interesting section, however, is devoted to British Menorca. Here, you'll find a sort of "speaking clock" of Menorcan words and phrases derived from the English language. Upstairs is devoted to 18th- and 19th-century Menorca, with cameos of islanders in traditional costume and temporary displays of modern, mostly local, art.

🏛 Plaça Espanya

Plaça Espanya is the central square of old Maó. A busy **fish market** occupies a circular bastion on the north side, offering countless varieties of fish, squid, shellfish and other seafood. From here, steps lead down to Maó's waterfront.

Fundació Teatre Principal

Costa d'en Deià 40. **Tel** 971 355 603.
W teatremao.com

Maó's theatre opened in 1829, and beats the Liceu in Barcelona and Teatro Real in Madrid to be Spain's first opera house. Built by the Italian singer and architect, Giovanni Palagi, it was often chosen by the big Spanish opera companies to premiere their Spanish tours. Today, it is used mainly as a cinema, but it also hosts some concerts and cultural events, including an annual musical festival in July and August and a week of opera in June and December.

Narrow alleys leading away from Maó's old centre

For hotels and restaurants in this region see pp150–51 and pp159–61

Façade of the Ajuntament opposite Església de Santa Maria

🏛 Santa Maria

Plaça Constitució. **Tel** 971 363 949. **Open** 8am & 7pm Mon–Sat; 8am, 11am, noon, 8:30pm Sun.

This church near the town hall was begun in 1287 on the site of a mosque, after the defeat of the Moors by Alfonso III. Rebuilt in a Neo-Classical style in the 18th century, it was remodelled several times after that. The large interior has retained much of its Catalan Gothic austerity and is devoid of any ornamentation, with only the transept and the vaults featuring rich Baroque decorations. The most striking elements are the Rococo main altarpiece and the vast organ, built in 1806 by the Swiss maker Johann Kyburz. It is a mighty piece with 3,120 pipes. Look out for the figures of trumpet-blowing angels.

🏛 Ajuntament

Plaça Constitució.

The town hall was built in 1613 and its façade remodelled in 1789, giving it a typically Spanish appearance. It features an orna-mental clock, presented to the town by Richard Kane, the first British governor of Menorca. Inside, the walls are lined with portraits of local notables, French and Spanish governors and, still hanging to this day, portraits of the British monarch George III alongside Queen Charlotte.

⚓ Harbour

The best way to arrive in Maó is by sea so that you catch your first sight of its magnificent natural harbour from the prow of a ship. Several centuries ago the famous Genoese admiral Andrea Doria concluded that June, July, August and Mahón were the best ports in the Mediterranean, by which he meant that outside the safe sailing season of the summer months, it was prudent to seek shelter here.

Today, the tranquil atmosphere of the harbour makes it difficult to imagine a time when this was once a vast British naval base.

Tours of the harbour in a glass-bottomed boat leave regularly from Maó and Es Castell.

Maó, perched on steep slopes, seen from the harbour

Mao

① Església del Carme
② Mercat Sa Plaça Carme
③ Centre d'Art i d'Història Hernández Sanz
④ Plaça Espanya
⑤ Teatre Principal
⑥ Santa Maria
⑦ Ajuntament
⑧ Harbour

Further Afield

Venturing outside Maó's centre involves a pleasant stroll along narrow avenues lined with quaint houses, and passing all the main historic sights of the town. The most interesting include the magnificent chapel of the Immaculate Conception in the church of **Sant Francesc**, built in an ornamental Spanish Baroque style. The **Museu de Menorca** is also well worth a visit if only for its extensive range of items from the Talayotic period. Another interesting place to see is the **gin distillery**.

For a longer hike, Maó is a good starting point for a walk along the coast – head north to **Cala Llonga**, or south right up to **Port de Malborough**.

Some of the Xoriguer Distillery's ancient gin-making equipment

🏭 Xoriguer Distillery

Moll de Ponent 91. **Tel** 971 362 197.
Gin production on the island is a legacy of the British occupation, although its local brands taste rather different to the ones currently produced in Britain. You can acquaint yourself with the gin distillation process by visiting the Xoriguer distillery, close to the harbour steps, which was founded in the 18th century.

As well as juniper, which is imported from the Pyrenees, gin contains a number of other aromatic herbs. Menorcan gin is sold only in Menorca and in a few restaurants in Mallorca.

The distillery also produces various liqueurs, including the *hierbas* that are believed by

Gobierno Militar, one of the most magnificent buildings in Maó

some to have therapeutic properties. All these drinks can be tasted on site, and of course bought in the shop.

⛪ Sant Francesc

Plaça d'es Monestir. **Open** 9:30am–12:30pm & 3:10–6pm Mon–Sat; 9am–12:30pm Sun.
The church of Sant Francesc, with its light-coloured Baroque façade (1719–92), stands at the end of **Carrer de Isabel II**.

The church's imposing interior has a vast, dark nave with a soaring Gothic altar at the end of it. The church's most outstanding feature is its octagonal chapel of the Immaculate Conception built in a fanciful Spanish Baroque style and decorated with stucco garlands of vine and roses. This is the most beautiful example of Baroque ornamentation in Menorca. Its creator is believed to be the talented painter, sculptor and architect Francesco Herrara.

Adjoining the south side of Sant Francesc is the monumental monastery, with an arcaded courtyard. Currently it houses the Museu de Menorca.

Ornament from Sant Francesc

🏛 Museu de Menorca

Avda Dr Guàrdia s/n. **Tel** 971 350 955. **Open** Jun–Sep: 10am–2pm & 6–8pm Tue–Sat, 10am–2pm Sun; Oct–May: 10am–2pm Tue–Sun (to 6pm Tue & Thu). **Closed** public hols. 🅿

This museum occupies the former cloisters of a Franciscan monastery. The collection includes works of art and archaeological relics. Many of the exhibits date from prehistoric times, and there is an extensive selection from the Talayotic period, as well as Roman, Byzantine and Arabic artifacts. Among the most interesting exhibits are a bronze statuette of a bull, Punic jewellery and some huge amphorae.

🏛 Gobierno Militar

Carrer de Isabel II. 🅿
The Military Governor's House and army headquarters are housed in one of Maó's most beautiful buildings. The palace was built in 1768, during the second British occupation. The building is still used by the army and can therefore be seen only from the outside, though the arcaded courtyard is well worth a peek.

🏛 Plaça Bastió

This small, irregular-shaped square has limited vehicle access, and serves as a good place for children to let off steam. Visitors who are fatigued by sightseeing often stop here for a rest.

Courtyard of the former Franciscan monastery

At the north corner of the square stands the medieval **Portal de Sant Roc** which is named after Saint Roch, a 14th-century hermit who was believed to be able to ward off the plague. Flanked by bulky twin turrets and a connecting arch, it is one of the few remaining fragments of Maó's medieval walls and was once the exit point from the city onto the road leading to Alaior. The fortifications did not stop Barbarossa from plundering the town, which he took in 1535, destroying most of the city's defences.

Portal de Sant Roc, viewed from the street leading to the town hall

⊞ Plaça Esplanada

Plaça Esplanada, with its flower-beds shaded by pine trees, is the biggest square in the city and was once used as a military parade ground. Now, it provides a popular meeting place for the locals, especially at the weekends. The ice-cream sellers and swings make it equally popular with local children. There is a market on Tuesday and Saturday mornings.

The square is flanked on three sides by low buildings, many of them housing bars, cafés and restaurants. The western section of the square features a huge Civil War memorial erected during the days of Franco. At the back of the square are army barracks built during the first British occupation of the island and now used by the Spanish Army.

Buses on their way to other island towns stop near here.

Mayonnaise

Following his victory over the British, Louis-François-Armand de Vignerot du Plessis, a cousin of Cardinal Richelieu, stopped at a local inn where he was served a tasty sauce. On his return to Paris, he introduced the sauce to the royal court, where the new garnish was an instant hit. Already known on the islands as *salsa mahonesa*, it became known in France as *mayonnaise*.

⊞ Ateneu Científic Literari i Artístic de Maó

Rovellada de Dalt 25. **Tel** 971 360 553. **Open** 4–9:30pm Mon–Fri. **Closed** Sat.

Menorca's Centre of Culture and Science has a collection of local ceramics, natural history exhibits (shells, birds, etc.), maps and charts, a library and permanent exhibitions of works by Spanish artists Pasqual Calbó, Màrius Verdaguer and Juan Vives Llull.

⬆ Sant Antoni Abat

Avinguda Vives Llull 15. **Tel** 971 350 636. **Open** 6–9pm Mon–Fri.

The 17th-century church of St Anthony was closed after it was pillaged during the Civil War. Following its restoration, it is now a venue for cultural events and exhibitions held by the Sa Nosta Foundation.

◪ Es Freginal

The park is a green oasis in the middle of town. During high season it serves as a venue for nightly cultural events. It also provides a stage for musicians taking part in the annual jazz festival.

Environs

About 2 km (1 mile) east of Maó, on the opposite side of the bay, are two swanky suburbs – **Sant Antoni** and **Cala Llonga**. A short distance further, at the end of the headland, stands the vast **La Mola** fortress, guarding the entrance to the inlet. During the days of Franco it was used as a jail for political prisoners.

Near Sant Antoni is the stately home of **Golden Farm** – a beautiful example of Menorcan Palladian architecture. Admiral Nelson is reputed to have first met his mistress Lady Hamilton here, although this is unlikely. Inside is a collection of mementos associated with the couple and an extensive library. The house is not open to the public.

Es Murtar, 9 km (6 miles) to the northeast, is a charming village of white houses standing at the foot of a rocky crag, on the shores of a bay. Neighbouring **Sa Mesquida** lies further along this rocky shoreline. The village is dominated by a well-preserved watchtower.

Plaça Esplanada, where locals come to relax

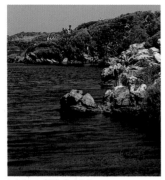

Lush shores of S'Albufera's Es Grau

❷ Es Grau

6 km (4 miles) north of Maó.

This small fishing village, fringed by dunes and pine forests, lies on the bay with a wide, sandy, horseshoe-shaped beach. Its safe shallow water is perfect for families with young children. At the weekend, the place becomes busier with day-trippers from Maó. From here you can take a cruise boat to nearby **Illa d'en Colom**, which has some nice beaches, the best of them being S'Arenal des Moro.

West of Es Grau is the fresh water lagoon, S'Albufera, the largest stretch of marshland on the island. The **Parc Natural S'Albufera**, where hunting and fishing are prohibited, is a UNESCO biosphere reserve and a magnificent area for hiking or birdwatching.

❸ Es Castell

2 km (1 mile) southeast of Maó.

Es Castell, once known as Villa Carlos, is a former garrison town. Originally called Georgetown, it was established in 1771 by the British and named for George III. The Georgian houses surrounding Plaça d'Esplanada serve as reminders of the British presence. One of the barrack buildings, Cuartel de Cala Corp, houses the small **Museu Militar de Menorca**, which has a collection of weapons and uniforms. Another sight is the parish church of **Nostra Senyora del Roser**.

🏛 Museu Militar de Menorca
Plaça Esplanada 19. **Tel** 971 362 100. 🖼

Environs
Illa Pinto was the site of the main British Navy base on the island, built in the 18th century. The local chapel is dedicated to Virgen del Camen, the patron saint of fishermen and the Spanish Navy. **Illa del Rei** is where Alfonso III landed in 1287 during the Reconquest. **Illa Plana**, the smallest island in the inlet, has the remains of a quarantine centre built in 1490 for those arriving at the island. **Illa Llazaret**, the largest of the islands, situated at the entrance to the inlet, was once a peninsula, until it was cut off from the mainland by the St George Canal in the early 1900s. On the nearby headland are the remains of **Fort San Felip**, a 16th-century fortress that once guarded the southern entrance to Maó's harbour. In its day, the fortress was one of the most highly advanced systems of defence in Europe and could house an entire garrison of soldiers underground. It was destroyed by the Spanish in 1782 and now only its ruins remain. On the opposite side of the bay, near the village of Sant Esteve, is **Fort Malborough**. Built by the British to back up Fort San Felip, it has since been restored and now

houses a museum and has a number of displays (some with loud sound effects) on Menorca's military history.

❹ Sant Lluís

5 km (3 miles) south of Maó.

This quaint little town, consisting of a square, a church and a few dozen whitewashed houses, was built by the French during the Seven Years' War (1756–63), as a quarters for Breton sailors. The French coat of arms on the church façade stands as a reminder of those days.

A windmill, **Moli de Dalt**, at the town's entrance, was built in 1762. Today, it is the only working windmill on the island and serves as the town's symbol. Next to it is a small museum with a collection of farm implements. The road into town bypasses the centre and heads towards the resorts of S'Algar, Cala d'Alcaufar, Punta Prima, Biniancolla, Binibeca Vell and Cap d'en Font.

French honeysuckle

Environs
Trepucó is a prehistoric site with a well-preserved *taula*. In the seaside villages of **S'Algar** and **Cala d'Alcaufar**, hotels stand side by side with fishermen's cottages. **Punta Prima** is the largest local resort. From here you have the view of the uninhabited island of **Illa de l'Aire**, with its lighthouse. West of town is a guard tower built by the Spaniards in the 18th century.

Colourful houses and apartments in Es Castell

Prehistoric Menorca

Menorca is exceptionally rich in megalithic structures. Most of the remains date from the Talayotic period – a civilization that flourished between 1500 and 123 BC. The period derives its name from the *talayots* (from *atalaya*, the Arabic word for a watchtower), the stone structures that are dotted around the island, mostly in former settlements. There are various theories as to what their original purpose was – they may have been used as defensive towers, burial sites or storehouses.

Huge *talayot* in the Trepucó settlement

Types of Structures

The ancient stone structures scattered throughout Menorca (and to a lesser extent found in Mallorca) fall into three main categories: *taulas*, *talayots* and *navetas*.

Taulas (table) consists of two slabs of rock, one placed on top of the other in a "T" formation. Some are up to 4.5 m (15 ft) high. Suggestions as to their original function range from a sacrificial altar to a roof support.

Talayots are circular buildings. Their purpose is a mystery – they may have been tombs, guard-houses, meeting places or even dwellings.

Navetas, shaped like an upturned boat or a pyramid, were probably built as a sepulchre or a dwelling. At least 10 of them remain in Menorca.

Spectacular 3-m- (10-ft-) high *taula* at Talati de Dalt settlement

Megalithic Sites

Menorca has an estimated 1,600 megalithic sites. Talayotic remains can be seen all over the island, usually in rural areas, but they are more highly concentrated on the plains of the more fertile south.

White houses and steeple in Binibeca Vell

❺ Binibeca Vell

9 km (6 miles) south of Maó.

Binibeca Vell stands out amid the similarity of many of Menorca's southern seaside resorts. Also known as *Poblat de Pescadors* ("Fishermen's Village"), it was built as a resort development in 1972 to resemble a traditional Menorcan coastal fishing village. It has whitewashed, two-storey houses, wooden balconies and a maze of streets that are so narrow you can touch the buildings on both sides with outstretched arms. The blaze of white walls, small patios and lush gardens enhance the Mediterranean atmosphere with a touch of Eastern influence. The "village" even has a church steeple, though no church. Nearby are a number of pleasant coves

and beaches, including **Cala Binibeca**, **Cala Binisafúller** and the smallest beach in Menorca – **Es Caló Blanc**.

Environs
The nearby resorts lack any distinguishing features, apart from the beaches and their associated attractions, so it is worth taking a trip to the village of **Sant Climent**, which has a small market and lovely 19th-century church. Sant Climent also has a venue, the Restaurant-bar Casino, which puts on jazz concerts twice a week. These concerts are popular, as long as you can hear the music above the noise from the nearby international airport. Nearby **Torelló**, right on the edge of the airport, has a *talayot* with aircraft warning lights.

❻ Cales Coves

11 km (7 miles) west of Maó.
🚌 Sant Climent.

This complex of prehistoric caves is best seen from the sea. Carved in the cliffs above a picturesque bay, the caves date from the Neolithic era. During the Talayotic period, the caves were used solely as burial chambers. Later they became the site of pagan rituals. On the shore are the remains of a Roman harbour

(some of the "newest" caves have Roman inscriptions). Nearby is a small beach.

❼ Cala en Porter

15 km (9 miles) west of Maó.

The seaside resort of Cala en Porter is one of Menorca's oldest holiday towns and is a sprawl of virtually identical holiday villas. Nevertheless, it provides good tourist facilities, including one of the loveliest beaches on the island, which is accessible via winding stairs and suitable for children. Its most unusual attraction is **Cova d'en Xoroi**, a huge cave, situated halfway down a steep cliff, which consists of several large chambers and tunnels. It has now been turned into a nightclub.

Environs
About 15 km (9 miles) northwest is the resort of **Son Bou**, with the ruins of an early Christian basilica (5th–6th century AD). The cliffs hide a number of caves that have been cut into them.

🎭 **Cova d'en Xoroi**
Tel 971 377 236. **Open** timings vary, please check website. ♿
🌐 covadenxoroi. com

❽ Alaior

🚌 🚲 Sant Llorenç (weekend after 10 Aug). 🌐 alaior.org

This market town, situated on a hill along the road from Maó to Ciutadella, is famous for its production of exquisite

Cala en Porter, one of the loveliest beaches in Menorca

Restaurant set in an old windmill in Es Mercadal

Menorcan cheeses. This is the dairy capital of Menorca (the island is also famous for its ice cream), with the biggest factories producing the famous *queso Mahón*, a white, half-fat cheese made of pasteurized cow's milk with added sheep's milk that gives it its distinctive flavour.

Besides buying cheese, you could also visit the fortified Baroque parish church of **Santa Eulàlia** (1674–90). The Munt de l'Angel **watchtower** stands on a hill behind the church and provides a beautiful view of the area. The huge fiesta celebrated on the day of St Lawrence includes riding shows, parades and horse races through the streets of the town.

Environs
Torralba d'en Salord, one of Mallorca's biggest Talayotic settlements, is situated along the road to Cala en Porter, about 3 km (2 miles) from Alaior. The local *taula* is one of the best-preserved and the tallest on the island. The rectangular temple has also survived in good condition. A bronze statuette of a bull discovered on this site can now be seen in the Museu de Menorca, in Maó (*see p100*).

Some 5 km (3 miles) to the south is **Torre d'en Galmés**, another settlement dating from the Talayotic period, which has a range of buildings including three *talayots*.

❾ Es Mercadal

🚍 🏠 Sun. 🎭 Sant Martí (3rd Sun in Jul).

Es Mercadal lies at the very heart of Menorca, along the Maó–Ciutadella road. Founded in the 14th century, the town has been largely overlooked by tourism and earns its keep through farming and a number of local industries. The town itself is charming, with trailing bougain-villea and the pretty 18th-century parish church of **Sant Martí**. Es Mercadal is known for its excellent Menorcan cuisine and you may like to stop for a snack or meal in one of its pleasant small cafés or in Ca n'Aguedet,

Detail from the façade of Santa Eulàlia

at Carrer de Lepanto 30, a restaurant that is very popular with the locals.

Environs
Some 3 km (2 miles) east, the convent of **Monte Toro** was built in 1670 on top of Monte Toro, which at 350 m (1,148 ft) is the highest point in Menorca. Occupied by the nuns of a Franciscan Order, it is regarded as the spiritual centre of Menorca and an ancient centre of pilgrimage.

Inside this 17th-century church is a statue of the Black Madonna – Verge del Toro – set within the main altarpiece, which depicts the Virgin Mary in a golden crown, holding the infant Jesus in her arms.

According to local tradition, the statue of the Virgin Mary has been worshipped here since the 13th century. These days, pilgrims visit Monte Toro, particularly on the first Sunday in May, to participate in the *Festa de la Verge del Toro*. Following mass in the church, the pilgrims then descend the stairs leading to Es Mercadal on their knees.

The old fortress, whose battered stonework is attached to the convent, has a military surveillance station. Nearby stands a huge stone statue of Christ, commemorating the Spaniards killed during the colonial war in Morocco.

Some 6 km (4 miles) north-east is **Son Parc** – the only golf course on the island.

Caldereta de Llagosta

This delicious lobster stew is the speciality of the northern regions on Menorca. Fresh lobsters are brought in every morning by local fishermen. The best stews are served in Fornells (*see p108*), which is famous for its seafood. The dish is extremely expensive but absolutely delicious. One popular way to enjoy it is to eat the gravy with bread, treating it as a soup, and have the lobster with mayonnaise as a main course.

Tempting lobster stew

Harbour and yacht marina in Fornells

⑩ Fornells

Fiesta de San Diego de Alcalá (13 Nov).

A picturesque fishing village, Fornells is situated 10 km (6 miles) north of Es Mercadal. During the summer season luxury yachts moor side by side with the fishing boats. The place has some excellent seafood restaurants. The local speciality is *caldereta de llagosta (see p105)* and it is thought to be so good

here that former King Juan Carlos frequently sailed over in his yacht from Mallorca just to eat in one of the waterfront restaurants. Once Fornells was a major port and you can still see the remains of fortifications built as a defence against Arab and Turkish pirates. At the entrance to the harbour is a large and conspicuous round watchtower. The village has no beach, but offers excellent facilities for diving, sailing and windsurfing.

In high season there are cruises to the small island of **Illa des Ravells**, with its ruins of an old English fort. Boat trips also go to **Illa dels Porros** and to the cape of **Na Guillemassa**, which has some interesting caves.

Environs

West of Fornells is **Cala Tirant** with a red sand beach. On

the east coast of the bay are luxury villas surrounded by masses of colourful flowers, shrubs and cacti. The view from here extends to Cap de Cavalleria.

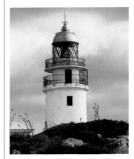

Cap de Cavalleria lighthouse rising above the rocks

⑪ Cap de Cavalleria

Cap De Cavalleria is situated 13 km (8 miles) to the north of Es Mercadal. This is the northernmost point of Menorca

Menorca's Beaches

Menorca has fewer easily accessible beaches than Mallorca or Ibiza. Some of the best ones are to be found at the eastern end of the south coast. These are small, sandy beaches, tucked away in coves. An increasing number of beaches are being developed west of Santa Galdana, and the resorts of Son Xoriguer and Cala en Bosch are gaining popularity. The rougher beaches on the northeastern coast are also popular.

② **Els Canutells**
A golden beach lies at the end of a narrow bay that cuts deep into the land. Small beaches on the eastern part of the bay are also good places for swimming.

Me-20

• Es Migjorn Gran

Me-18

Sant Tomás

① • Son Bou

③ **Cala Binisafúller**
This 40-m- (130-ft-) long beach is situated next to the road between Cap d'En Font and Punta Prima. It is mainly used by holidaymakers staying at the nearby apartments and bungalows.

① **Son Bou**
Some 3 km (2 miles) long, Son Bou is the longest beach in Menorca. At its eastern end are the ruins of an early Christian basilica.

Key

▬ Scenic route

═ Other road

and of all the Balearic islands: a tall, rocky headland swept by the northern wind – the "tramontana" – and battered by the rolling waves of the sea. The steep cliffs provide nesting grounds for peregrine, sea eagle and kite. The road leading to Cap de Cavalleria runs through lovely picturesque countryside.

The large dirt car park beside the road on the way to the cape marks the start of the footpath that leads to the **Platja de Cavalleria**. This is a long, wide and very appealing double-curved beach of reddish sand framed by low-lying hills. There's rarely much of a crowd here, but you can continue west on foot to two even more secluded coves. These are the **Platja de Binimel-Là**, a shale beach about 2.8 km (1.7 miles) further west, where the waters are clear and good for swimming and snorkelling, though seaweed can be a problem; and, 2 km

Magnificent beach in Sant Tomàs near Es Migjorn Gran

(1.2 miles) further along, **Cala Pregonda**, a sea-stack-studded bay with a wide sandy beach. There are no facilities on any of these beaches, so bring your own food and drink.

⑫ Es Migjorn Gran

11 km (7 miles) south of Es Mercadal. 🏠 Wed. 🎭 San Cristobal de Ses Corregudes (end Jul or early Aug). 🌐 ajmigjorngran.org

A small, tranquil village set among fertile fields, Es Migjorn Gran has a sleepy, provincial flavour. From here you can take a 5-km (3-mile) walk to the seashore. The route leads through the **Barranc de Binigaus** canyon filled with fragrant wild herbs and flowers. You could stop on the way to see the limestone walls and caves, including the biggest of them – **Cova des Coloms**.

Environs

Some 11 km (7 miles) south is **Sant Tomàs** resort. A dozen or so hotels line its main street, but there are no all-night clubs, and few restaurants. However, there is a great beach.

④ Cala Binibeca
This wide beach is near Binibeca Vell. The beach has hardly been developed. A restaurant is by the car park.

⑥ Cala Alcaufar
The beach runs along the bay, on the south-east coast. The northern shore of the bay is densely built up.

⑤ Punta Prima
This southernmost beach of Menorca is one of the most popular on the island. The beach overlooks the rocky island of Illa de l'Aire.

Me-12

Sant Climent

Me-8

Sant Lluís

S'Algar

a en Porter

⑥ Alcaufar

②

③

Binibeca ④

⑤

Biniancolla

0 kilometres 2

0 miles 2

Turquoise waves lapping on Santa Galdana bay's sheltered beach

🏛 Centro de Geologia de Menorca

C/ Mallorca 2. **Tel** 971 374 505.
Open May–Sep: 10am–2pm &
6–8pm Tue–Sun; Mar, Apr, Oct
& Nov: 10am–2pm Tue–Sat.

⓮ Santa Galdana

5 km (3 miles) south of Ferreries.

The only way to get to
Santa Galdana is by car from
Ferreries or on foot, along the
d'Algendar canyon. Situated
on a beautiful bay, the resort's
popularity is growing, and a
number of high-rise hotels
have popped up. Most of
the other buildings are villas,
set among the trees. The main
tourist attraction is the beach,
with its white sand and
turquoise water, sheltered
from the wind by high cliffs
and a pine forest.

It is worth taking a walk
west from here to the
charming **Cala Macarella**.
The adjacent **Cala Macarelleta**
has a nudist beach. Both
beaches are well estab-
lished and can be
accessed by steps
carved into the rock.
Further west is
Cala Turqueta,
probably the
most beautiful
bay on this part
of the coast.
Another beach,
situated in a
charming cove
east of Santa Galdana, is **Cala
Mitjana**, which is a lovely spot,
though it can get busy during
the summer months.

⓭ Ferreries

Tel 971 363 790 (Maó). 🚌
10:30am–1:30pm & 5:30pm–8:30pm
Sat. 🎉 Sant Bartomeu (23–25 Aug).

Ferreries is situated at the foot
of the S'Enclusa hill. At 142 m
(466 ft) above sea level, this
picturesque little town is
the highest settlement in
Menorca. Its name derives
from the many blacksmiths
(*ferreries*) who once worked
around here. At the heart
of the village is the **Plaça
d'Espanya**. Here, at a weekly
Saturday market, you can
buy leather goods as well as
produce brought in by local
farmers, including vegetables,
fruit, cheese and honey. In
Plaça l'Església is the parish
church of **Sant Bartomeu**
(1705) and the town hall. It
is also worth stepping into
the **Centro de Geologia de
Menorca**, to see a selection of
the island's natural wonders.

Environs

About 6 km (4 miles) north of
Ferreries are the ruins of **Santa
Agueda** castle. Not much remains
of this Moorish stronghold, but
the view from the top of the
second-highest mountain in
Menorca justifies the effort of
the 260-m (853-ft) climb.

The strategic advantages of
the hill were well-known to the
Romans, who, in the 2nd
century, chose it as the
site for their first fortress.
The Moors adapted
the site to build
a summer
residence for
the Menorcan
governor and
improved the
surrounding
fortifications.
The fort was the
last strong hold to
surrender during
the Reconquest.
Ferreries is the centre of the
leather industry. Along the road
to Maó are several shops selling
Menorcan footwear.

Remains of the Moorish
castle of Santa Agueda

Carrer Fred, close to the main square
in Ferreries

Gin in Menorca

One legacy of the 100-year rule of Menorca by the
British is the tradition of producing and drinking gin,
which was a popular drink with the many British
sailors stationed here. Unlike the rest of Spain, where
wine is the most popular tipple, Menorcans have
taken to gin in a big way. A wide selection of gin and
other local liquors can be purchased at the 18th-
century Xoriguer distillery, next to the landing stage
in Maó (*see p100*). The gin produced by the Xoriguer
distillery is the most popular brand on the island and
is sold in *canecas* – ceramic bottles reminiscent of
the clay jugs that were once used by British sailors.

Gin from the distillery in Maó

⑮ Western Coast of Menorca

The region between Ciutadella and Cap d'Artutx is excellent for exploring. Whether walking, cycling or driving, you can enjoy the best of the island, including a nature reserve near Son Xoriguer, the Son Olivaret megalithic remains and the churches and museums of Ciutadella, the former capital of Menorca. Parts of this unspoiled region can even be explored on horseback.

⑤ Sa Caleta
Near the beach, at the entrance of Cala Santadria bay, is a former defence tower, Es Castellar.

④ Cala Blanca
This small beach is tucked away between bungalows, villas and a cluster of narrow streets. Visited mainly by locals, it is uncrowded and has safe swimming.

③ Son Olivaret
The two sets of megalithic structures – Son Olivaret Nou and Son Olivaret Vell – include both *talayots* and *taulas*.

⑥ Son Oleo
On the outskirts of Ciutadella is a small beach, lying at the end of a long narrow bay. It is fairly quiet and used mainly by the locals.

⑦ Ciutadella
Take at least one day to explore the former capital of Menorca. From here you can make trips north to Cala en Blanes or to Cala Morell.

② Cala en Bosch
This harbour, situated in a sheltered bay, has a landing stage for pleasure boats. Next to the harbour there is a shopping centre.

① Son Xoriguer
Son Xoriguer is also the starting point for trips on horseback to the neighbouring reserve. The route leads past two beaches and then along the seashore.

Tips for Drivers

Length: 16 km (10 miles).
Stopping-off points: Stop off for refreshments at one of the restaurants in Cala en Bosch or Ciutadella. A good place for swimming is Cala Blanca, halfway along the route.

Key
■ Suggested route
= Other road

⑯ Ciutadella

A picturesque town with narrow, winding streets, handsome palaces and a busy harbour, Ciutadella has always competed with Maó. In the days of Arab rule it was the island's capital, and in 1558 it was invaded by the Turks, who killed many of its inhabitants and carted off some 3,500 more to slave markets in Istanbul. Of its buildings, only the cathedral remained. Those who survived were determined to rebuild Ciutadella. Most of the Menorcan aristocracy continued to make it their home, even after Maó became the capital.

Neo-Gothic canopy above the Cathedral altar

Plaça d'es Born, the town's principal square

Exploring Ciutadella

Though there are few traces of Arab rule, Ciutadella has much to offer in the way of architecture. Numerous opulent palaces and Gothic and Baroque churches reveal just how successful the restoration of Ciutadella in the 17th and 18th centuries was. The main square in town is Plaça d'es Born, a characterful area close to the Gothic cathedral. The Museu Municipal holds a wide collection of prehistoric artifacts gathered from all over the island and is well worth a visit.

🏛 Plaça d'es Born

This is a former Arab military drill ground and was rebuilt in a grand Neo-Classical style in the 19th century. It is said to be one of Spain's most beautiful squares. At its centre stands an **obelisk** marking *Any de la Desgràcia* – the "Year of Calamity", when Turkish corsairs invaded Ciutadella. The square is lined with historic buildings, including the **town hall**, a former palace of the Moorish governor, as well as the late 19th-century **Teatre Municipal d'es Born** and 19th-century palaces with Italian-style

façades. The most imposing of these are the **Palau Salort** and the adjoining **Palau de Torre-Saura**. The latter is embellished by two handsome loggias and its frontage proclaims the family coat of arms above a forbidding wooden door that leads into a courtyard. The aristocratic interior is, however, out of bounds. The square also holds several appealing bars and restaurants, perfect for a relaxing break.

🏛 Cathedral

Plaça de la Catedral. **Tel** 971 356 523.
Open 10am–4pm Mon–Fri, 10am–2:15pm Sat. ⭑
Work on the cathedral began towards the end of the 13th

century on the site of a mosque. Although it suffered fire damage, it escaped much of the destruction during the Turkish raid but was heavily remodelled after 1558. During the Civil War the Republican militia destroyed most of its furnishings.

One of the oldest parts of the cathedral is the Gothic south entrance that bears stone carvings of weird creatures and the heraldic crests of the Menorcan knights and nobility. The main Neo-Classical entrance dates from the early 1800s. Inside, light filters through the stained-glass window to bathe the nave in a gentle glow.

🏛 Església del Roser

C/ Roser. **Tel** 971 383 563.
The façade of this small church includes a beautiful 17th-century Spanish Baroque-style doorway. Destroyed during the Civil War, the church was rebuilt and is now used as a municipal exhibition hall.

🏛 Can Saura and Palau Martorell

C/ Santissim.
These two adjacent palaces were built in the 17th century.

Cafés spilling onto the pavements at Plaça Nova

Their distinctive façades reflect the character of the town's noble mansions built during that period.

🏛 Claustre de Convent de Sant Agustí

C/ Seminari 7. **Tel** 971 481 297. **Open** 10:30am–1:30pm Tue–Sat.

The museum at the Convent de Sant Agustí occupies the old cloisters. Its collection of prehistoric and modern artifacts includes a miniature statuette of a bull and a bronze casting of a mermaid. It also has a collection of Catalonian paintings, and some sacred objects made of precious metals, including chalices and Communion cups. Next to the cloisters is the Baroque **Església de Socors**.

⌂ Sant Crist

Near the bank building that was formerly the house

Ses Voltes' arches line the walkway leading to the Cathedral

of Menorcan aristocrat, Joan Miquel Saura, stands the Baroque Capella del Sant Crist, built in 1667. Its fanciful façade is decorated with stone carvings of fruit garlands and masks. The statue of Christ above the high altar is said to have dripped with sweat in 1661 and became the

VISITORS' CHECKLIST

Practical Information
Town Hall, Plaça des Born 15.
🏘 29,000. **Tel** 971 484 155.
📮 Fri & Sat. 🎆 Festa Sant Joan (23–24 Jun). 🌐 ajciutadella.org

Transport
🚌 🚢

object of a folk cult. Standing near the chapel is a column topped with a bronze figure of the Lamb of God, the work of local artist Matias Quetglas.

🏛 Plaça Nova

This small square is the site of the town's most popular cafés and bars. Ses Voltes, an arcaded walkway which runs from here to the cathedral, is one of the main streets of the Old Town. The Moorish vaulted arches that line the street hide a good selection of patisseries and souvenir shops.

🏛 Plaça Llibertat

This charming square situated at the rear of the former Augustinian monastery is well known to all who shop for food. Its two covered markets, selling fresh meat, fish, fruit and vegetables, are popular with the locals.

Arcades of the covered market in Plaça Llibertat

Ciutadella

① Plaça d'es Born
② Catedral
③ Església del Roser
④ Can Saura and Palau Martorell
⑤ Claustre de Convent de Sant Agustí
⑥ Sant Crist
⑦ Plaça Nova
⑧ Plaça Llibertat
⑨ Santa Clara
⑩ Museu Municipal
⑪ Plaça Alfons III
⑫ Plaça de s'Esplanada and Plaça dels Pins
⑬ Harbour

```
0 metres        200
0 yards         200
```

⌂ Santa Clara
Carrer Santa Clara. **Closed** to the public.

The original church and convent of Santa Clara was founded in 1287 by Alfonso III. Destroyed during the Turkish raid in 1558, it was rebuilt in the 17th century only to be destroyed again during the Spanish Civil War. A community of nuns still lives here. The wood carving depicting the *Adoration of Shepherds*, owned by the convent, was stolen by the Turks and taken to Istanbul but subsequently recovered.

Statue of a horse, the star of the Festa de Sant Joan

⌂ Museu Municipal
Plaça de sa Font s/n. **Tel** 971 380 297. **Open** 10am–2pm Tue–Sat (from 6–9pm May–Sep). 🗹 (free on Wed)

The museum occupies a bastion of the former town fortifications built in 1677. This is the only preserved fragment of the town's fortifications. Founded in 1995, the Museu Municipal has a good collection of Talayotic, Roman and Muslim artifacts, most of which are kept in a large, vaulted room. There are crafted beakers and tumblers, bowls and jugs, bronze weapons and jewellery (with a distinct Phoenician influence). There is also an odd collection of human skulls, showing the damage caused by the practice of trepanning.

⌂ Plaça Alfons III
This modest square is on the outskirts of the Old Town, by Avda de la Constitució. Several cafés and restaurants shelter under the trees. The square can be seen from some distance and you can't miss the old windmill, the only survivor from a platoon of windmills that once dotted the town.

⌂ Plaça de s'Esplanada and Plaça dels Pins
These two adjacent green squares are the lungs amid the historic buildings of Ciutadella. The many bars and restaurants provide pleasant places in which to relax and people-watch, especially when the light breezes from the west blow in at sunset. In the evening there are jazz concerts here.

⌂ Harbour
Moll Comercial.

Ciutadella's shallow harbour was the main reason the British moved the island's capital to Maó. Now that a bigger and better harbour has been built 4 km (2.5 miles) outside of town, the old harbour accommodates yachts and assorted leisure craft, plus a scattering of fishing boats. Having descended from Plaça d'es Born to the old harbour, it is worth taking a walk along the bay to soak up some of the harbourside activity. Early in the morning you can see fishermen returning with their catch, the first bars opening and the town waking up to a new day.

Windmill and tourist office in Plaça Alfons III

From **Punta na Mari**, at the entrance to the harbour, you can see Castell de Sant Nicolau. On the other side of the harbour bay, about 500 m (1,640 ft) further on, is **Cala des Degollador**'s tiny beach. The beaches of **Platja Petita** and **Sa Platja Gran** are several hundred metres further on.

A phenomenon peculiar to Ciutadella harbour is the mysterious *rissaga* wave. No one is able to predict when this event will take place, but it can cause flooding of the port to a height of several metres. The last big *rissaga* occurred in 1984 and left the harbour under 2 m (7 ft) of water.

Further Afield
The boundaries of the Old Town are defined by the wide avenues of Avda del Capità Negrete, Avda del Jaume I and Avda de la Constitució. Outside these limits there are a few interesting sights, principally **La Ermita de Sant Joan de Missa** and the **Castell de Sant Nicolau**. A stroll along the north side of the harbour will take you to **Punta na Mari**. Ciutadella, situated on Menorca's west coast, makes a good base from which to explore the area. From here you can get to **Cala Morell** in the north, or **Cap d'Artrutx** 10 km (6 miles) to the south.

Georgian town hall on Plaça de s'Esplanada

⬆ La Ermita de Sant Joan de Missa

Carrer de Comte Cifuentes.
The chapel, 8 km (5 miles) southeast of the town centre, is an important venue for the Festa Sant Joan celebrations. Vespers are sung here on the evening of 23 June. The nearby road, which leads to Macarella, Macarelleta and Cala en Turqueta beaches, is transformed into a racecourse during the two days of celebrations.

Fishermen in the harbour preparing their nets

🏰 Castell de Sant Nicolau

Plaça Almirall Farragut.
The 17th-century Castell de Sant Nicolau was built as a watchtower to protect the harbour. You can still enter the stronghold via a draw-bridge and in the evening the castle remains open to provide a vantage point for the spectacular sunsets over the har-bour. It also serves as a venue for temporary exhibitions.

Standing near the castle is the statue of a four-star admiral of the United States Navy, David Farragut, hero of the American Civil War and son of an immigrant from Menorca. The admiral is depicted in his uniform with epaulettes, holding a telescope. When he returned to Menorca in 1867, he was awarded hon-orary citizenship and a huge crowd turned out to greet him.

Environs

Naveta d'es Tudons, 5 km (3 miles) east of town, is Menorca's best-preserved prehistoric ruin. The Bronze Age

Festa de Sant Joan

This midsummer festival (23–24 June) has provided the citizens of Ciutadella with an opportunity to go wild since the 14th century. St John's Day begins with Mass in the cathedral, but fireworks, jousting and the carrying of a live sheep through the streets are also part of the fun. For most, the highlight of the day is the *caixers* (horsemen). Representing the medieval social classes, they ride among the noisy crowds.

Prancing horse in the streets of Ciutadella

structure, built of stone blocks, is 7 m (23 ft) high and 14 m (46 ft) long and was used as a burial chamber. When it was excavated, in the 1950s, more than 50 bodies were discovered. In **Torre Llafuda**, about 3 km (2 miles) away, amid the shade of olive groves, stands one cracked *taula* and a well-preserved *talayot*. The pleasant setting and the surrounding fertile farmland make this a good place to stop and relax. Travel southeast of Ciutadella and you find a number of beautiful beaches hidden in small coves. These include **Cala des Talaier**, dominated by a

stone watchtower. Along the road leading to **Son Saura** is Son Catlar, Menorca's biggest prehistoric settlement. Its wall is several metres high and built of enormous stone blocks. Inside, amid the sea of ruins you can distinguish one *taula* and five *talayots*.

A short way to the north of Ciutadella are two large resorts – **Cala en Blanes** and **Los Delfines** (which has a small aqua center). Eight kilometres (5 miles) northeast is the tourist village of **Cala Morell**. The man-made prehistoric caves are dug into rocks and were used for burials in the late Bronze and Iron Ages. They are now open to the public.

🏊 Aqua Center

Urb los Delfines. **Tel** 971 388 705.
Open mid May–Sep: 10:30am–6:30pm daily. 🅿 🆆 aquacenter-menorca.com

Castell de Sant Nicolau guarding the entrance to the harbour

IBIZA

Despite its reputation as a party island, Ibiza has maintained much of its rural charm. Fields of almonds and figs, olive groves, the relentless munching of the flocks of sheep – all are part of modern-day Ibiza. However, there is no denying that the island is a magnet for clubbers, who flock here every summer attracted by the loud music, lovely beaches, high-energy nightlife and extraordinarily tolerant attitude of the locals.

The closest of the Balearic Islands to mainland Spain, Ibiza is intersected by a modest range of mountains and surrounded by scores of islets and protruding rocks. Its 200-km- (125-mile-) long coastline is extremely varied, with small coves hiding beautiful beaches and mysterious caves.

Together with Formentera and a number of outlying islets, Ibiza belongs to the group of islands dubbed by the Greeks as the Pitiusas, or "pine tree islands". Besides the Greeks, Ibiza's visitors included the Phoenicians, the Carthaginians and the Romans. The last big invasion took place in the 1960s, when the island was "discovered" by hippies, and subsequently began to appear in all the European holiday brochures. Tourism took a firm and

rapid hold on the economy, and during the 1990s Ibiza gained entry into the *Guinness Book of Records* as the entertainment island of the world. Famous for its nightlife, thousands of visitors fill the resorts, and big-name nightclubs offer a wealth of DJs and dancing.

Away from the bustling clubs, the north of the island is a rural patchwork of almond, olive and fig groves. The most distinctive features of the southern region are the expansive salt lakes where sea salt is extracted to this very day.

Dalt Vila, the old part of Eivissa, is one of the best-preserved medieval towns in Europe, despite its influx of pleasure seekers. For many locals time still moves at a gentle pace on the island.

An alley in Sa Penya, in the old district of Eivissa

◀ A sunny morning on Calle de Santa Cruz

Exploring Ibiza

Ibiza has much to offer holidaymakers. It is the Mediterranean's club capital and the majority of visitors come here to enjoy the delights of over 50 local beaches in sheltered coves, as well as to revel in the nightclubs of Eivissa and Sant Antoni. Everyone should visit Dalt Vila, Eivissa's Old Town, for its Gothic cathedral and to see and be seen in one of the many swanky restaurants and chic bars. Those in search of tranquillity can head for the island's interior, where the hilly countryside is peppered with old stone cottages. For the energetic, the rugged coastline to the northwest provides excellent walking.

Locator Map

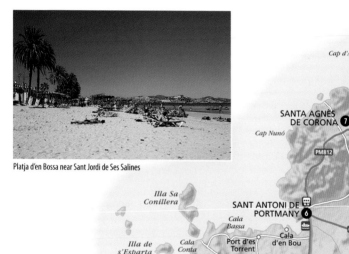

Platja d'en Bossa near Sant Jordi de Ses Salines

0 kilometres   5
0 miles   5

Getting There

Ibiza has fewer scheduled flights than Mallorca, but the island is still very well connected by plane. During holiday weekends, Ibiza's airport becomes one of the busiest on the planet. The planes landing here are mainly from the UK, bringing tourists for a week or two of partying. Barcelona and Madrid also have frequent flights to the island. Ferries from Eivissa and Sant Antoni de Portmany harbours sail for Mallorca and Formentera, as well as to Barcelona and Dénia.

Cala d'en Ferrer seen from the top of Sant Miquel, near Na Xamena

Sights at a Glance

1. Eivissa *pp120–23*
2. Sant Jordi de Ses Salines
3. Ses Salines
4. Sant Josép de sa Talaia
6. Sant Antoni de Portmany
7. Santa Agnès de Corona
8. Els Amunts
9. Sant Joan de Labritja
10. Portinatx
11. Sant Vicent de Sa Cala
12. Santa Eulària des Riu
13. Jesús

Tours

5. *West Coast of Ibiza pp130–31*

Plaça des Parque in Eivissa

Key

— Major road
═ Minor road
— Scenic route
△ Summit

For keys to symbols *see back flap*

❶ Street by Street: Eivissa

Attracted by the hilltop site and sheltered harbour, the Phoenicians founded Eivissa in the mid-7th century BC. The Puig de Molins necropolis dates from those days. Dalt Vila (Upper Town) is the oldest remaining part of Eivissa and since 1999 has been a UNESCO World Heritage Site. Strengthened by fortifications begun by the Emperor Charles V, it once guarded the entrance to the bay. Sa Penya, at the end of the harbour under Dalt Vila, was once the fishermen's quarter and is still one of the more colourful parts of town. La Marina, stretching out along the waterfront, is the place to go for night-time entertainment.

★ **Portal de ses Taules**
A broad paved drive leads from Sa Penya to Portal de ses Taules – the main town gate.

Museu d'Art
Contemporani d'Eivissa

Plaça del Sol's shady square looks out over the harbour and is full of shops and cafés.

Capella de Sant Ciriac
A Mass is celebrated here each year in August to mark the capture of the town by Jaume I in 1235.

Plaça de la Vila
The main square of Dalt Vila is lined with shops, restaurants and cafés to tempt passing visitors.

Key

━ Suggested route

Dalt Vila
The Upper Town, built on a hill, is best seen from the harbour shore where its strategic importance is obvious.

Museu Arqueològic

City walls

SA CARROSSA

IGNASI RIQUER

G. BALANSAT

PERE TUR

CARRER DE PONENT

PLAÇA DE LA CATEDRAL

Sa Carrossa
Quiet by day, Sa Carrossa is popular with Eivissa's gay visitors and is a hip night-time hangout in the summer.

Castell Almudaina

★ Cathedral
The cathedral, dedicated to Our Lady of the Snows, was completed in 1592. It is Dalt Vila's most impressive building.

Reial Curia
The modest house of the former Royal Tribunal of Justice, standing near the cathedral, has a fine Gothic doorway.

Vast city walls surrounding Dalt Vila

Exploring Eivissa

Eivissa is the largest and most beautiful town on the island. To avoid the crowds, visit early in the morning. For a romantic stroll, visit after dark, when it is a bit cooler. In Sa Penya and Sa Marina, the harbour district, you can take a break and see evidence of present-day Eivissa. The place is full of bars, restaurants, clubs and market stalls. As night falls, the streets outside Dalt Vila become one huge dance floor.

⛫ Cathedral
Plaça de la Catedral.

The Cathedral Church of Santa María de las Nieves (Our Lady of the Snows) stands at the highest point in Dalt Vila, near the severely dilapidated medieval castle (Castell).

Ibiza's consecutive rulers used this place as the site for their temples in Punic times. In AD 283, on the orders of the Roman Emperor Marcus Aurelius, a temple was built here and dedicated to the god Mercury. Following the conquest of the island by the Catalans, work began to build a Christian church, which was completed in 1592. The only remains of the original Gothic structure are the tower and the vestry portal. In the 18th century, the cathedral was remodelled in a heavy Baroque style. The vestry houses a small museum with a collection of beautifully embroidered chasubles (priestly garments), as well as Gothic and Baroque paintings. On the first floor is a collection of altar pieces in silver and gold plate.

⛫ Fortifications

The present city walls surrounding Dalt Vila were erected in the 16th century during the reign of Felipe II, according to plans by the Italian architect Giovanni Battista Calvi. In 1585, with the completion of the impressive Portal de ses Taules (decorated with the coat of arms of Felipe II and replicas of ancient Roman statues), the city's defences were in place.

The view from the northern bastion of Santa Llucia encompasses the new town, the harbour docks and the nearby island of Formentera.

🏛 Museu Arqueològic
Plaça de la Catedral 3.
Tel 971 301 771. **Open** Apr–Sep: 10am–2pm & 6–8pm Tue–Sun; Oct–Mar: 9am–3pm Tue–Sun.

The archaeological museum houses a collection of prehistoric artifacts and relics dating from the times of the island's Carthaginian, Roman and Moorish rulers. On display are tombstones, statuettes and coins, as well as glass and ceramic objects. The museum building is itself impressive, and was the home of Ibiza's government for 300 years.

🏛 Museu d'Art Contemporani d'Eivissa
C/ Ronda Narcis Puget. **Tel** 971 302 723. **Open** timings vary, please check website. **Closed** public holidays.
W eivissa.es/mace

The Modern Art Museum in Portal de ses Taules consists of two underground galleries of the former arsenal, built within the city walls. The museum was founded in 1969 and includes several hundred works by artists living in Ibiza. Some works are for sale, but prices can be rather steep.

Replica Roman statue at Portal de ses Taules

🏛 Plaça de Espanya

The **Ajuntament** (town hall) dominates this square and occupies a building that was once a Dominican monastery and a school for the town's poor. Adjacent to it is the church of Santo Domingo, with its later Baroque façade (entrance from Carrer Balansat).

The local *chiringuito* bar, open 24 hours, serves Balearic snacks and specialities. Carrer Pere Tur features splendid 18th-century mansions. Among them is **Casa Riquer**,

Fresh fruit at a stall in Es Mercat Vell

Sa Torre bastion guarding the harbour

once home to Antoni Riquer, the most famous buccaneer in Ibiza.

Santo Domingo
Carrer Balansat.
Below the city walls is the late 16th-century church of Santo Domingo, commonly known as El Convent.

It is worth visiting this to see the lovely paintings covering the vaulted ceilings, and the ceramic tiles lining the walls and floors. The Capella del Roser has an interesting Baroque altar.

Es Mercat Vell
Plaça de la Constitució.
The old market building lies north of Portal de ses Taules. The hall, resembling an ancient Greek temple, was built in 1873. Every morning it is packed with vendors selling fresh fruit and vegetables. A short distance further on is the **Sa Peixateria** fish market.

Sa Penya
The Sa Penya district, situated between Dalt Vila and the harbour, was once inhabited mainly by fishermen and has always been a fairly "picturesque" part of town. Even today, it does not enjoy a good reputation and when venturing here you should take extra care of your wallet and any valuables you might have. During high season, the streets get very crowded. The place is full of cafés, bars and clubs. Life in Sa Penya only starts in earnest after dark.

Sa Marina
Like Sa Penya, Sa Marina was originally a working-class district and sprang up as overcrowding in Dalt Vila forced many people to live outside the city walls. Now the area around the harbour provides ferry links to mainland Spain and is packed with restaurants, cafés, bars and shops. Its narrow alleys are full of stalls selling clothes and souvenirs. Many of these offer items reminiscent of the days when the island was a favourite with hippies.

Sa Torre
A small military defence tower stands at the end of Carrer Garijo. The bastion was restored in 1994 and is a relic of the fortifications that once guarded the entrance to the harbour. Today, it affords a view over the entire bay and the harbour and on to Formentera.

Monument als Corsaris
Passeig des Moll.
In the early 19th century, the inhabitants of Ibiza, tormented by constant pirate raids, enrolled the help of Antoni Riquer, a buccaneer who fought battles with the pirate ships that brazenly attacked the passing merchant vessels.

His struggles with Novelli, a buccaneer in the pay of the British who commanded the large brig *Felicity*, became the stuff of legend. Despite being hugely outgunned by Novelli, Riquer sank the enemy vessel after a fierce battle, for which the grateful Ibizans erected this monument. It is believed to be the world's only monument that is dedicated to a pirate.

Teatro Pereyra
C/Comte Rosselló 3.
Built in 1898, this was the first theatre in Ibiza. Now the Neo-Classical building houses the Teatro Pereyra café, which is worth dropping into in the evening for live music or stand-up comedy.

Neon sign of Teatro Pereyra café

Passeig de Vara de Rey
Eivissa's main street is named after General Joachim Vara de Rey, a Spanish general who perished in Cuba during the Spanish-American war in 1898. The street's many bars and restaurants are very popular in the evenings.

Puig des Molins
Via Romana 31. **Tel** 971 301 771.
Open Oct–Mar: 9:30am–3pm Tue–Sat, 10am–2pm Sun; Apr–Sep: 10am–2pm & 6–8pm Tue–Sat, 10am–2pm Sun.
Many of the objects associated with Phoenician culture on display in the Museu Arqueològic were unearthed from this ancient burial site. The "Hill of the Windmills" was one of the Mediterranean's top burial sites and the remains of the nobility would have been brought here from all over the Carthaginian empire. Ibiza, being free of snakes and scorpions, was attractive to the Carthaginians, whose religion specified a burial site for their dead that was free of poisonous creatures.

Environs
There are several beaches near Eivissa served by local buses. **Playa de Talamanca** is not large, but is nearest to the town. On the opposite side of the capital, at its southern end, is **Platja de ses Figueretes. Es Cavallet**, a short way down the coast, is very popular, especially with gay visitors. **Ses Salines'** beach, a little further on, is favoured by many people staying in Eivissa, and has regular bus links to the city.

Monument to General Vara de Rey

Nightlife in Ibiza

In the early 1960s, Ibiza became a popular haunt of hippies who were drawn to this isolated Spanish outpost by the beauty of the scenery and the relaxed way of life. They brought with them valuable foreign cash and the local bars, shops and businesses started to prosper. At times, though, even the islanders' legendary tolerance was strained and in 1968 the loud music, drugs and sex on the beach resulted in the deportation of 41 people. Where hippies led, however, the rest have followed, and Ibiza is today the club capital of the world.

People queueing outside the popular DC10 club in Sant Jordi, Ibiza

Promoting Pacha's Flower Power Party on the beach

Birth of Club Culture

The pioneers of clubland were **Pacha** and **Amnesia**, which opened in the early 1970s. The Ku club, currently known as **Privilege**, joined the scene shortly afterwards. Banking on the popularity of the party scene at the time, they offered their own more stylish and restrained version. Gradually, word spread and the clubs became fashionable with the rich and the famous.

The 1980s and 1990s heralded the emergence of DJs who decamped to Ibiza for the summer and forged a new type of dance music. Some became stars in their own right, performing to crowds of 3,000 or more. From then on, the club scene in Ibiza gained its own momentum and it is now a major part of the island's economy.

Clubs

There are eight major clubs on the island, each capable of accommodating several thousand people. The biggest of them, **Privilege**, can host parties for up to 10,000 guests. Every night they offer new attractions, including parties in foam, Brazilian nights, ghost nights and "Flower Power" balls. In addition, the clubs make their premises available to other promoters that operate on the continent. On Mondays from June to September, the best party is Circoloco at **DC10**. Admission charges are high and may be anything up to €50. Drinks are also expensive.

Smaller clubs are cheaper. They do not offer such elaborate entertainment, but have their own unique charm. They tempt their guests in with free drinks and various fun gimmicks. In the Sa Penya and La Marina districts of Eivissa, revellers often end up partying on the streets. During high season, special night-bus services run between Eivissa and Sant Antoni, where most of the clubs are concentrated.

Neon sign of a club in Eivissa

Clubbers

People of all ages can be found in Ibiza's many clubs because there are no age limits, although young people prevail. Many come to party, others are drawn by sheer curiosity. For some, the Ibiza club scene is simply a way of life. The clubs are most frenetic during summer weekends, when they are invaded by clubbers from all over Europe. The rule is to visit several clubs each night. As is usual at such hectic events, there may be an occasional petty theft or scuffle. You may also come across drug dealers and con artists offering various goods at bargain prices to drunken passers-by. Nevertheless, generally speaking, the clubs have tight security and are safe places.

Revellers dancing under coloured lights at El Divino, in Eivissa

Music and Dancing

Dancing in the local clubs is led by some of the world's top DJs. They include Fatboy Slim, Paul van Dyk, Mark Spoon, Carl Cox and John Digweed, to mention but a few. These DJs dictate which music will later find its way into the clubs of London, Paris and Berlin. Each year they try to surprise their fans with something new.

As the party season ends in Ibiza, most of the top clubs and their associated DJs go on worldwide tours, promoting their latest music. Individual clubs also produce CDs of last season's hits.

Although many kinds of music can be heard in Ibiza, the clubs have become famous for their summer anthems and for a unique Balearic Beat that is a fusion of electronic music with Latin and funk rhythms. Much of it is based on drum machines pounding out four beats to the bar, but Ibiza is known for its eclectic tastes and has produced a more subtle sound often branded as "chillout".

Posters advertising club nights in Ibiza

No one style of dancing prevails in the clubs and you will often see a free-form frenzy. Many people just copy the podium dancers.

Clothes

It is not necessary for people to wear any special clothes to be admitted to an Ibizan club, the exception being theme parties, when you are expected to wear appropriate costume and come dressed as a "Flower Child" or an astronaut, for example.

Club-goers who frequent venues where they might be playing in foam or jets of water tend to be scantily dressed. Regular clubbers are usually fashionably dressed, with clothes that are often sexy. As with the music, club fashions change every year.

DJ Sonique at the decks in Es Paradis

Before and After

Most clubbers do not wait until midnight to begin partying. After a day spent relaxing on the beach, many people start their evening in cafés, bars and pubs. The first to open their doors are the small clubs. By the time **El Divino** or **Amnesia** open their doors, the party on the island is already in full swing. Even at dawn, it is common to still see people dancing in the streets of Eivissa. Some beaches have daytime dance cafés and clubs, such as Bora-Bora opposite the flamboyant **Space** club on Platja d'en Bossa. Space hosts a party that begins at 8am.

Dancing crowds at Amnesia, one of Ibiza's most venerable clubs

❷ Sant Jordi de Ses Salines

4 km (2 miles) southwest of Eivissa.
🚌 Sat.

The small village of Sant Jordi de Ses Salines lies along the road leading from Eivissa to the airport. It was established in the 15th century, but there is not much evidence left of its ancient pedigree. The most important local sight is the modest white church of **Sant Jordi** that stands surrounded by a high wall. A quirky Saturday market takes place here from 8am and has a good mix of cheap jewellery, clothes and second-hand books.

Environs

A little further on is **Platja d'en Bossa**. The local beach is popular with young people, especially the southern end where a dynamic club scene has developed. Much of this is based around Space, a huge club that opened in 1988 *(see pp124–5)*. Close to this is Bora-Bora, a club-bar where parties spill out onto the sand.

Children are also catered for here. Behind the beach is a large waterpark, **Aguamar**, with numerous pools and slides.

A short way south of Sant Jordi is a hippodrome where you can bet on trotting races, popular throughout the Balearic Islands.

🏊 **Aguamar**
Platja d'en Bossa. **Tel** 971 396 790.
Open May–Oct: 10am–6pm daily. 🚫

Ses Salines, a haven for many species of bird

❸ Ses Salines

10 km (6 miles) southwest of Eivissa.

Situated at the southern end of Ibiza are the saline lowlands – Ses Salines. These natural salt-pans are extremely important for the local wildlife and were known as the "Salt Gardens" in Phoenician times.

They are sheltered to the north by the Serra Grossa hills that rise up to 160 m (520 ft) in some places; to the south they are flanked by the wooded areas of Faló and Corbari. In 1992, the area was given special protection as a nature reserve.

For centuries, the revenue from the local salt production provided a large chunk of the island's income. Until quite recently, the place was served by a narrow-gauge railway carrying salt to La Canal – a small port at the southern end of the peninsula. Salt production still continues here, though not on such a grand scale – some 70,000 tonnes of the stuff are exported each year.

Built between the salt lakes is the village of **Sant Francesc de S'Estany**, where some salt workers still live. It has a small picturesque church. The asphalt road that passes the church leads to a 16th-century watch-tower, **Torre de sa Salt Rossa**, 2 km (1 mile) away. From here there is a fine view over nearby Illa Sal Rossa island, the wide beaches of Figueretes lying to the south of the capital and Dalt Vila in Eivissa.

Ses Salines' beach, **Platja de Ses Salines**, is one of the island's most fashionable spots. One section of this beautiful, long sandy beach has been set apart for nudists.

❹ Sant Josep de sa Talaia

🏘 25,000. 🚌 ℹ Plaça Església s/n, 971 801 627. 🎉 Sant Josép (19 Mar).

The small town of Sant Josep de sa Talaia, 13 km (9 miles) west of Eivissa, is the municipal capital of the southwestern region and is off the beaten track. Its pace of life is slow. It is worth visiting the local traditional tavern, Bernat Vinya, where men gather to play cards and chat over a glass of wine. The only historic relic to visit is the **church**, built in the typical island style.

Environs

The town lies at the foot of Ibiza's highest mountain, **Sa Talaiassa** (475 m/1,558 ft). Keen walkers can make the two-hour hike to the peak along a well-marked trail that starts in Sant Josép. From the top there is a magnificent panorama of the

Slides in Aguamar, near Sant Jordi

district, including the rocky islet of **Es Vedrà**. In order to take a closer look at Es Vedrà you need to drive along the coast up to the sandy bay of **Cala d'Hort**, with its pleasant sandy beach and several terraced restaurants.

According to legend, Es Vedrà was once the home of the sirens who lured Odysseus. Sailors and divers experience a strange magnetic anomaly here, and some believe the island to have been a landing site for aliens. This lofty rock, now inhabited only by birds and flocks of wild goats and sheep, makes an extraordinary impression. Occasionally, in calm weather, it even blows off a plume of steam.

Some 5 km (3 miles) from Sant Josép, situated to the right of the road that leads to Eivissa, is **Cova Santa**. The main attractions of this cave, which is the largest in Ibiza, are its huge stalactites, some of which are a dozen or so metres long.

Fountain in Passeig de ses Fonts, Sant Antoni de Portmany

❺ West Coast of Ibiza

See pp130–31.

❻ Sant Antoni de Portmany

🏙 23,000. 🚌 🚲 🚢 Passeig de Ses Font s/n, 971 343 363. 🎉 Sant Antoni (17 Jan), Sant Bartolome (24 Aug).

The second-largest town in Ibiza was known as Portus Magnus by the Romans. The large bay that provided a natural harbour for ships now boasts yacht marinas and a ferry terminal. Once upon a time this was a small fishing village, until it was transformed in the 1960s into a busy, commercialized summer resort with scores of hotels. Regular bus services run from here to Eivissa and Santa Eulària des Riu. Amid the sea of high-rise hotel buildings stands the 14th-century church of **Sant Antoni Abat**. This fortified parish church, now standing

in Plaça de Església, was built on a hill, away from the harbour, and served as a shelter for the local population during pirate raids. Originally, there were defensive guns positioned on the church roof.

The bustling fishing harbour is popular with visitors. A palm-fringed promenade runs along the bay. At one end is a large flowerbed with sculptures made in Sant Rafael, including the ingenious *Columbus' Egg*. The famous entertainment district between Carrer de Mar and Carrer Ample comes to life only after dark. The local clubs, including Es Paradis, are among the island's best *(see pp124–5)*.

Columbus' Egg in Sant Antoni

Of the nearby beaches, **Cala Bassa** and blue-flag **Cala Conta** are probably the best. **Port d'es Torrent** is also popular, especially with families *(see p131)*.

❼ Santa Agnès de Corona

8 km (5 miles) northeast of Sant Antoni de Portmany. 🚌

Santa Agnès de Corona has maintained its old-world atmosphere. There is not much here apart from a small quaint church, a shop and a bar where you can quench your thirst and enjoy a plate of tapas. You can take a walk from here to the nearby summit of **Es Camp Vell** and on to the neighbouring village of **Sant Mateu d'Aubarca**.

Environs
Southwest of Santa Agnès de Corona is an original early Christian chapel of **Santa Agnès**, discovered in 1907 in a grotto. Local legend says that a sailor was saved from drowning by St Agnes during a fierce storm, and built a chapel to her on the spot where he was washed up by the waves. On St Agnes's Day, local people make a pilgrimage to this site.

Village church in Santa Agnès de Corona

Sunset at Eivissa, the charming capital of Ibiza ▶

❺ West Coast of Ibiza

The main attraction of Ibiza's west coast is its magnificent beaches, many of which are tucked away in small coves and offer family-friendly facilities and safe bathing. Some of the resorts have become built up in recent years, but the west coast remains one of the island's most beautiful areas, with a romantic coastline, pristine waters and remote mountains clad in pine trees. The mysterious islet of Es Vedrà *(see p127)*, just off the coast, is a remarkable sight and featured in the film *South Pacific* as Bali Ha'i. The route suggested here cuts across the Serra de Sant Josep in the south and bypasses the highest peak on the island, Sa Talaiassa (475 m/1,558 ft).

Illa Sa Conillera

Illa de s´Esparta

⑥ Cala Molí
This small resort is flanked by steep cliffs and consists of modest villas and pensions surrounded by green pine trees. Its beach is regarded as one of the most beautiful on the island.

⑤ Cala Vedella
This little resort is slowly becoming fashionable. Situated at the mouth of a narrow inlet, it has a wonderful beach and plenty of low-rise hotels and apartments. The resort is unlikely to be spoiled as there is no room for large hotels.

③ Mirador des Savinar
The best way to reach nearby Torre de Pirata, a former watchtower and now a viewpoint, is on foot. A drive over the bumpy road may damage your car. The point provides the best view of Es Vedrà.

Illa es Vedrà

Illa Vedranell

④ Cala d'Hort
This is the southernmost resort on the western coast. Many visitors come to this beach, far from the main resorts and towns, to admire the view of Es Vedrà, others to enjoy the exquisite local paella.

② Cap Llentrisca
The rough track leading along the craggy cliffs is fairly difficult, but from here you can see the entire south coast of the island.

⑦ Cala Tarida

Another beautiful cove, Cala Tarida has golden beaches and a number of family-friendly hotels. Until recently a quiet corner of the island, it is beginning to get busy, especially during high season.

Tips for Drivers

Length: About 20 km (12 miles).
Stopping-off points: All resorts have bars and restaurants. Overnight accommodation may be difficult to find during peak season.
Additional information: There are no petrol stations along the entire route. The nearest one is in Sant Josep de sa Talaia. Some places can be reached by bus.

⑧ Port d'es Torrent

Here you can join an organized canoe trip to Illa Sa Conillera and Cala Bassa. Several of the nearby villas are owned by the rich and famous, including Claudia Schiffer.

⑨ Cala Bassa

One of the most beautiful and popular beaches in the region of Sant Antoni de Portmany; it can be reached by bus. Numerous cruising boats visit the local harbour.

① Es Cubells

This village has a beautifully simple church and a modest restaurant. It offers a magnificent view over Cala d'Es Cubells. On a clear day you can see Formentera from here.

Sant Antoni de Portmany

Sant Antoni de Portmany

PM 803

• Sant Agustí des Vedrà

Sant Josep de sa Talaia
PM 803

Eivissa ↓

Vista Alegre

Key

▬ Suggested route
═ Other road
▬ Scenic road

0 kilometres   2
0 miles   2

Sheep grazing in Sant Mateu d'Aubarca

❽ Els Amunts

Ibiza's spectacular mountain range, Els Amunts, is situated in the northern part of the island and stretches from Sant Antoni de Portmany in the west to Sant Vicent de Sa Cala in the northeast.

Rarely visited by tourists, the region has maintained its unspoiled charm. Pinewood hills are interspersed with fertile valleys full of olive, almond and fig groves, as well as the occasional vineyard. The shore rises steeply and the roads leading to the water's edge are narrow, unmade and rugged, presenting a challenge even to four-wheel-drive vehicles. The area is a hiker's paradise; walking around you are likely to meet only the local shepherds.

Except for the small resorts, such as Port de Sant Miquel, Portinatx or Cala de Sant Vincent, the inland towns, including Sant Joan de Labritja and Santa Agnès de Corona (see p127), have maintained their traditional, rural character. A good example of this is the little village of **Sant Mateu d'Aubarca**, where you can see flocks of sheep and goats grazing in the orchards.

Near Sant Llorenç lies the fortified settlement of Balàfia. Believed to be the island's only surviving Moorish hamlet, the whitewashed interlocking houses with flat roofs and amber-coloured watchtowers once acted as fortresses during pirate attacks.

❾ Sant Joan de Labritja

16 km (10 miles) north of Eivissa. 🚌 🚖 Sant Joan (24 Jun), Santa Maria (5 Aug). W sanjuanibizatravel.com

This quiet little town in the north of the island lies in the shadow of the Es Fornás mountain (410 m/1,345 ft). The only buildings of note in town are the **Ajuntament** (town hall) and a small 18th-century **church**. The local cafés and restaurants are well worth visiting. Sant Joan was popular with hippies in the 1960s, and you can stock up on beads, Roman-style sandals and magically endowed crystals at the New Age Bazaar.

Environs
About 7 km (4 miles) west of town is the small village of **Sant Miquel de Balansat**. It has an impressive 16th-century fortress-church that provided shelter during the frequent raids by pirates, who once ventured deep into the island's interior in search of loot and slaves. Every Thursday at 6pm from May to October, there is a music and dance show performed by a local folklore group in front of the church. Dressed in traditional costumes, they entertain people with lively dances to tunes played on traditional instruments, including drums and local flutes (xeremia).

Hibiscus flower in full bloom

Port de Sant Miquel is 4 km (2 miles) north of Sant Miquel. It has a fishing harbour and a handful of hotels. The resort is popular with families and has facilities for water sports as well as a diving centre. Nearby, on top of a hill, stands one of the island's most exclusive hotels – Hacienda Na Xamena. The top of the 200-m- (656-ft-) high cliff provides a magnificent view over the surging waves below.

To the north of the town is the **Cova de Can Marça**. This cave, which was used by tobacco and liquor smugglers, is one of the most beautiful of its kind on the island, and is on a par with the caves found in Mallorca. There is an entrance fee which buys you a sound and light show and a 40-minute guided tour.

East of Port de Sant Miquel is **Cala de Benirràs**. It gets very busy in the evenings, when visitors arrive to admire one of the most beautiful sunsets on the island. At other times it is relatively quiet. On Thursday nights it becomes a venue for hippy concerts and dances.

🐾 **Cova de Can Marça**
Port de Sant Miquel. **Open** 10:30am–1:30pm & 2:30–8pm daily (Nov–Apr: 11am–5:30pm). 🅿 ♿ 🚻 ⏱

❿ Portinatx

8 km (5 miles) north of Sant Joan de Labratija. 🚌

The northernmost holiday village of Ibiza was built as a family resort. It consists solely of hotels,

Lighthouse on Punta de Sa Galera, near Portinatx

Coastal boulevard in Sant Vincent de Sa Cala

have neither telephones nor any other modern conveniences. The island authorities set up the **Camp d'Aprenentatge** here, where pupils from local schools learn about the old ways of rural life and about Ibiza's natural environment.

Environs

About 3 km (2 miles) east of town is **Cala de Sant Vicent**. This beautiful cove has become a modern resort, with quiet hotels and good restaurants. Visitors love the beach with its clean water and rugged scenery, surrounded by green pine forests.

From here, signposts point towards the famous **Cova d'es Culleram**, discovered in 1907, which was a temple to the goddess Tanoit during the days of the Carthaginian rulers. The caves can be visited and the finds unearthed here can be seen in the Museu Arqueològic at Dalt Vila, in Eivissa *(see p122)*.

Another interesting destination for a walk is **Punta Grossa** – a headland situated a little way to the east, which has a lighthouse. The view from here includes the **Illa de Tagomago** and the eastern cost of the island. **Tagomago** island lies 6 km (4 miles) southeast of Cala de Sant Vicent. It is uninhabited and has no regular ferry links with the main island but it is often visited by cruise boats and yachts. The clear waters around the island are popular with scuba divers.

Cova d'es Culleram
Open Apr–Dec: Tue–Sun.

apartments, souvenir shops, restaurants and numerous cafés.

It is an attractive, quiet place with four beaches – Sa Torre, S'Arenal Petit, S'Arenal Gran and Es Portitxol – separated from each other by rocky protrusions. It can become busy during high season, but instead of baking on a beach you may prefer to go water-skiing or take a trip in a glass-bottomed boat to admire the life lurking beneath the clear waters.

Environs

Nearby, just 4 km (2 miles) west of Portinatx, is **Cala Xarraca**, a beautiful beach with views along the north coast. The beach provided the setting for the film *South Pacific*.

⓫ Sant Vicent de Sa Cala

8 km (5 miles) east of Sant Joan de Labratija.

Sant Vicent de Sa Cala lies along the main road leading from Sant Joan de Labratija to the east

coast of Ibiza. Running to the south of it is the range of the Serra de Mala Costa mountains. The only local historic building is the modest 19th-century **parish church**, open only during service hours.

Sant Vicent de Sa Cala is nevertheless worth visiting for a different reason. The passage of time seems almost to have ground to a halt here. The locals work on the land using age-old methods and tools, and they

Hippies

Hippies began arriving in Ibiza in the 1960s, drawn by the beaches, people and unhurried lifestyle. It soon became the "in" place and tour operators were quick to catch on. Most of the hippies moved on long ago, but the hippy style – or, rather, its New Age descendant – has found its way into the island's culture. A small number of New Age families still live on the island; one community is near Balàfia.

Stall selling jewellery

Fortified church at the top of Puig de Missa in Santa Eulària des Riu

⓬ Santa Eulària des Riu

🏘 35,000. 🚌 ℹ C/Mariano Riquer Wallis 4, 971 330 728. 🎪 Santa Eulària (12 Feb).

Ibiza's third-largest town stands on the banks of the island's only river, the Riu de Santa Eulària. The town's main shopping street is Passeig de s' Alamera. This **Ramblas** connects the main street with the coastal prom-enade. During the day, the palm trees provide welcome shade. At night there are many lively clubs, restaurants and cafés to enjoy.

You can escape the town by by walking up nearby **Puig de Missa** (67 m/219 ft). At the top is a 16th-century **fortified church**, regarded by many as the loveliest and best-preserved example of its kind in Ibiza. This whitewashed building, once used by the town's inhabitants as a shelter from pirates, is surrounded by a handful of picturesque local houses and a small cemetery. The adjacent flat-roofed building houses the modest **Museu Etnològic**. Just a short walk away is the **Museu Barrau**, which has a collection of paintings, furniture and drawings by the Spanish Impressionist Laureá Barrau.

Environs

Es Canar, a popular resort 4 km (2 miles) north of Santa Eulària des Riu, lies on the shore of a pine-fringed bay with a beautiful beach. The local hippy market (Apr–Oct:

Wed) is the best known and biggest in Ibiza. Held in the grounds of the Punta Arabi club, it attracts large crowds. Here, you can buy jewellery and unusual clothes and T-shirts, though much of the stuff on sale is not made locally. Nearby are two large camp sites and a couple of beaches – **Cala Nova** and **Cala Llenya**. During the summer there is a daily boat trip to Formentera.

Anita's Bar in **Sant Carles de Peralta**, a little town 8 km (5 miles) northeast of Santa Eulària, was the cradle of the island's hippy culture and still remains popular. Two kilometres (1 mile) south of Sant Carles is a hippy bazaar, Las Dalias. On Saturdays and Sundays, the colourful stalls display every-thing from beads and bangles to bongos and intricate water pipes. There is also a café-bar here.

About 5 km (3 miles) south of Santa Eulària is **Cala Llonga**. This is one of the most popular resorts on the southeastern shores of the

Town hall in Plaça de Espanya

island. Its beautiful sandy beach makes it an ideal place for families with young children.

🏛 Museu Etnològic
Puig de Missa. **Tel** 971 332 845. **Open** Apr–Sep: daily; Oct–Mar: Tue–Sun.

🏛 Museu Barrau
Puig de Missa. **Tel** 971 330 072. **Open** 9:30am–1pm Tue–Sat.

Arcaded entrance to a church garden in Jesús

⓭ Jesús

2 km (1 mile) north of Eivissa. 🚌

This modest village is situated near Eivissa, on the road to Santa Eulària. The church of **Nostra Mare de Déu de Jesús** has a unique early 16th-century Gothic-Renaissance altar of the Virgen de los Angeles. Painted by the Valencian artists Pere de Cabanes and Rodrigo de Osona, it illustrates scenes from the life of the Virgin Mary, Christ and the Apostles. There are a couple of cafés opposite the church.

Environs

A short way to the south and within walking distance of Eivissa is **Talamanca**. Its main attractions, beside the 2-km (1-mile) sandy beach, are the Aqualandia waterpark and some good fish restaurants.

Ibiza's Beaches

Apart from the clubs, Ibiza's main attraction is its beaches. There are over 50 of them, adding up to over 50 km (30 miles) of stunning coastline. Many of the most popular ones are on the southeast coast, between Santa Eulària des Riu and Cala de Sant Vicent, and have excellent facilities. It is still possible to find a quieter spot. The delightful Cala d'en Serra, for instance, near Portinatx, has a *chiringuito* ("refreshment shack") and little else.

① Cala es Figueral
A long, sandy beach with small, rocky islets near the shore. The northern portion is used as a nudist beach.

Es Figueral

Sant Carles de Peralta

La Joya

PM 810

S'Argamassa

Santa Eulària des Riu

PM 810

PMV 810-1

0 km   1
0 miles   1

Key

■ Major road
■ Scenic route
= Other road

② Cala Boix
Surrounded by green hills, this beach remains relatively deserted even during high season. It is situated near Punta Prima, offering a view of Illa de Tagomago.

③ Platja des Canar
This popular resort has a small beach, situated near the pleasure-boat harbour. The surrounding area is full of shops, bars and restaurants.

④ Platja des Niu Blau
This pine-fringed beach in a cove with shallow water is a particular favourite of families.

⑥ Cala Llonga
Situated between Puig de ses Torretes and Punta Roja, on a 300-m- (1,000-ft-) wide bay, Cala Llonga is a friendly resort and attracts hundreds of holidaymakers.

⑤ Platja del Pinos
The beach, close to Santa Eulària, is situated at the mouth of the seasonal Riu de Santa Eulària that dries up in the summer.

FORMENTERA

The tiny island of Formentera, 4 km (2 miles) south of Ibiza, is just 85 sq km (32 sq miles) in area, including its two satellite islets, Espardell and Espalmador. A sense of peace and tranquillity pervades the island. The beaches are secluded, the grassy farmland is serene and the tiny clusters of whitewashed houses that make up the island's villages are positively slumberous.

It is the very lack of high-profile tourist facilities that attracts visitors. Its beaches are some of the emptiest and cleanest to be found anywhere in Spain, high-rise hotels are nowhere to be seen and the main means of transport on the island are bicycles and scooters – the tourist office will encourage you to cycle rather than hire a car.

The Greeks called it Snake Island (although snakes are rarely seen), but never settled here. The more practical Romans left settlers on the island to grow cereals and other crops, and named it *Frumenteria* (Wheat Island), giving rise to its present name.

Following the fall of the Roman Empire, the island became a refuge for outlaws and pirates. For two centuries it was ruled by the Arabs. Throughout the Middle Ages, Formentera remained practically deserted. The second major wave of settlers arrived in the late 17th century. It was at that time that several defensive watchtowers were built, although only a handful of them survive today.

Ever since that time, Formentera has managed to maintain its unique character as a virgin island. The quiet farmsteads and villages appear to have remained unaffected by modern living, and the loveliest corners of the island are only reached by rough, unpaved roads. For the peace-loving visitor, it is a tranquil idyll. Even so, the island's economy is entirely dependent upon its summer visitors, most of whom come for day trips. Each summer the island's population doubles, but there are still plenty of quiet spots to be found.

Century-old stone windmill on the island of Formentera

◀ Beautiful, rugged coastline of the small island of Formentera

Exploring Formentera

With few hotels and plenty of seclusion on offer, Formentera is a paradise for those seeking a quiet holiday, free from distractions. The coastline is stunning, with crystal-clear turquoise waters and pristine beaches. The nightlife is calm and unhurried in the bars and restaurants of Sant Francesc – the island's tiny capital. Es Pujols is the main resort. It too is small-scale, but it is a lively, fun place to be with some good bars and a couple of laid-back clubs. For a little gentle sightseeing, the island has a handful of ancient defensive towers, pretty village churches and some prehistoric ruins in Ca Na Costa.

Lonely lighthouse at the end of the road on Cap de Barbària

Sights at a Glance

1. Sant Francesc
2. Cap de Barbària
3. La Savina
4. Illa Espalmador
5. Ses Salines
6. Ca Na Costa
7. Es Pujols
8. Platja Migjorn
9. El Pilar de la Mola

Key

— Major road

= Minor road

Catamarans with sails aloft on the beach in Es Pujols

For hotels and restaurants in this region see p151 and p163

Locator Map

Platja Migjorn, the longest beach on Formentera

Quiet beach in Cala Saona, used by the guests of the only hotel

Getting There

There is no airport on Formentera, but the island has good sea links with Ibiza. Most services run between La Savina and Eivissa. The voyage takes about one hour (fast ferries take 25 minutes), although journey times can vary. Santa Eulària des Riu also has ferry links with Formentera and with Dénia during the summer. Buses from La Savina harbour go to various parts of the island, but the best way to travel is by scooter or bicycle. The main road cuts across the island, connecting La Savina to Punta de sa Ruda. There are also good roads leading to Es Pujols, Cala Saona and Cap de Barbària.

Plaça de la Constitució in Sant Francesc

❶ Sant Francesc

🏠 3,400. ℹ️ Plaça de la Constitució s/n, 971 323 620. 🚌 Sant Francesc Xavier (3 Dec). 🌐 **formentera.es**

Formentera's tiny capital is a mere 3 km (2 miles) from La Savina harbour and contains most of the island's historic buildings. In Plaça de la Constitució is an imposing fortified church dating from 1729, which was used by the many of the island's inhabitants as a shelter from the frequent pirate raids that ravaged the island. Now it houses the local government offices and a post office. Nearby is the **Museu Etnòlogic**. Carrer de Jaume I and its adjacent streets are full of market stalls selling clothes and souvenirs. Among them, you can find New Age stalls offering jewellery.

The oldest building in town is the 14th-century **Capilla de sa Tanca Vell**, a stone structure with no windows and covered with a barrel roof, which was also often used as a refuge from pirates. Also worth visiting is the local restaurant, Es Pla, situated along the road to Cala Saona, which is famous for its Indian cuisine and large selection of beers.

Environs
Some 3 km (2 miles) to the east is **Sant Ferran**. This modest village with a lovely church was once the centre of alternative culture, taken over by large numbers of hippies. The legendary Fonda Pepe bar and the library, run by an American called Bob, were hippy meeting places in the 1960s. It is worth going there

for a drink, just to savour the hazy atmosphere of "flower power" nostalgia.

Not far from Sant Ferran is **Cova d'en Xeroni**, a limestone cave, discovered by accident in 1975. The cave has been illuminated with 1970s disco lights, which only adds to the charm of the guided tour.

🦇 **Cova d'en Xeroni**
Ctra Sant Ferran–La Mola, 6 km (4 miles). **Open** May–Oct: 10am–1:30pm & 5–8pm Mon–Sat. Call 971 328 214 to arrange a visit. 🎫

❷ Cap de Barbària

8 km (5 miles) southwest of Sant Francesc.

A bumpy road leads from Sant Francesc southwards, across an area of wild desert, to the distant Barbària headland. This is the southernmost point of Formentera and it features an 18th-century defence watchtower, **Torre des Garroveret**, as well as a lighthouse warning passing ships of the numerous rocks that jut from the sea at the island's tip. Nearby are the unearthed

remains of a fortified megalithic settlement. The area is also rich in sculptures built of stones placed one by one by passing visitors. The most typical and eye-catching features of this windswept desert are pine trees twisted into weird shapes by the wind, and rocks eroded by centuries of wind and water.

Environs
Travelling from Sant Francesc, you pass the little road leading to **Cala Saona**. Here, positioned in a small cove, are a beautiful sandy beach, a handful of restaurants and a solitary hotel.

Moored boats in the Estany d'es Peix lake

❸ La Savina

3 km (2 miles) north of Sant Francesc. 🚢

The only harbour in Formentera providing ferry links with Ibiza is situated in the northern part of the island. Apart from when visitors are spilling on or off the ferries, La Savina is a fairly sleepy, unassuming place. Nevertheless, it is possible to find several shops and supermarkets here, as well as car, scooter and bicycle hire. Buses to Sant Francesc, El Pujols and other villages depart from stops behind the ticket offices. There is also a taxi stand here. In view of the small distances involved, cab rides are not very expensive. La Savina adjoins the protected saltwater lagoons of **Estany Pudent** and **Estany d'es Peix**. The latter has a fishing harbour that is always full of boats seeking shelter in the shallow, calm waters of the lagoon; drying nets can be seen hanging along the shore.

Torre des Garroveret in Cap de Barbària

For hotels and restaurants in this region see p151 and p163

The southern coast of Illa Espalmador as seen from Formentera

❹ Illa Espalmador

This small, 3-km- (2-mile-) long island is situated between Formentera and Ibiza. There is no regular ferry service; however, during high season the island is visited by pleasure boats sailing from La Savina.

The tiny island is popular with day-trippers from Ibiza, who flock here for the chance to sunbathe on the shores of **s'Alga**, a large natural harbour situated at the southern end of the island. This is also a favourite spot for yachts cruising the archipelago. A short walk north of the beach is a sulphurous mud pool where you can indulge in a bath of warm, sticky ooze (get there early to avoid the rush). The island's only monument is the **Torre de sa Guardiola**, an 18th-century defence tower that has recently been restored.

At low tide, some people attempt to walk across the sound to Formentera, although this is prohibited by the notice boards displayed at the tip of the **Es Trucadors** peninsula – the only traces of man's presence on this spit of white sand are the fragments of boats, nets and buoys washed ashore by the sea.

❺ Ses Salines

3 km (2 miles) north of Es Pujols.

The flat, salty marshes found along the road leading from La Savina to Es Pujols are famous for their birdlife. The most common species include the heron and the fen-duck. During the summer season, the grounds are also visited by flamingoes. Until recently it was commercially viable to produce salt here, but in 1955 the area was declared a listed zone in view of its ecological importance. Now the area including Ses Salines, Estany Pudent and the Punta de sa Pedera headland to the west of La Savina island forms a nature reserve.

Situated to the north of Ses Salines are **Platja de ses Illetes** and **Platja de Llevant**, which are considered to be among the loveliest beaches the Balearic Islands have to offer. The adjacent 200-year-old saltmill now houses a restaurant.

Salt was valued for centuries, not only as a condiment but also as legal tender. Even today it is still being produced in the traditional way in many places throughout the Balearic Islands. Seawater floods the shallow lagoons and then evaporates when heated by the sun, leaving behind pure salt. This creates a specific environment on which salt-loving flora and fauna thrive. Salty shrimps are the favourite food of many birds, including the black-winged stilt.

❻ Ca Na Costa

1.5 km (1 mile) north of Es Pujols.

Situated close to the Es Pujols resort is the megalithic burial chamber of Ca Na Costa (1800–1600 BC), a circle of seven vertical limestone blocks. The simplicity of the stone ring belies its historical importance, as it is the only structure of its kind in the Balearic Islands and the most precious historic relic on Formentera. It is also the only evidence of prehistoric human habitation remaining on the island.

The excavations were begun in 1974 and unearthed a number of objects, including ceramic and bronze vessels and axes, which are now on display in Eivissa's Museu Arqueològic (see p122).

Picturesesque Ses Salines

Popular beach in Es Pujols

❼ Es Pujols

7 km (4 miles) northeast of Sant Francesc. 🚌 🚢 Virgen del Carmen (16 Jul).

The small resort of Es Pujols is the island of Formentera's main holiday centre. It is a low-key, relaxed kind of place with a small marina at the eastern end of the town. Some of the island's best beaches are within easy walking distance, and the nightlife in the bars, restaurants and clubs, for otherwise sleepy Formentera at least, is quite lively.

Environs
A short way east of Es Pujols, standing on a peninsula, is a 17th-century watchtower – **Torre de Punta Prima**; next to it is one of the best hotels on the island – the luxury Punta Prima Club. A little further along the coast, among the rocks, is **Cova de ses Fumades Negres**.

❽ Platja Migjorn

This lovely beach is a 5-km- (3-mile-) long stretch of fine sand, with pale turquoise waters. It is fringed by pine forests and is the longest beach on the island. At its eastern end is the **Torre d'es Català**; at its western end are the **Cova d'es Ram** caves. The holiday village of **Maryland** in the east and **Es Ca Marí** in the west have numerous hotels and apartments tucked away in the woods. The central section of the beach is the most pleasant and secluded. A handful of bars and restaurants are set back from

the beach and are more easily accessible by car. The most popular of them, the Blue Bar, doubles up as a low-key nightclub.

Rocky Platja Migjorn in the vicinity of Es Arenals

❾ El Pilar de la Mola

11 km (7 miles) southeast of Sant Ferran. 🚌

Situated at the heart of the La Mola plateau, El Pilar de la Mola is a fairly sleepy little place and makes a good stopping-off point on a trip to Formentera's 19th-century lighthouse, **Faro de la Mola**. El Pilar de la Mola's most interesting historic building is the

whitewashed church of **Nostra Senyora del Pilar**, built in 1784. The town is best known for its craftsmen, whose workshops are open to visitors. The popular Wednesday and Sunday markets sell jewellery, good-quality leather goods and excellent local cheese (which goes perfectly with a glass of the local dry red wine).

Environs
Es Caló is a small fishing village on the north coast of the island. Unusually, it has no harbour and the boats have to be pulled ashore on special rails. When travelling from here towards La Mola, it is essential to stop at the **El Mirador** bar, which offers a magnificent panoramic view of Formentera. Some 2 km (1 mile) north of El Pilar de la Mola rises the 133-m- (436-ft-) high Ferrer hill. A little further on, to the west, is the **Cova d'es Fum**, a large cave where the locals hid their treasures during a Viking raid in 1118. Unfortunately for them, the Viking pirates discovered the hiding place and, having smoked them out, slaughtered the defenders and made off with the loot.

Travelling 3 km (2 miles) east, you arrive at **Punta de sa Ruda** – a rocky crag that drops steeply towards the crashing sea, over 100 m (320 ft) below. The views of the island from here are stunning. The Faro de la Mola lighthouse, built in 1861, is situated at the edge of the crag and was the inspiration for "the lighthouse at the end of the world" in Jules Verne's *Journey Around the Solar System*.

Nostra Senyora del Pilar in El Pilar de la Mola

Formentera's Beaches

The beaches of Formentera can easily rival those of Ibiza. The unspoiled natural environment, magnificent sand and clean waters attract an increasing number of visitors. Most have no hotels or clubs nearby and only a few feature bars or restaurants, which for many people only adds to their charm. The roads leading to some of the beaches (even the popular ones) can be quite rough and, as a consequence, they are never as busy as elsewhere on the Balearic Islands.

① Platja de ses Illetes
The most popular beach in Formentera. Stretching to the north of it is the Es Trucadors peninsula.

Key
⬛ Major road
═ Other road

② Platja de Llevant
This beach, occupying the eastern side of the peninsula, is much quieter than Platja de ses Illetes. Its northern end is a favourite spot for nudists.

③ Platja de sa Roqueta
Situated next to the only hotel in this area, you can walk along the shore to Es Pujols or Platja de Llevant from here.

④ Platja de Tramuntana
A number of small beaches are tucked among the rocks. This spot is popular with nudists and anyone who wants to escape the bustling atmosphere of Illetes and Platja Migjorn.

0 kilometres   2
0 miles   2

⑤ Es Caló de Sant Augusti
Several beaches are situated to the west of town. They can be reached via the footbridges that cross the thickets covering the dunes.

TRAVELLERS'
NEEDS

WHERE TO STAY

The Balearic Islands are one of Europe's most popular holiday destinations. Their magnificent climate, fine beaches and close proximity to mainland Europe mean that visitors arrive in thousands between June and September. Unsurprisingly, a large number of hotels have been developed to cater for the demand.

Until recently, this has meant that much of the accommodation has been fairly formulaic, although a rise in rural tourism has seen a boom in bright B&Bs away from the coast. Mallorca has the best-developed hotel facilities, while Formentera has the fewest hotels. Visitors should also note that many hotels close down during low season.

The exclusive Hotel La Residencia *(see p148)* in Deià, Mallorca

Hotels

Most hotels on the Balearic Islands are situated along the coast, around the old town centres and harbours, and are usually within easy reach of the beaches. There are more hotel beds in the Balearics than in the whole of Greece. Even so, at the height of the season it can be difficult to get a room unless you have booked well in advance. The most popular resorts are so densely packed that finding a quiet hotel with a sea view is virtually impossible in the high season. As an alternative, some historic buildings have been turned into luxury hotels, particularly in the major towns. These offer a higher standard and bags of old-world charm but often at a higher price.

Many hotel developments are located in remote spots. Most provide a range of attractions. These include evening entertainment as well as recreation facilities such as tennis courts, swimming pools and gymnasiums. It is certainly advisable to check in advance to find out whether these facilities are included in the basic price.

Fincas

As elsewhere, rural hotels and apartments are becoming popular on the Balearic Islands, especially with those seeking quiet, out-of-the-way places. This type of holiday is offered by *fincas*. These are hotels that occupy former country mansions or farmhouses, predominantly in the island's interior. Mostly found in Mallorca, they are not necessarily a cheap option

but can provide a degree of authenticity not found elsewhere. Rooms are mostly furnished with period furniture, which accentuates the character of the place.

Some *fincas* are very high-class, and cater for the wealthy. Others are in ordinary country houses and may be surrounded by holiday bungalows and apartments. When choosing to stay in a *finca*, you should bear in mind that they are typically far from the beaches and town nightlife. Most of the larger tourist information offices have lists of organizations offering this type of service, but the Internet is a much better source of information and listings.

Camp Sites

Those who enjoy camping or caravanning will have difficulties in the Balearics. There are few camp sites and those that do exist are generally situated in unattractive locations. Before travelling, check the facilities on the island you intend to visit. Camping on unauthorized sites is allowed with some limitations. You are not allowed to pitch a tent in town, on military grounds, tourist sites or within 3 km (2 miles) of an official camp site.

Historic Hotels

The Balearic Islands do not have the equivalent of the state-run parador hotels that can be found elsewhere

Courtyard of the Cap Rocat hotel *(see p148)*, Mallorca

◄ Tourists at a cafe in Cova d'en Xoroi, a picturesque cliff on the south coast of Menorca

The elegant Hotel Formentor *(see p149)*, a one-time favourite of the rich and famous

in Spain, but along with *fincas* it is possible to find accommodation in places with more history, such as convents and monasteries. This is mainly true of Mallorca, where the most popular hotel of this type is the Santuari de Lluc. These inexpensive rooms are intended for people who are prepared to put up with a certain lack of luxury (it is a monastery after all). However, they are very popular with visitors and you may have problems finding a monastery room during the high season.

Pool of the Hotel Hacienda Na Xamena *(see p151)*, Ibiza

Prices

The price you pay for a hotel room depends on the season. Although the main holiday season coincides with the summer months, prices only peak during the month of August. Out of the tour operators' peak season, rates are generally much lower. When enquiring about prices, you should remember that hotels can quote their tariffs in a variety of ways. Some are per room; others, per person, per night. Always check what is included in the price. In many cases, breakfast has to be paid for separately. Many resorts offer an all-inclusive service, in which all meals and soft drinks are included in the price.

Some of the Balearic Islands' hotels and apartments are block-booked in advance by travel agents and tour operators. Booking this way can prove much cheaper than trying to book directly with the hotel. You should also note that some smaller *pensiones* may not accept credit cards.

Booking

Accommodation may be booked in writing or via the hotels' websites. Obviously, you can also book over the phone, but it is always preferable to have a piece of paper to confirm your reservation. It is relatively easy to find accommodation off-season, even at short notice. If you are visiting during the peak season, you should book well in advance.

Some hotels require a deposit or even full payment at the time of booking, in which case you should take your receipt with you. Despite the set price lists, try haggling over the price, particularly out of season.

The charming patio of the Hotel Born *(see p148)*, Palma

Recommended Hotels

In this book we have chosen hotels that we believe stand out from the rest. Many of these may not adhere to the commonly accepted criteria of what makes a "good hotel", and instead may brim in history, great service or be the type of place where location rules over mod cons and designer details.

The very best of these have been given a DK Choice symbol. They generally carry four or five stars and range from boutique urban boltholes to chic rural retreats. Do book well ahead, as for many people a stay at these destination hotels is the main reason to visit.

DIRECTORY

General Accommodation

- w interhotel.com
- w mallorcahotelguide.com
- w visitmallorca.com
- w visitmenorca.com

Hotel Chains

- w amic-hotels-mallorca.com
- w barcelo.com
- w iberostar.com
- w insotel.com
- w riu.com
- w solmelia.es

Fincas

Asociación de Agroturismo Balear
Avda Gabriel Alomar
i Villalonga 8A, 2nd floor, Palma.
Tel 971 721 508.
- w holidaylettings.co.uk
- w ruralhotelsmallorca.com
- w rusticbooking.com
- w rusticrent.com
- w toprural.com

Camp Sites

- w campingsonline.com
- w fedcamping.com

Federación Española de Empresarios de Campings
C/Valderribas 48, Esc 3, 1º C,
28007 Madrid.
Tel 914 481 234.
- w guiacampingfecc.com
- w infocamping.com
- w vayacamping.net

Where to Stay

Mallorca

ALCÚDIA: La Victoria Petit Hotel €
Historic
Carretera Cabo Pinar, km 6, 07400
Tel *971 549 912*
W lavictoriahotel.com
Simple and comfortable rooms in a renovated hermitage that dates back to the1400s.

ANDRATX: Son Esteve €€
Historic
Barri Cas Vidals 42, 07150
Tel *655 572 630*
W sonesteve.com
Rustic rooms in rolling countryside, that can be explored on horseback. Stylish contemporary suites.

BANYALBUFAR: Sa Baronia €
B&B
C/Baronia 16, 07191
Tel *971 618 146*
W hbaronia.com
A rambling extension to an old 17th-century watchtower on the fabulous northwest coast.

CALA BLAVA: Cap Rocat €€€
Historic
Ctra d'Enderrocat s/n, 07609
Tel *971 747 878*
W caprocat.com
An atmospheric hotel in what was once an old fortress standing guard over the bay.

CALVIÀ: Hospes Maricel & Spa €€€
Boutique
Crta s'Andratx 11, 07181
Tel *971 707 744*
W hospes.com
Modern, understated rooms, some with sea views. Enjoy the fabulous, sea-facing infinity pool.

CAPDEPERA: Casas de Son Barbasa €€
Boutique
Cala Mesquida, 07580
Tel *971 565 776*
W sonbarbassa.com
Smart rooms retaining a rustic charm. Beautifully situated in Parque Natural de Llevant.

DEIÀ: Hotel La Residencia €€€
Luxury
Son Canals s/n, 07179
Tel *971 639 011*
W hotellaresidencia.es
With an award-winning spa, this is a popular celebrity getaway. Spacious and well-decorated bedrooms.

ILLETES: Hotel Roc Illetes Playa Resort €
Passeig Illetes 62, 07181
Tel *971 402 411*
W roc-hotels.com
Seafront hotel with access to a spectacular beach. Large, airy rooms and two pools.

INCA: Finca Son Vivot €€
Boutique
Ctra Palma–Alcúdia, km 30, 07300
Tel *971 880 124*
W sonvivot.com
Fourteenth-century country house with period decor but modern facilities.

DK Choice

LLUC: Sanctuari de Lluc €
Historic
Plaça Pelegrins, 1, 07315
Tel *971 871 525*
W lluc.net
Tranquil rooms within a sanctuary that dates back to the 13th century. Wonderful views of the Tramontana mountains.

MANACOR: Son Amoixa Vell €€€
B&B
Ctra Manacor–Cales de Mallorca, km 5.4, 07500
Tel *971 846 292*
W sonamoixa.com
This restored 16th-century finca is set amid lush green trees. Eat from an a la carte menu and enjoy the extensive wine list.

MOSCARI: Son Ametler €€
Rural
C/Son Riera s/n, 07314 Caimari
Tel *971 515 419 or 687 934 435*
W whotelsonametler.com
In the foothills of the Serra de Tramuntana, this well-run hotel

offers eight guest rooms in a sympathetically modernized old finca. There's an outside pool and a residents' restaurant, where the food is simply outstanding.

PALMA: Hotel Born €
Historic
C/Sant Jaume 3, 07012
Tel *971 712 942*
W hotelborn.com
Spacious rooms set around the leafy patio of what was originally a medieval mansion.

PALMA: Brondo Architect Hotel €€
Boutique
C/C'an Brondo 4, 07001
Tel *971 720 507*
W brondoarchitect.com
Lovely bohemian decor and private balconies in a medieval townhouse.

PALMA: Hotel Feliz €€
Boutique
Avinguda Joan Miró 74, 07015
Tel *971 288 847*
W hotelfeliz.com
Charming hotel with small but inviting rooms with an eclectic 1970s ambience.

PALMA: Hotel San Lorenzo €€
Historic
San Lorenzo 14, 07012
Tel *971 728 200*
W hotelsanlorenzo.com
Quaint hotel with a rooftop pool and terrace, besides a separate swimming pool. Excellent views.

Outdoor seating area of Hotel La Residencia, Deià

**PALMA: Hotel
Santa Clara**   €€
Boutique
C/San Alonso 16, 07001
Tel 971 729 231
w santaclarahotel.es
A historic mansion tastefully
converted into a smart urban
hotel. Spa and views of the bay.

PALMA: Hotel Tres   €€
Boutique
C/Apuntadores 3, 07012
Tel 971 717 333
w hoteltres.com
With parts of a 16th-century
palace within, Hotel Tres
has superb views over
the old town.

PALMA: Puro Hotel   €€
Boutique
C/Montenegro 12, 07012
Tel 971 425 450
w purohotel.com
Chic hotel with a faux-Asian
decor. Popular with young
people and groups.

PALMA: Hotel Can Cera   €€€
Luxury
C/Sant Francesc 8, 07001
Tel 971 715 012
w cancerahotel.com
Gothic and Renaissance
architecture with lavish
interiors. Spacious and
bright bedrooms.

**PALMA: Hotel Convent
de la Missió**   €€€
Luxury
C/de la Missió 7a, 07003
Tel 971 227 347
w conventdelamissio.com
Elegant 17th-century convent,
imaginatively converted. The
crypt now houses a spa.

**PALMA: Palacio Ca
Sa Galesa**   €€€
Luxury
C/Miramar 8, 07001
Tel 971 715 400
w palaciocasagalesa.com
Majestic 16th-century mansion
with 12 individually-designed
rooms. Excellent spa and
wellness facilities.

DK Choice

PALMA: Portixol Hotel   €€€
Boutique
C/Sirena, 07006
Tel 971 271 800
w portixol.com
In the small fishing port of
Portixol, this outstanding hotel
offers a splendid choice of
rooms, impeccable service
and a great Scandinavian vibe.

POLLENÇA: Hotel Desbrull   €
Boutique
C/Marqués Desbrull 7, 07460
Tel 971 535 055
w desbrull.com
Period architecture, avant-
garde decor combined with
innovative technology.

POLLENÇA: Posada de Lluc   €€
Boutique
C/Roser Vell, 11, 07460
Tel 971 535 220
w posadalluc.com
Classic 15th-century building with
modern amenities and a pool.
Rooms are cheerful and bright.

POLLENÇA: Son San Jordi   €€
B&B
Calle Sant Jordi 29, 07460
Tel 971 530 389
w hotelsonsantjordi.com
Four-poster beds, an outdoor
pool and full kitchens. Ideal
for families.

POLLENÇA: Hotel Llenaire   €€€
Rural
Camí de Llenaire s/n, 07470
Tel 971 535 251
w hotellenaire.com
A handsome manor house with
views over the bay has been
turned into a charming country
hotel. There are 11 rooms, an
infinity pool and a sauna.

DK Choice

POLLENÇA: Son Brull   €€€
Boutique
Crta. Palma–Pollença PM 220, km
49.8, 07460
Tel 971 535 353
w sonbrull.com
Sophisticated spa-hotel with 23
luxurious rooms, located in a
sensitively-restored 12th-century
monastery. The restaurant
serves creative organic fare.

**PORT D'ALCÚDIA:
Condes de Alcúdia**   €
Resort
Avda de la Platja 4, 07410
Tel 971 545 920
w hotelesglobales.com
Excellent family getaway, with
rooms large enough for a couple
and two children.

**PORT D'ALCÚDIA:
Grupotel Amapola**   €
Resort
Urb. Las Gaviotas s/n, Circuito
Del Lago 49, Platja de Muro, 07458
Tel 971 890 551
w grupotel.com
This deluxe, modern hotel, with
all facilities, is excellent for family
holidays. It is set just back from

Vibrant, colourful interiors of the dining
area in Portixol Hotel, Palma

the seashore, on the southern
end of this sprawling resort. It
is also near the lake defining
the S´Albufera region.

**PORT DE POLLENÇA:
Hotel Formentor (Barceló)**   €€€
Resort
Playa de Formentor s/n, 07470
Tel 971 899 100
w barcelo.com
Once a celebrity haunt, this
elegant retreat has the beach
at its doorstep.

**PORT DE POLLENÇA:
Hotel Illa d'Or**   €€€
Resort
Paseo Colón 265, 07470
Tel 971 865 100
w hotelillador.com
This well-equipped seashore
hotel is set in its own grounds.
Dating back to the 1920s, it
is built in traditional Spanish
style, though the interior is
ultra-modern.

**PORT DE SÓLLER:
Citric Hotel Soller**   €
Resort
Cami del Far s/n, 07108
Tel 971 631 352
w citrichotels.com
Modern-themed hotel on the
water's edge with a large terrace
overlooking the bay.

DK Choice

**PORT DE SÓLLER: Hotel
Espléndido**   €€€
Resort
Es Traves 5, 07108
Tel 971 631 850
w esplendidohotel.com
Perched on the water's edge at
Sóller, this stunning destination
hotel has a vintage decor.
Excellent spa facilities and
an intimate bistro.

For more information on types of hotels see page 147

PORTO CRISTO:
THB Felip Class €
Resort
Burdils 41, 07680 Porto Cristo
Tel *971 820 594*
W thbhotels.com
Rooms at this hundred-year-old
hotel on the seafront have
attached balconies. There is also
a well-equipped wellness zone.

**PUIGPUNYENT: Gran Hotel
Son Net** €€€
Historic
C/Castillo de Sonnet s/n, 07194
Tel *971 147 000*
W sonnet.es
A getaway fit for royalty, the
elegant Son Net is replete with
gardens and mountain views.
Two restaurants on site offer
gourmet Mediterranean dishes.

SANT LLORENÇ:
Hotel Son Trobat €€
B&B
*Carretera Manacor–Sant Llorenç,
km 4.8, 07530*
Tel *971 569 674*
W sontrobat.com
A handsome finca surrounded by
orange and lemon groves, the
Son Trobat has a spa, a heated
pool and a restaurant. Some of
Mallorca's best golf courses are
only a short drive away.

SINEU: Hotel Son Cleda €
Boutique
Plaça es Fossar 7, 07510
Tel *971 521 027*
W hotelsoncleda.com
Originally a 16th-century town-
house, the hotel has a terrace
overlooking the village square.

SÓLLER: Hotel La Vila €
Historic
Plaza Constitución 14, 07100
Tel *971 634 641*
W lavilahotel.com
Pretty *fin de siécle* architecture
accompanies personalised service
here. The hotel has a great location,
overlooking the main square.

SÓLLER: L'Avenida Hotel €€
Boutique
Gran Via 9, 07100
Tel *971 634 075*
W avenida-hotel.com
Cosmopolitan ambiance in a
small-town setting. The hotel
offers beautiful mountain views.

SÓLLER: Finca Can Coll €€
B&B
Cami de Can Coll 1, 07100
Tel *971 633 244*
W cancoll.com
Stylish little hotel with an
outdoor pool and lovely
views of the countryside.

Exterior of Son Granot *(see p151)*, Es Castell

SÓLLER: Finca Ca N'Ai €€€
B&B
*Cami Son Sales 50, Vall de Sóller,
07100*
Tel *971 632 494*
W canai.com
This beautifully renovated, 300-
year-old country mansion is
surrounded by orange groves.
Facilities include an outdoor pool.

SÓLLER: Gran Hotel €€€
Luxury
C/Romaguera 18, 07100
Tel *971 638 686*
W granhotelsoller.com
Spacious rooms that look out
over the town and surrounding
countryside await at this elegant
19th-century hotel. The wellness
area includes a heated pool,
sauna and massage room.

DK Choice

SON SERVERA:
Finca Son Gener €€€
Luxury
*Ctra. Vella Son Servera, Artà km 3,
07550*
Tel *971 183 612*
W songener.com
Spanish architect Toni Esteve
converted this 18th-century
farmhouse into one of the
best hotels in Mallorca. Rooms
have terraces with great views
of the surrounding almond
and olive groves.

VALLDEMOSSA:
Cases de C'as Garriguer €€
Boutique
*Ctra Valldemossa a Andratx, km 2.5,
07170*
Tel *971 612 300*
W vistamarhotel.es
The ancient Son Olesa country
estate is now a peaceful rural
hotel with antique furnishings
in the bedrooms.

Menorca

CALA EN PORTER:
Sa Barrera €€
Boutique
Carrer Sa Barrera 12, 07712
Tel *971 377 126*
W hotelsabarrera.com
Moroccan-influenced decor,
elegant rooms and a lovely
bay just a short walk away.

**CIUTADELLA: Hotel
Sa Prensa** €
B&B
Carrer Madrid, 70, 07760
Tel *971 382 698*
W saprensa.com
Great port views from the
terraces of some rooms. Situated
just a stone's throw from the
seafront. Book ahead.

DK Choice

**CIUTADELLA: Agroturisme
Biniatram** €€
Boutique
*Ctra Cala Morell s/n, Cala Morell,
07760*
Tel *971 383 113*
W biniatram.com
This small, family-run finca
offers apartments with self-
catering facilities, in addition
to rooms with balconies.
The beach is located within
walking distance.

**CIUTADELLA: Hotel Rural
Sant Ignasi** €€
Historic
*Ronda Norte s/n, Ciutadella,
07760*
Tel *971 385 575*
W santignasi.com
A grand country mansion with
vast grounds, gardens and
vineyards. Traditionally
decorated rooms.

CIUTADELLA:
Hotel Tres Sants €€
Boutique
C/Sant Cristofol 2, 07760
Tel *626 053 536*
W grupelcarme.com
Chic interiors, an enticing rooftop
terrace and a Turkish bath.
Apartments are also available.

**CIUTADELLA: Morvedra
Nou Ciutadella** €€
Historic
*Camí de Sant Joan de Missa, km 7,
07760*
Tel *971 359 521*
W morvedranou.es
This classy rural hotel was a
cottage in the 1600s. Set in
gorgeous grounds.

DK Choice

ES CASTELL: Son Granot €€€
Luxury
Carretera de Sant Felip s/n, 07720
Tel *971 355 555*
🅦 songranot.com
A lovely 18th-century Georgian home with a delightful entrance staircase, this hilltop hotel has interiors that combine period detail with modern elements.

ES MERCADAL: Hostal Jeni €
B&B
C/Mirada del Toro 81, 0740
Tel *971 375 059*
🅦 hostaljeni.com
Charming town-centre hotel with a terrace garden which includes a jacuzzi and pool with a retractable roof.

SANT LLUÍS: Biniaroca Hotel Rural €€
B&B
Camí Vell 57, 07710
Tel *971 150 059*
🅦 biniarroca.com
Run by a local artist, this private cottage has a nice garden and antique-filled rooms.

Ibiza

DK Choice

EIVISSA: Ibiza Gran Hotel €€€
Boutique
Paseo Juan Carlos I, 17, 07800
Tel *971 806 806*
🅦 ibizagranhotel.com
This fashionable hotel offers chic rooms and terrific wellness facilities: a spa, pool, gym and wetdeck. Visiting celebrities are often seen working on their tans.

Deck chairs lining the outdoor swimming pool at Ibiza Gran hotel, Elvissa

EIVISSA: Mirador de Dalt Vila €€€
Historic
Plaça d'España 4, Ibiza, 07800
Tel *971 303 045*
🅦 hotelmiradoribiza.com
Luxurious 19th-century palace in the heart of the city with just 12 elegant rooms and suites, which come complete with choice furnishings and beamed ceilings.

PORTINATX: Cas Mallorqui €
B&B
Cala Portinatx s/n, 07810
Tel *971 320 505*
🅦 casmallorqui.com
Comfortable rooms with views of the beach. Ideal for watersports and diving enthusiasts.

SAN MIGUEL: Hotel Hacienda Na Xamena €€€
Luxury
Urbanización Na Xamena, 07815
Tel *971 334 500*
🅦 hotelhacienda-ibiza.com
A superb retreat for an unparalleled Balearic lifestyle experience.

SANT GERTRUDIS DE FRUITERA: Cas Gasi €€€
Boutique
Carretera Viejo de Sant Mateu s/n, 07814
Tel *971 197 700*
🅦 casgasi.com
Deep in the countryside, this handsomely converted old farmhouse with period touches and a modern extension sits in beautiful grounds.

SANT JOAN: The Giri Residence €€€
Boutique
C/Principal 3–5, 07810
Tel *971 333 345*
🅦 thegiri.com
This hotel offers Morroccan interiors with a pleasing Mediterranean ambiance.

SANT JOAN DE LABRITJA: Finca Can Marti €€
B&B
Venda de Ca's Ripolls, 29, 07810
Tel *971 333 500*
🅦 canmarti.com
A finca and working farm that offers an eclectic, apartment-style stay.

SANT JOSÉP DE TALAIA: Ses Pitreras €€€
Boutique
C/Valladolid 1–3, 07839
Tel *971 345 000*
🅦 sespitreras.com
A delightful, compact hotel with plush rooms, set in a 1970s building.

SANTA EULÀRIA DES RIU: Aguas de Ibiza €€€
Resort
C/Salvador Camacho 9, 07840
Tel *971 319 962*
🅦 aguasdeibiza.com
Spa and wellness facilities at this premium resort on the beachfront.

Formentera

EL PILAR DE LA MOLA: Es Ram Resort €€€
Boutique
Camino Es Ram, Route de la Mola
Tel *971 948 427*
🅦 esramresort.com
Independent mini-villas with charming terraces, set between pine forests and the beach.

DK Choice

ES CALO: Hostal Entre Pinos €
B&B
Ctra La Mola, km 12.3, 07872
Tel *971 327 019*
🅦 hostalentrepinos.com
Close to the beaches of Es Caló and Arenal, this family-run hotel has a lovely terrace-bar, pool and garden. The outdoor spaces are great for children.

LA SAVINA: Hostal Bellavista €
B&B
Puerto de La Savina, 07870
Tel *971 323 324*
🅦 hostal-bellavista.com
A no-frills option in front of the port of La Savina. Some rooms have balconies with views.

LA SAVINA: Hostal La Savina €
B&B
Avenida Mediterránea 20–40, 07870
Tel *971 322 279*
🅦 hostal-lasavina.com
Lovely, family-run hotel with white-washed rooms right on the water's edge. Gorgeous sea views.

PLATJA MIGJORN: Riu La Mola €€€
Resort
Playa de Mitjorn s/n, Sant Francesc Javier, 07860
Tel *971 327 000*
🅦 riulamola.com
Family-friendly resort on the mystical Migjorn beach. Good amenities, including a spa.

SANT FERRAN DE SES ROQUES: Hostal Illes Pituïses €
B&B
Avda Juan Castelló Guasch 48, 07871
Tel *971 328 189*
🅦 illespitiuses.com
En-suite rooms with balconies or terraces. Pleasant gardens.

For more information on types of hotels *see page 147*

WHERE TO EAT AND DRINK

The resorts and large town centres found in the Balearic Islands offer a good selection of restaurants, able to satisfy even the most demanding of palates. While the resorts do, of course, cater to visitors who have come for the beaches rather than the food, good-quality local cuisine is always available. Restaurants serving local specialities can be easily spotted (not having an "international" or photo menu is a good rule of thumb) and many are open all year.

Stay *(see p159)* restaurant in Port de Pollença, Mallorca

Local Cuisine

A number of the Balearic dishes are Catalan in origin. *Ensaimadas*, delicious spiral pastries that are dusted with icing sugar, are commonplace. So, too, are the spicy pork pâtés *(sobrasadas)*. Rustic "one-pot" dishes and soups are also popular. The best known of these is *caldereta de llagosta (see 105)*.

With the exception of cheaper varieties such as sardines, the price paid for local fish and seafood is the same as elsewhere in Spain, though you'll always find a cheaper daily special.

When to Eat

As with the rest of Spain, lunchtime in the Balearic Islands is usually between 1:30pm and 3pm. It may be that restaurants are full and you may have to wait a long time to be served. Outside traditional mealtimes, the menu selection can be limited. Some restaurant kitchens may be closed after 3pm. As an alternative, bars can provide a good variety of food and snacks while beachside restaurants are good for snacks at any time of the day.

Dinner on the islands usually starts after 8pm, when the temperature drops. This is when the restaurants, cafés, gardens and bars fill up. For Spaniards this is a time to meet with friends. Restaurants also tend to fill up for Sunday lunch and booking is recommended at this time.

Places to Eat

There is a boundless choice of places to eat in the Balearic Islands. This is especially true during the high season, when many restaurants that are

A modest restaurant in Estellencs

closed during the other months of the year open. In the cheaper bars it is worth trying *tapas* or *raciónes* (small plates), as these are most likely to be freshly prepared (a *ración* is often enough for two).

When venturing into a bar that is popular with the locals, you should try the set price *menú del día* (menu of the day). This is a full three-course meal, accompanied by a drink. Often these menus are very good value and may cost as little as €10.

Many visitors prefer to use their hotel's restaurant for breakfast and dinner, and take their lunch in bars and restaurants close to the beach. Some hotels have wonderful restaurants; others are merely adequate. One point in hotel restaurants' favour is that they can offer a wide selection of food, low prices, fast service and a friendly atmosphere. Most of them serve a safe, international cuisine and you are likely to see paella, pizza, fish and chips, roast chicken and curry all on the same menu. These restaurants successfully compete with the popular fast-food chains. Restaurants that are near or on less crowded beaches tend to offer much better food, but the choice may be limited.

Vegetarians

The food of these islands tends to be on the heavy side and is based mainly on pork and fish, but it also has a lot to offer vegetarians. It is easy to make a meal of *tapas* consisting of vegetables such as artichokes, broad beans, aubergines, peppers, tomatoes or *tortilla española* (Spanish omelette). One of the simplest vegetarian dishes is *tumbet* (a tomato-rich vegetable stew). Local vegetarian cuisine worth recommending includes *eggs al modo de Sóller* and Mahón-style beans. Most restaurants offer some vegetarian dishes. If there are none on the menu you can always ask for a salad (specify that you don't want meat or fish in it) or a *macedonia* (fruit salad), or even a *gazpacho* (the traditional Spanish cold tomato soup). Local cheeses are also great. Try the creamy, nutty queso *mallorquín* and the cured cheese from Maó.

The elegant interiors of Fosh (see p158), Palma

Booking

There are a large number of restaurants on the Balearic Islands and there should not be any problem in finding a table. Nevertheless, it is worthwhile booking a table in advance to avoid disappointment, particularly when you want to dine in reputable rural restaurants such as those attached to hotels, or those in a remote location.

Disabled Persons

New restaurants are obliged to have disabled access, but many older establishments remain inaccessible; they may not have wheelchair ramps and the tables tend to be placed close together. The most accessible

are the bars and small restaurants situated along seaside promenades, with outside tables.

Traditional paella is served throughout the region

Prices and Tipping

In beachside restaurants, prices are reasonable. A lunch will cost around €20 to €25. The *menú del día* may be even cheaper. The sky is the limit on prices charged by some of the top restaurants. Some regional dishes and seafood may be expensive. The price of the latter will depend on the weight of the ordered lobster or fish.

Mallorca and Ibiza tend to have the highest prices. The final bill includes service charges and tax and is, therefore, higher than the sum of the menu items. Normally, the tip does not exceed 10 per cent; it is usual to round up the bill.

Most restaurants welcome credit cards, though American Express is less common. Some bars take Visa, but small sums are normally paid in cash. Some small restaurants, especially those not geared up for tourists, may not accept credit cards at all – so it is best to check in advance.

Recommended Restaurants

The *nueva cocina* food phenomenon that has swept Catalonia is making headway in the Balearics. Mostly it is found in owner-run establishments, where the chef takes time-honoured recipes, the finest local ingredients and gives them a contemporary, personal twist, both in taste and presentation. At the other end of the spectrum, home-cooked meals prepared in family-run restaurants can provide an equally memorable meal.

Both these categories, and more, have been considered when choosing the restaurants featured in this guide. They span a wide choice of budget ranges and tastes, and cover something for everyone. For the "best of the best", we've marked recommended restaurants as DK Choice. These are the island's most outstanding establishments, offering singular experiences that are unrivalled by anything on the mainland.

Juan y Andrea (see p163) in Formentera, Platja Illetes

The Flavours of the Balearics

This quartet of beautiful islands, strategically positioned on ancient trading routes, has been fought over for thousands of years. Each occupying force – Arabs, Catalans, French and British among them – has left its mark, and the local cuisine reflects this. Mediterranean seafood, particularly spectacular lobster and crayfish, remains the most prominent local ingredient, but the islands are also known for their delicious pastries and desserts, like the feather-light *ensaimada* from Mallorca and the typical Ibizan *flaó*. Cured meats *(embutits)* and traditionally made cheeses are also local specialities.

Locally grown oranges

Mediterranean sea produce in a Mallorcan fish market

Mallorca and Menorca

Seafood predominates in the Balearic Islands. Menorca is renowned for *caldereta de llagosta* (spiny lobster stew), once a simple fishermen's dish but now a delicacy *(see p105)*. The classic Mallorcan dish is *pa amb oli*, a slice of toasted country bread rubbed with garlic and drizzled with local olive oil. Menorca's creamy garlic sauce *all i oli* is a delicious

accompaniment to meat and seafood dishes, and the island also produces fine cheese, *formatge de Maó*.

Ibiza and Formentera

Seafood also reigns supreme on Ibiza and its quieter little sister, Formentera, especially in *calders* (stews) such as *borrida de rajada* (skate with potatoes, eggs and pastis) and *guisat de peix*. Pork is

the staple meat. For a picnic, try *cocarrois*, pastries filled with meat, fish or vegetables, and *formatjades*, soft-cheese-filled pastries flavoured with cinnamon. Delicious local desserts include *gató* (almond cake served with ice cream) and Ibizan *flaó*, made with creamy cheese and eggs, and flavoured with mint.

Ensaimadas

Cuscussô Menorquin (bread pudding)

Flaó Ibicenco

Galletas de Alaior (aniseed biscuits)

Formatjades

Gató (almond tart)

Selection of delicious Balearic pastries

Regional Dishes and Specialities

Fish and shellfish (particularly the revered local lobster) are omnipresent in the Balearics, particularly along the coast. Try them simply grilled to fully appreciate their freshness (many seaside restaurants have their own fishing boats), but you will also find wonderful, slow-cooked stews which are bursting with flavour. The rugged inland regions provide mountain lamb and kid, along with pork, which is also used to make *embutits*, including spicy Mallorcan *sobrasada* which is delicious with *pa amb oli*.

All i oli (garlic and olive oil sauce

The tourist industry has not killed the longstanding farming tradition on the Balearics, which produce plentiful fruit and vegetables. Mallorca makes its own robust wines, particularly around the village of Binissalem, while Menorca, thanks to the long British occupation of the island, makes its own piquant gin.

Tumbet de peix A fish pie, made with layers of firm white fish, peppers, aubergine (eggplant) and sliced boiled egg.

Where to Eat and Drink

Mallorca

ALARÓ: Traffic €
Regional
Plaça de la Vila, 7, 07170 Alaró
Tel *971 879 117* **Closed** *Tue*
Located in an old manor with a
pleasant terrace by a garden
and pool. The *lechona* (suckling
pig) is a speciality.

**ALCÚDIA: Meson de
los Patos** €€
Seafood
*Cami de Ca'n Blau 42, Parque
Natural de S'Albufera, Bahía
d'Alcúdia, 07410*
Tel *971 890 265* **Closed** *Mon;
6 Jan–mid-Feb*
This eatery is located in the
beautiful Parc Natural de
S'Albufera. The menu includes
a variety of outstanding fish
dishes and an excellent
selection of island wines.

**ALCÚDIA: Restaurante
Jardín** €€€
Regional
C/ Tritones s/n, 07410, Port d'Alcúdia
Tel *971 892 391* **Closed** *Nov–Mar*
Michelin-starred fine dining with
a choice of service indoors, or
in the pretty outdoor garden.
Well-planned and beautifully
designed menu.

BINISSALEM: Es P'dal €
Bistro
Passeig des Born 8, 07350
Tel *971 511 061*
A pub-style old bar serving
quality pizzas and tapas with a

The elegant interiors of Restaurante Jardín,
a Michelin-starred restaurant in Alcúdia

good selection of beers and
local wines. A good place to
have a drink or a coffee.
Occasional live music.

BINISSALEM: Can Arabí €€
Mediterranean
Cami Bellveure, km 1.200, 07350
Tel *971 313 505* **Closed** *Mon*
Enjoy appetizing Mallorcan
and Mediterranean cuisine at
this country-style restaurant.
The daily menu is prepared
using fresh, locally sourced,
organic ingredients.

BUNYOLA: I un poc mes €
International
Santa Bàrbara 3, 07110
Tel *971 148 378* **Closed** *Sun dinner
& Mon*
A small cantina serving fresh
local fare in creative dishes
with Asian influences.

DK Choice

CAIMARI: Ca Na Toneta €€
Regional
Horitzó 21, 07314
Tel *971 515 226* **Closed** *winter:
Mon–Thu*
In a stylishly renovated
country house, Maria and
Teresa Solivellas treat their
customers like old friends.
Located amid the untouched
landscape near the village of
Caimari, Ca Na Toneta works
closely with local producers and
farmers to provide authentic
homecooking, though the
dishes have a contemporary
touch. The six-course menu is
worth the indulgence.

CALA RAJADA: La Casita €
Regional
C/ es Farallo 6, 07590
Tel *971 563 731* **Closed** *Tue*
The chef at this delightful restaurant serves meat and fish
prepared to his own exacting
recipes. The restaurant also
has a *bodega* with a range
of island wines.

**CALA RAJADA:
Cavall Bernat** €€€
Fusion
*C/ Maressers 2, Cala Sant Vicenç,
07469*
Tel *971 530 250* **Closed** *Nov–Apr:
Sun*
Offering a mix of classic Mallorcan
dishes and international recipes
(with a *cocina nueva* touch),
Cavall Bernat is a stylish, slightly
formal establishment.

Price Guide
For a three-course meal for one,
including half a bottle of house wine,
service and tax.

€	up to €30
€€	€30–€60
€€€	over €60

CALA RAJADA: Ses Rotges €€€
French
C/Rafael Blanes 21, 07590
Tel *971 563 108* **Closed** *Jan–mid-
Mar; Sun dinner;*
Mallorcan-influenced, classic
French dishes and great
home-made desserts. The
terrace overlooks a lovely
subtropical garden.

CALVIÀ: Lila Portals €€
Contemporary
Passatge Mor 1, Portals Nous, 07181
Tel *971 676 894*
Splendid terrace overlooking
the beach, this place serves
creative Mediterranean dishes
and surprising desserts. Tapas
dishes are served all day.

**CAMPANET: Es Mirador
Monnaber** €€
Contemporary
Possessió Monnaber Nou, 07310
Tel *971 877 176*
Attached to a regal country
house hotel, Es Mirador Monnaber
offers a choice of classic dishes
with a modern touch.

**COLÒNIA DE SANT JORDI:
Pep Serra** €€
Seafood
C/ Gabriel Roca 87, 07638
Tel *971 655 399* **Closed** *Mon–Fri;
Oct–Mar;*
Enjoy freshly caught fish and a
selection of other sea produce at
this charming seafront restaurant.
Don't miss the outstanding
langoustine paella.

**COLÒNIA DE SANT JORDI:
La Playa** €€€
Seafood
C/ Mayor 25, 07638
Tel *971 656 555* **Closed** *Mon lunch*
In a typical Mallorcan house
on the beach, this hotel and
restaurant serves paella, lobster
salad and fresh fish straight off
the boat.

DEIÀ: Café Miró €€€
Regional
Cami de Son Canals s/n, 07179
Tel *971 636 046* **Closed** *Sun*
Located in a splendid 17th-
century country house, this
bistro serves excellent local,
island cuisine.

For more information on types of restaurants *see page 153*

Charming indoor seating at the well-reviewed Santi Taura in Lloseta

DEIÀ: El Olivo €€€
Mediterranean
Son Canals s/n, 07179
Tel *971 639 011*   **Closed** *Winter: Mon & Tue*
Set inside a former olive mill, with additional seating out on a lovely terrace, this famous restaurant offers delightful options. The *menú degustación* is a memorable feast. Dress formally.

ESCORCA: Es Guix €€
Regional
Urbanización Es Guix, 07315
Tel *971 517 092*   **Closed** *Tue; Jan & Mar: Mon–Thu*
Outstanding traditional restaurant overlooking a rock pool in a lovely forested setting. Located near the Santuari de Lluc.

ESPORLES: Meson de la Villa €€
Regional
C/ Nou de Sant Pere 5, 07190
Tel *971 610 901*   **Closed** *summer: Sun & lunch; winter: Wed & Sun–Tue dinner; July*
This townhouse restaurant prides itself in being the first truly Castilian grill in Mallorca. Food is prepared in a rustic wood-burning grill.

FELANITX: Sa Llotja €€€
Mediterranean
C/Pescadors s/n Porto Colom, 07670
Tel *971 825 165*   **Closed** *Mon; Nov–Dec*
Appetizing Mediterranean cuisine based on fresh seasonal fare, particularly fish and vegetables. The restaurant occupies a beautiful 15th-century building overlooking the harbour.

INCA: Celler Ca'n Ripoll €
Regional
C/ Jaume Armengol 4, 07300
Tel *971 500 024*   **Closed** *Sun dinner*
A winery from the 1760s, Celler Ca'n Ripoll is an atmospherically

restored national heritage building. Try the island classics, such as the roast milk lamb, and for dessert, anything with fresh almonds.

INCA: S'Angel €
Tapas
Plaza del Ángel 2, 07300
Tel *971 880 473*
This place is renowned for its wide-ranging choice of innovative Mediterranean dishes and *pintxos*, plus its amazing selection of gin and tonics.

INCA: Cellar Can Amer €€
Regional
C/ Pau 39, 07300
Tel *971 501 261*   **Closed** *May–Sep: Sat & Sun; Winter: Sun dinner*
Hidden away in Inca's market, this award-winning restaurant serves classic Mallorcan cuisine. The recipes have been developed over decades of research into the origins of Mallorcan food.

DK Choice

LLOSETA: Santi Taura €€
Regional
C/Joan Carles I 48, 07360
Tel *656 738 214*   **Closed** *Mon lunch, Tue & Sun dinner; Aug: 2 weeks*
Local chef Santi Taura is a food anthropologist of sorts – he unearths old island recipes and reinterprets them. The restaurant offers a tasting menu, which changes weekly. With each course, the waiter (or often Santi himself) explains the cultural history of what's on your plate. Book in advance.

MANACOR: La Reserva Rotana €€€
International
Cami de Bendris, km 3, 07500
Tel *971 845 685*   **Closed** *lunch; mid-Nov–mid-Feb*
On the patio of this handsome 17th-century hotel, chef Cristian Denz combines Mallorcan and

international recipes to create wonderful gourmet delights, all presented with panache.

MONTUÏRI: Pizzeria Es Moli €
Bistro
C/ es Molinar 51, 07230
Tel *971 646 508*   **Closed** *Wed*
A pleasant restaurant set in an old windmill with fantastic views. Delicious home-made pizzas, fresh pasta and Italian salads on offer.

PALMA: Bar Cuba Colonial €
Mediterranean
C/ Sant Magí 1, 07013
Tel *971 452 237*
A lovely café with tables on the street. At night, it becomes a bar and salsa club with an à la carte menu on offer.

PALMA: Bon Lloc €
Vegetarian
C/ San Feliu 7, 07012
Tel *971 718 617*   **Closed** *Sun & Mon–Wed dinner*
One of the rare vegan and vegetarian restaurants in Mallorca, Bon Lloc offers a choice of light meals, cooked using local ingredients.

PALMA: Ca'n Torrat €
Regional
Carretera Maravillas, 25. Exit 11, Autopista de Palma (3 km from the airport) S'Arenal, 07610
Tel *971 262 055*   **Closed** *Wed*
Famed for its wood-fired barbecue and grill, Ca'n Torrat offers traditional local dishes such as suckling pig, roast lamb and fried fish.

PALMA: Café L'Antiquari €
Tapas
C/ Arabi 5, 07003
Tel *871 572 313*   **Closed** *Sun*
A relaxed place with an interesting decor and a friendly, almost hippy, vibe. Helpings are sizable but not too large, and the brunches are absolutely delectable.

Lovely outdoor seating under the trees at El Olivo, Deià

PALMA: Can Punta €
International
C/ Vicario Joaquin Fuster 105, 07006
Tel 971 274 334   **Closed** Summer: Mon; Winter: dinner (except Fri & Sat & Tue)
Pretty café and restaurant on the waterfront at Portixol. The menu includes Greek-inspired salads, tapas, and coffee and snacks throughout the day.

PALMA: Cappuccino €
Café
C/ de Sant Miquel 53, 07002
Tel 971 719 764   **Closed** Sun
In the heart of Palma, this stylish café offers great morning coffee, light lunches and wonderful evening drinks.

PALMA: Club Nautico Cala Gamba €
Seafood
Passeig Cala Gamba s/n, 07007
Tel 971 262 372   **Closed** Mon
With its nautical theme and large windows that overlook the marina, this restaurant is a must-visit. The menu includes an interesting choice of locally-caught fish.

PALMA: Fibonacci Pan €
Bistro
C/Vicario Joaquin Fuster 95, 07006
Tel 971 264 258
Scandinavian bakery that offers excellent sandwiches, cakes, croissants and top-rate coffee. Also serves light salads and soups at lunchtime.

PALMA: Koh €
Asian
C/de Servet 15, 07013
Tel 971 287 039   **Closed** Sun & lunch
In Palma's Santa Catalina district, Koh serves tasty and tangy dishes – curries, noodles, barbecued meats and Vietnamese rolls. Street-food nights on Wednesdays.

PALMA: Molta Barra €
Tapas
Carrer del Pes de la Farina 12, 07001
Tel 971 076 767   **Closed** Sun & Mon
With delightful tapas and pintxos at good prices, this popular eatery is an integral part of the night scene in the buzzing Sa Gerreria area.

PALMA: Quina Creu €
Bistro
C/ Corderia 24, 07001
Tel 971 711 772   **Closed** Sun
Views of an ancient street to accompany good, unpretentious bistro fare. Eclectic, retro decor and a friendly ambience.

La Taberna de la Bóveda, Palma, offering food from Castile and the Basque Country

PALMA: La Taberna de la Bóveda €
Tapas
Passeig Sagrera 3, 07012
Tel 971 720 026   **Closed** Sun
Popular tapas bar with pretty period decor. Serves large helpings of Basque Country and Castilian favourites.

PALMA: Tast €
Tapas
C/ de la Unió 2, 07001
Tel 971 729 878   **Closed** Sun
Popular local place that serves top-quality tapas and pintxos, with bite-sized canapés made with farmhouse cheese and charcuterie (cooked cold meats).

PALMA: La Bodeguilla €€
Tapas
C/ Sant Jaume 3, 07012
Tel 971 718 274
A superb tapas bar with a dining room upstairs, this Palma institution serves typical Mallorcan cuisine.

PALMA: Forn de Sant Joan €€
Regional
C/ Sant Joan 4, 07012
Tel 971 728 422
One of Palma's best restaurants, in an old bakery spread over four floors. It serves imaginative dishes with a modern touch.

PALMA: El Gallego €€
Seafood
C/ Carmen 16, 07003
Tel 971 710 313   **Closed** dinner (except Thu–Sat)
Popular noisy eatery that serves Galician seafood specialities. Try the steamed mussels, octopus or cod with salsa verde.

PALMA: Nassau Beach Club €€
Seafood
Passeig de Portitxol 5, 07004
Tel 664 449 053
Nassau Beach Club is popular with both locals and visitors, who come here to enjoy salads and ciabattas, or sushi and fresh fish, while lounging on a deck chair on the beach. The Sunday brunches have live DJs.

PALMA: Las Olas Bistro €€
Fusion
C/ Can Fortuny 5, 07001
Tel 971 214 905   **Closed** Sun, Mon & Tue
This smart little eatery leads a double life: it serves French-Mediterranean lunches by day and Asian cuisine by night, with a special focus on Vietnamese and Cambodian dishes.

PALMA: Toque €€
Belgian
C/ Federico García Lorca 6, 07014
Tel 971 287 068   **Closed** Sun & Mon
Toque is a family restaurant serving delicious mussels, escargots in green sauce, steak tartare and premium desserts; all accompanied by a good selection of Belgian beers, French and local wines. Book in advance.

PALMA: Wasabi Blue €€
Fusion
C/ Trafalgar 41, El Molinar, 07007
Tel 971 264 602   **Closed** Oct–Mar; Tue & Sun dinner
A renowned fusion restaurant by the seafront, Wasabi Blue serves remarkable sushi and uses local fish to make a variety of makis, rolls and sashimi.

Selecting a suitable wine match at La Bodeguilla tapas bar, Palma

For more information on types of restaurants see page153

The modern interiors of Fosh in the hotel Convent de la Missió in Palma

DK Choice

PALMA: Fosh €€€
Mediterranean
C/ de la Missió 7A, 07003
Tel 971 720 114
British chef Marc Fosh has
garnered a reputation of
being one of the island's
finest chefs. Fosh is a stylish
restaurant located in the hip
Convent de la Missió hotel,
where Fosh makes use of local
ingredients to create the most
extraordinary Mediterranean
delights. The menu changes
seasonally. It offers a good
wine list and a truly memorable experience.

POLLENÇA: Manzanas y Peras €
Tapas
C/ Martell 6, Plaça Seglars, 07460
Tel 971 532 292
On a little square at the foot of
the Via Crucis, this boho café-
restaurant has every reason to
be proud of its fresh and tasty menu,
featuring a delicious range of
home-made tapas.

POLLENÇA: Clivia €€
Regional
Avinguda Pollentia 5, 07460
Tel 971 533 635
An excellent range of Spanish
dishes are available here – try
the squid in ink. If you choose
fish, the waiter will show you
the raw fish first.

POLLENÇA: Il Giardino €€
Italian
Plaça Major 11, 07460
Tel 971 534 302 **Closed** Nov–Feb
One of the best restaurants in
Pollença, this bistro-style place
offers top Italian fare prepared
with quality local ingredients.
The ravioli stuffed with wild
mushrooms is particularly good.

POLLENÇA:
3/65 Restaurant €€€
Regional
Crta Palma–Pollença PM 220,
km 49.9, 07460
Tel 971 535 353 **Closed** daily
lunch & Tue (except Aug); Dec–Jan
Part of the chic boutique
hotel Son Brull, this elegant
restaurant serves gourmet
cuisine created from fresh
local ingredients and produce
of the hotel's own certified
organic farm.

PORT DE POLLENÇA:
Bellaverde €
Vegetarian
C/ Monges 14, 07470
Tel 675 602 528 **Closed** Mon
An outstanding vegetarian and
vegan café-restaurant with a
delightful shaded courtyard
and a simply superb menu:
try, for example, the pumpkin
lasagne with goats' cheese,
or the beetroot fusilli.

Diners at the busy Hell's Kitchen in
Port de Pollença

PORT DE POLLENÇA:
Hell's Kitchen €
International
C/ Verge del Carme 8, 07470
Tel 971 867 163 **Closed** Winter: Mon
& Tue
A friendly café run by expats that
offers home-made cuisine, from
curries to pasta, and even British
staples such as a Sunday roast.

PORT DE POLLENÇA: Laguna €
International
Edificio Bonança, C/ El Faro 15, 07470
Tel 971 864 919 **Closed** Nov–Mar
Delicious cocktails and appet-
izing meals by the pool, in
keeping with the laid-back,
tropical ambience.

PORT DE POLLENÇA: Neptuno €
Seafood
C/ Migjorn 8, 07470
Tel 971 867 859
A bright, nautical-themed eatery
serving tapas and home-made
meals. It also has a children's
menu. Reservations essential.

PORT DE POLLENÇA:
Corb Mari €€
Seafood
Passeig Anglada Camarassa 91, 07470
Tel 971 867 040 **Closed** Mon
(except Jun–Aug); Dec–mid-Mar
While it specializes in grilled
meat, Corb Mari also whips
up some of the best paellas
in Pollença. Don't forget to
try the barbecued prawns,
squid kebabs and monkfish.

PORT DE POLLENÇA: Iru €€
Contemporary
Paseo Anglada Camarasa 23, 07470
Tel 971 867 002 **Closed** Tue
(except in summer); mid-Nov–Feb
Innovative fish and meat dishes,
served on a sunny terrace near
the Port of Pollença. Reasonably
priced, with light pastas and
salads at lunchtime.

PORT DE POLLENÇA:
La Llonja €€
Seafood
Moll Vell s/n, 07470
Tel *971 868 430* **Closed** *Nov–Mar: Tue*
An elegant place with a weekly menu that is based on what the fishermen bring in. Try the legendary lobster stew – it is absolutely divine.

PORT DE POLLENÇA: Stay €€
International
Muelle Nuevo s/n, 07470
Tel *971 864 013*
A charming glass-fronted restaurant with great views that sits right on the port. It serves delicious fish, pasta and salads.

PORT DE SÓLLER:
Muleta de Ca S'Hereu €€
Regional
Camp de sa Mar s/n, 07100
Tel *971 186 018*
Rustic eatery at a charming rural hotel ; serves modest salad lunches but generous home-cooked meals in the evenings.

PORT DE SÓLLER: Es Fanals €€€
Seafood
C/ Belgica s/n, 07108
Tel *971 637 886*
Part of the luxurious Jumeriah resort, this lunch-only, alfresco restaurant serves stellar seafood against a spectacular Mediterranean backdrop.

PORTO COLOM:
Sa Sinia €€
Seafood
C/ Pescadores 28, 07670
Tel *971 824 323* **Closed** *Mon; Nov–Jan*
Among the finest restaurants in Mallorca, Sa Sinia is well-known for its unique seafood creations, home-made desserts and warm, friendly service.

DK Choice

SA COMA:
Es Molí d'en Bou €€€
Regional
C/ Liles s/n, 07560
Tel *971 569 663* **Closed** *Mon, Tue–Fri lunch & Sun*
Es Molí d'en Bou has been awarded a Michelin star in recognition of chef Tomeu Caldentey's subtle, creative interpretations of Mallorcan cuisine. Enjoy the artistry of the tasting menu or dishes such as suckling pig with apples and *sobrasada* or *solomillo* with white asparagus and clams.

SÓLLER: El Guia €
Regional
C/ Castañer 2, 07100
Tel *971 630 227*
El Guia is the dining room of an old-fashioned, family-run hotel in the heart of Sóller; in addition to a friendly ambience, it offers a number of well-prepared classic dishes.

SÓLLER: Sa Cova €€
International
Plaça Constitució 7, 07100
Tel *971 633 222* **Closed** *Sun dinner*
Enjoy rabbit in garlic sauce, crab with snails, or couscous with vegetables and meats. A range of vegetarian dishes is also available.

SÓLLER: Bens d'Avall €€€
Regional
Urb. Costa Deià. Ctra Sóller–Deià, 07100
Tel *971 632 381* **Closed** *Mon & Tue lunch; Winter: Mon–Thu*
This restaurant sits in a wonderful setting and enjoys stunning views of the coast and Deià. The food builds upon the best of local ingredients.

VALLDEMOSSA:
C'an Costa €€
Regional
Carretera Deià, km 2.5, 07170
Tel *971 612 263* **Closed** *Nov–Mar; Tue*
Charming and rural, this restaurant wows diners with simple, rustic-style cooking. The suckling pig is a speciality.

Menorca

ALAIOR: Ca'n Jaumot €
Tapas
C/ Sant Joan Baptista 6, 07730
Tel *971 378 294* **Closed** *May–Aug: Sun*
A popular local rendezvous, offers a wide assortment of tapas, pizzas, salads and sandwiches, together with a good collection of wines.

ALAIOR: Es Forn de Torre Solí Nou €€
Regional
Urb Torre Solí Nou, 07730
Tel *971 372 898*
Excellent meat and poultry *a la brasa* (char-grilled). The best tables in this attractive restaurant are those on the breezy terrace.

CALA EN PORTER: Sa Païssa €
Bistro
Av da Central 54, 07730
Tel *971 377 389*
Conveniently located in the centre of Cala en Porter in an eponymous hostel, Sa Païssa offers a fairly good selection of well-cooked dishes. Breakfast, lunch and dinner available.

CIUTADELLA:
Bar Aurora €
Tapas
Plaça Alfons III 3, 07760
Tel *971 481 994*
Located in one of Ciutadella's most charming squares, Bar Aurora is a tapas institution and local favourite. Try the meatballs and grilled squid.

CIUTADELLA: Sa Xarxa €
Regional
C/ Sebastià 3, 07760
Tel *971 480 323*
This informal café-bar serves a good selection of tapas and snacks, all at fairly low prices (starting from €6). Its pavement terrace, just off the main drag, is a good place for people watching in the evening.

CIUTADELLA:
Es Tastet €
Regional
C/ Carnisseria 9, 07760
Tel *971 384 797* **Closed** *Feb; summer: Sun lunch; winter: Sun dinner*
A wonderful, friendly place for breakfast, as well as creative tapas, pasta and fish through the day. The owner takes pride in cooking with fresh market produce.

The stunning outdoors at Es Forn de Torre Solí Nou, Alaior

For more information on types of restaurants *see page 153*

Table laid out at the Son Granot restaurant, part of a beautiful rural hotel in Es Castell

CIUTADELLA: Cas Ferrer de Sa Font €€
Regional
C/ Portal de Sa Font 16, 07760
Tel *971 480 784* **Closed** *Nov–Mar; Jun–Aug: Sun lunch*
Spread out over three rooms of an imposing 17th-century mansion, this restaurant offers a small but worthy menu. The dishes are mostly island specials, cooked using organic produce from its own kitchen garden.

CIUTADELLA: Pins 46 €€
Mediterranean
Plaça dels Pins 46, 07760
Tel *971 481 674*
This smart restaurant – a branch of a small, local chain – offers a well-chosen menu featuring such delights as lobster with onion or grilled local prawns. Eat either inside or outside, in the garden courtyard.

CIUTADELLA: Es Tast de na Silvia €€
Mediterranean
Passeig de Portixol 21–22, 07760
Tel *971 387 895* **Closed** *Wed; Nov–Mar*
Enjoy top-notch Mediterranean cuisine served in a romantic ambience. Es Tast ranks as one of the best among a series of touristy restaurants in the area.

CIUTADELLA: Café Balear €€€
Seafood
Pla de Sant Joan 15, 07760
Tel *971 380 005*
Formerly a fishermen's quayside inn, Café Balear even has its own boat, which goes out every morning to catch the day's menu. This is one of the best fish eateries on the entire island of Menorca.

ES CASTELL: Sant Joan de Binissaida €€
Regional
Cami de Binissaida 108, 07720
Tel *971 355 598* **Closed** *Nov–Apr*
Savour traditional Menorcan dishes in the stone-walled dining room, or in the lush gardens of this beautiful rural hotel.

ES CASTELL: Son Granot €€
Regional
Carretera Sant Felip s/n, 07720
Tel *971 355 555*
Family recipes for traditional fare prepared with vegetables from the kitchen garden of this country hotel. The Georgian-style building dates back to 1712.

ES MERCADAL: Es Moli d'es Racó €€
Regional
C/ Major 53, 07740
Tel *971 375 275*
No-frills country restaurant that makes good use of an old wind-mill. Top-class traditional food and a good choice of island wines.

ES MIGJORN GRAN: S'Engolidor €€
Regional
C/ Major 3, 07749
Tel *971 370 193* **Closed** *Nov–Mar; Mon & daily lunch*
Found behind the simple façade of a four-room hotel, S'Engolidor is a real treat. The menu features delicious Menorcan dishes – try the tender baby lamb and aubergine stuffed with fish.

FERRERIES: Liorna €
International
C/ Econòm Florit (C/ de Dalt) 9, 07750
Tel *971 373 912* **Closed** *summer: Mon; winter: Mon–Thu*
Damia Coll's restaurant doesn't just look like an art gallery – it is one. Options include pizzas, sushi and Thai specials.

FERRERIES: Meson El Gallo €€
Regional
Ctra Cala Galdana, km 1.5, 07750
Tel *971 373 039* **Closed** *Mon; summer: lunch (except Sat & Sun); winter: dinner (except Fri & Sat); Dec & Jan*
The signature dish of this farmhouse restaurant just outside Ferreries is *gallo* (rooster) paella. Also popular are the lip-smacking steaks, best relished with Mallorcan cheese.

FORNELLS: Ca Na Marga €€
Regional
Urbanización "Ses Salines", Parc núm. 1, 07748
Tel *971 376 410* **Closed** *Nov–Apr; lunch*
Family-run restaurant in Ses Salines, where fish, meat and vegetables *a la brasa* (char-grilled) is the mainstay.

FORNELLS: Sa Rumbada €€
Seafood
C/ Gumersindo Riera 27, 07748
Tel *971 376 777* **Closed** *Nov–Apr*
This attractive seaside restaurant has a splendid terrace and a laid-back ambience. Don't miss the famed, delicious lobster stew.

MAÓ: Sa Gavina II €
Regional
Moll de Llevant 157, 07701
Tel *971 350 691*
Small restaurant serving traditional food and home-made bread. Ask for the *raciones* (portions) menu to try more than one dish.

MAÓ: Restaurante Way €
Japanese
Moll de Llevant 216, 07701, Port de Maó
Tel *971 143 692*
A matchless Japanese restaurant where the sushi, maki and tempura are made using local catch. They also serve Chinese cuisine.

Key to Price Guide *see page 155*

MAÓ: Cap Roig €€
Seafood
Ctra Sa Mesquida 13, 07589, Sa Mesquida
Tel *971 188 383* **Closed** *mid–Oct–Easter*
Named after the star of its menu – scorpion fish – Cap Roig is highly recommended. Its *caldereta de llagosta* (lobster stew) is another excellent option, as is the Norway crab or crayfish, when available. Enjoy your food with stunning sea views from the cliff-top location.

MAÓ: Casa Sexto €€
Seafood
C/ Vassallo 2, 07703
Tel *971 368 407* **Closed** *Sun dinner*
Casa Sexto produces delectable Galician specialities using fresh regional ingredients, including a variety of seafood, shellfish and cheese.

DK Choice

MAÓ: La Minerva €€€
Regional
Moll de Llevant 87, 07701
Tel *971 351 995* **Closed** *Mon; Jan*
A classic hangout for the island's yacht club crowd, La Minerva is the place to be seen. If you are lucky enough to get a table on the floating terrace in the harbour, you will be served the longest menu in Menorca. A wide range of meat dishes are on offer, as well as fish, notably the seafood *zarzuela* (stew). There is also a good fixed-price menu.

SANT LLUIS: Pan y Vino €€
Regional
Cami de la Coixa 3, Torret, 07710
Tel *971 150 201* **Closed** *Tue; Dec–mid Feb; Sun dinner; winter: Fri lunch*
French chef Patrick James uses seasonal produce to prepare elaborate local dishes with a French touch in this charming restaurant that is based in an old farmhouse.

SANTA GALDANA: El Mirador €€
Regional
Platja Cala Galdana s/n, 07750
Tel *971 154 503*
This charming eatery, located on a rocky headland, offers gorgeous views and delicious house specials, which usually include paella and fresh fish-of-the-day. It also has an excellent wine list.

Ibiza

EIVISSA: Locals Only €
Mediterranean
Plaça del Parc 5, 07800
Tel *971 301 997* **Closed** *Mon*
Opened by Tito Piazza, former chef of the famous Cipriani restaurant in New York, Locals Only serves classic island cuisine. Cocktails and brunch are also available.

EIVISSA: La Masia d'en Sort €
Contemporary
Ctra de Sant Miquel, km 1, 07800
Tel *971 310 228* **Closed** *Mon (except Aug); daily for lunch*
A handsome 200-year-old country house with lovingly prepared island classics, to be enjoyed under lemon trees.

EIVISSA: Ca n'Alfredo €€
Seafood
Passeig Vara de Rey 16, 07800
Tel *971 311 274* **Closed** *Mon & Sun dinner; Nov: 2 weeks*
The oldest restaurant in Eivissa, located in a mansion on the port. Its menu is largely based on fish and rice.

EIVISSA: La Brasa €€€
International
Carrer de Pere Sala 3, 07800
Tel *971 301 202* **Closed** *winter: Sun*
This incredible restaurant, with a pleasant garden, is part of a villa in the old town.

EIVISSA: Las Dos Lunas €€€
International
Ctra Ibiza–San Antonio, km 5.4, 07840
Tel *971 198 102* **Closed** *Nov–April*
One of the most exclusive restaurants in Ibiza, Las Dos Lunas has an Italian and Mediterranean menu. Get a chance to rub elbows with many visiting celebrities.

EIVISSA: El Faro €€€
Seafood
Plaça Sa Riba 1, 07800
Tel *971 313 233* **Closed** *Oct–Apr*
Large terrace and palm-shaded garden. One of the best places to eat fish in Ibiza.

EIVISSA: El Olivo €€€
French
Plaça de la Vila 9, 07800
Tel *971 300 680* **Closed** *mid–Oct–mid–Apr; lunch*
Popular restaurant with a trendy terrace in the fashionable Dalt Vila. The cuisine is Ibizan-French with a *cocina nueva* edge.

EIVISSA: Sa Punta €€€
Fusion
Es Puet de Talamanca, 07819, Bahía de Talamanca
Tel *971 193 424* **Closed** *Nov–Mar*
This is the place to be seen in Sa Punta. Dishes combine island cuisine with ritzy flourishes of Italian, Thai and Japanese.

FIGUERETAS: Soleado €€
Seafood
Passeig Ses Pitiusas s/n, 07800
Tel *971 394 811* **Closed** *Nov–Apr*
On the palm-lined seafront, this terrace restaurant reflects its French owners' culinary heritage.

SANT ANTONI DE PORTMANY: Rincon de Pepe €
Tapas
Sant Mateu 6, 07820
Tel *971 340 697* **Closed** *Nov–Mar*
Original quayside tapas bar and restaurant with a good variety and a point-at-what-you-want system that works well.

SANT ANTONI DE PORTMANY: Es Rebost de Ca'n Prats €€
Regional
C/ Cervantes 4, 07820
Tel *971 346 252* **Closed** *Tue; Jan*
This family-run restaurant is the place for an authentic Ibizan dining experience in Sant Antoni.

SANT ANTONI DE PORTMANY: Sa Capella €€€
Regional
Ctra Sant Antoni–Santa Agnès, km 1, 07820
Tel *971 340 057* **Closed** *Nov–Mar; daily for lunch*
This 16th-century chapel has been transformed into a lovely restaurant with a terrace and *Modernista* decor.

Seating at Soleado, overlooking the Figueretas seafront

For more information on types of restaurants *see page 153*

The dining area at Sant Josep de Talaia's Es Torrent, located on the beach

SANT CARLES DE PERALTA:
Anita's Bar €
Tapas
Lugar Barri, Sant Carles s/n, 07850
Tel *971 335 090*
With its vine-covered patio and a range of tapas and pizzas, this hippy bar, a big player in Ibiza's counterculture, remains a firm local favourite.

SANT JOSEP DE SA TALAIA:
El Destino €
Tapas
Calle de Talaia 15, 07830
Tel *971 800 341*   **Closed** *Sun; Nov–Mar*
The diverse patronage furthers El Destino's reputation as the most famous tapas bar and restaurant in Ibiza. Tapas come with a twist of Moroccan and hints of Asian flavours, crossed with traditional island cuisine. Book in advance.

SANT JOSEP DE SA TALAIA:
Sa Caleta €€€
Seafood
Playa de es Bol Nou, 07830
Tel *971 187 095*   **Closed** *winter: dinner*
A beach club with a garden and sunloungers, Sa Caleta is an idyllic spot for a drink. The menu includes delicious grilled fish and seafood.

SANT JOSEP DE TALAIA:
Es Torrent €€€
Seafood
Cala d'es Torrent, Ctra Porroig to Sant Josep, 07839
Tel *971 802 160*   **Closed** *Nov–Easter*
With tables right on the beach, this eatery serves superb fish, seafood and rice dishes. It is very popular with the locals.

SANT JOSEP DE SA TALAIA:
Es Xarcu €€€
Seafood
Cala Es Xarcu, Porroig, 07839
Tel *971 187 867*   **Closed** *Nov–Easter*
This informal eatery located on the beach of a small, tranquil bay serves local fish, hand-cut *jamón* (ham) and tapas under grass parasols.

SANT LLORENÇ:
Cami de Balafia €€
International
Ctra Sant Joan de Labritja, km 15.4 (Ctra Sant Llorenç), 07812
Tel *971 325 019*   **Closed** *Mon*
A hacienda-type patio under the stars, this is a family-run restaurant that serves juicy steaks and grilled meat dishes.

DK Choice

SANT LLORENÇ:
La Paloma €€
Mediterranean
C/Can Pou 4, 07812
Tel *971 325 543*   **Closed** *Oct–Jun: Mon; Nov*
Garden restaurant surrounded by fruit orchards. In winter, it moves indoors to the renovated *finca*. A small range of Italian-inspired dishes is made with local, organic ingredients. The café, also on the premises, is great for breakfasts and lunches.

SANT RAFAEL: El Ayoun €€€
Moroccan
C/ Isidor Macabich 6, 07816
Tel *971 198 335*   **Closed** *lunch*
This is as authentic as a Moroccan restaurant gets in Ibiza. On the menu are variations on couscous and tagine, with some spicy starters.

SANT RAFAEL: El Clodenis €€€
International
Plaça d'Església s/n, 07816
Tel *971 198 545*   **Closed** *Apr–Jun: Sun; winter: Sun–Wed*
This venerable Ibizan restaurant in a great, whitewashed island house with a terrace serves Provençal cuisine and traditional island dishes. Simple and good, just like the atmosphere.

SANT RAFAEL:
L'Elephant €€€
Fusion
Plaça de l'Església s/n, 07816
Tel *971 198 056*   **Closed** *Nov–Apr; lunch*
The French fusion menu at L'Elephant includes a good choice of fish, though there are also meat and vegetarian options. The decor is stylish and minimalist, and there is a lovely rooftop terrace.

SANTA EULÀRIA DES RIU:
Can Cosmi €
Regional
C/ Sant Jaume 44, 07840
Tel *971 807 315*   **Closed** *winter: Tue dinner; mid-Dec–mid-Jan*
Historic institution that serves some of the best tortillas in Ibiza. Admire the work of local artists displayed on the walls.

SANTA EULÀRIA DES RIU:
El Bigotes €€
Seafood
Cala Mastella, Sant Carles, 07850
Tel *650 797 633*   **Closed** *Nov–Mar; daily for dinner*
Perched overlooking a *cala* (cove) with crystalline waters, El Bigotes serves fresh-off-the-boat fish in a picturesque outdoor setting.

The garden restaurant at La Paloma in Sant Llorenç, surrounded by fruit orchards

Bartender serves wine to customers at Bar Costa, a typical village inn in Santa Gertrudis de Fruitera

SANTA EULÀRIA DES RIU: Es Caliu €€
Regional
C/Sant Joan, km 10.8, 07840
Tel *971 325 075* **Closed** *Jul–Aug; lunch; end-Dec–end-Jan*
This country-style eatery is well established on Ibiza's culinary map. Specialities include grilled steaks, suckling pig and rabbit.

SANTA EULÀRIA DES RIU: Can Pep Salvado €€
Regional
Ctra Es Canar, km 2.5, 07840
Tel *971 338 171* **Closed** *Mon*
Traditional Ibizan dishes such as mixed fish with *all i oli* and Spanish staples draw patrons to this roadside restaurant.

SANTA EULÀRIA DES RIU: La Casita €€
Bistro
Urbanización Valverde–Cala Llonga 60, 07849
Tel *971 330 293* **Closed** *Feb; Tue; lunch (except Sat & Sun)*
A country restaurant with a beautiful garden. The Summer menu includes green fig soup, goat's cheese and pesto salad.

SANTA GERTRUDIS DE FRUITERA: Bar Costa €
Tapas
Plaça de l'Església s/n, 07819
Tel *971 197 021* **Closed** *Tue*
Famous for its *bocadillos* (hearty sandwiches) and art-adorned walls, Bar Costa is in every way a typical *venta* (country inn).

Formentera

ES CALÓ: Es Caló €€
Regional
C/ Vicari Joan Mari 14, Es Caló de Sant Agustí, 07872
Tel *971 327 311* **Closed** *Nov–Mar*
With stunning views over the sea and the cliffs of La Mola,

this elegant beach restaurant has an open-air wood and stone dining room. Highlights on the menu include delicious regional specialities, such as fresh seafood and rice. The desserts are absolutely fabulous.

ES CALÓ: Restaurante Pascual €€€
Seafood
Carrer des Vicari Joan Mary 2, 07872, Pilar de la Mola
Tel *971 327 014*
A large terrace and lovely gardens lend this eatery a beautiful ambience. The menu offers varieties of fresh fish.

LA MOLA: Blue Bar €
Bistro
Platja Es Migjorn Gran, Ctra Sant Ferran de Ses Roques–La Mola, km 8, 07871
Tel *666 758 190* **Closed** *Nov–Mar*
One of the original 1960s hippy beach bars; serves modest salads, tasty pasta, fish and a host of vegetarian options.

LA MOLA: Es Mirador €€
Seafood
Carretera de la Mola, km 14.3, 07860
Tel *971 327 037* **Closed** *mid-Oct–Apr*
This charming restaurant can be found at the easternmost promontory of the island, with views of Ibiza in the distance. Apart from its spectacular setting, Es Mirador offers tasty island fare such as paella and fresh fish.

LA SAVINA: Aigua €€
International
Port de la Savina s/n, 07870
Tel *971 323 322*
The menu at this beach club ranges from Italian-inspired dishes to sushi, with cocktails served at the gin bar late into the evening.

LA SAVINA: Bellavista €€
Seafood
Port de La Savina, 07870
Tel *971 323 324*
One of Ibiza's best restaurants away from the beach, Bellavista has a large terrace offering views of the port.

DK Choice

PLATJA ILLETES: Juan y Andrea €€€
Seafood
Platja Illetes s/n, 07860
Tel *971 187 130* **Closed** *Oct–Apr*
From fresh fish and shellfish to lobster (caught by the restaurant's fishing boat), Juan y Andrea serves excellent food. Local rice dishes are a speciality, as are the grilled prawns and the lobster *ajillo* (chopped garlic). The eatery overlooks Platja de Illetas, one of the wildest and most beautiful beaches in the Mediterranean.

A retro snooker table in the eclectic interiors of Blue Bar, La Mola

For more information on types of restaurants *see page 153*

SHOPPING IN THE BALEARIC ISLANDS

As elsewhere in Spain, the islands produce a wide variety of good leatherware, with Inca, in Mallorca, having a worldwide reputation for footwear. Those looking for items of clothing often head to Ibiza, which is known for its "ad-lib" fashion trends and the prevalence of jewellery stalls. Locally produced ceramics also make good souvenirs and are available on all of the islands, as are other island crafts including embroidery and basketwork. Local produce should also not be ignored, and bringing home a string of garlic, some spicy sausages or a good bottle of Mallorcan wine is as good a way as any of remembering the holiday.

Ceramics shop in Maó, Menorca

Where to Buy

Souvenirs of the Balearic Islands can be bought almost anywhere and the number of small shops offering all sorts of knick-knacks and mementos is truly amazing. They can be found in the historic parts of towns, in tourist centres and near harbours and beaches. Almost every hotel has its own boutique. There are also numerous shops selling clothes and anything that may be useful on the beach, including mattresses, mats, hats, beach balls and sun-block creams.

The items offered by boutiques can also be found in larger shopping centres, where you can buy food and various factory products. Palma has the largest choice of shops while Maó, in Menorca, has quite a few outlets and can cater for most holidaymakers' tastes.

Factory shops are good places to buy souvenirs.

They offer slightly lower prices and a much larger selection of goods. The specialist centres are also great places to hunt for souvenirs including pottery or synthetic pearls.

Opening Hours

The large shops in tourist centres are usually open from

Boutiques and restaurants along a seaside promenade

9am until 9pm. Some close for a siesta between 2pm and 5pm. Boutiques have similar opening hours. Shops along the beaches open virtually non-stop. These are the most reliable places to buy food and other basic articles. During high season most shops remain open seven days a week.

Provincial towns and villages do not have such regular opening hours and are more attuned to the pace of life of the local people than to holiday-makers. Shops in small villages may also close at weekends.

How to Pay

When shopping in small shops, food stores and markets, it is customary to pay in cash. Elsewhere, all major cards are widely accepted.

Markets

Markets are an integral feature of the Mallorcan scenery. They are held at weekly intervals, mostly in the provincial towns and villages of the island. They mainly serve the local population, although during high season they also offer many goods aimed at tourists. Besides everyday domestic items, most of them sell fruit, vegetables and sometimes locally produced sauces and preserves. Markets tend to start in the mornings and end early in the afternoon.

Hippy markets are held mainly on Formentera and Ibiza. Aimed squarely at visitors, they offer colourful clothes reminiscent of the fashions popular in the 1960s, as well as every type of ornament, including brooches, earrings, necklaces, belts and bracelets made of shells. These bustling markets are organized during the high season only and, unlike traditional Mallorcan markets, they are held every day.

Food

The Balearic Islands offer a number of unique food products that are specific to the region. The delicious *ensaimada* pastry, popular with tourists, is packed in distinctive octagonal boxes, making it easy to transport. Gourmets may be tempted by *sobrasada* – a spicy pork sausage produced in several varieties and used in many Balearic dishes. Strings of dried peppers, or olives prepared in a variety of ways, attract those who wish to bring back culinary souvenirs. All these products can be bought in markets and food stores. Shops that sell exclusively Balearic food are very attractive. The sheer number and variety of colourful products on display will tempt anyone to step inside.

Hippy bazaar in San Francesc on Formentera

The most popular alcohols produced on the islands include gin from Maó and herb liqueurs. You can taste the local gin in the Xoriguer Distillery in Maó *(see p100)*. Liqueurs are produced in a great number of varieties on all the islands and can be sampled in the shops that sell them. Balearic wines are also well worth trying. The best wines come from the Binissalem region on Mallorca, where a grand wine festival is held every year in September. There are two main wine-producing regions in the Balearic Islands – Binissalem and Pla i Llevant, both on Mallorca. Wines that are especially worth sampling include those from the cellars of Jaume de Puntiró, Macià Batle, Vins Nadal, Ànima Negra, Pere Seda and Miquel Gelabert.

Dried peppers

Souvenirs

These days it can be difficult to buy genuine local handicrafts on the Balearic Islands. Sometimes you can find them in markets, but you may find they have been largely replaced by factory-made articles that imitate handicrafts. These include ceramics decorated with traditional patterns, typical of the islands. The most characteristic pottery items – the *siurells* produced mainly on Mallorca – are colourful whistles in the shape of people or animals, painted in white, red and green. They can be bought in many places at the markets, in small shops and in large stores that sell Balearic pottery. Popular, but expensive, is the glassware produced by the three glassworks on Mallorca. At the Ca'n Gordiola glassworks near Algaida you can witness the production process *(see p91)*. Equally popular are articles made of olive wood, such as bowls and mortars produced by the Olive-Art factory near Manacor.

Also close to Manacor is Perlas Majorica, a shop selling high-quality simulated pearls that can be bought in smart boutiques all over Europe, as well *(see p85)*.

Items of clothing are popular souvenirs. Espadrilles (traditional canvas footwear) can be found in Ibiza. Leather goods such as wallets, handbags, jackets and sandals are prevalent in Menorca. T-shirts and baseball caps with humorous slogans and pictures abound on all the islands.

Shop selling local delicacies in Palma

What to Buy in the Balearic Islands

The choice of souvenirs in the Balearic Islands is considerable, but it can be difficult to find genuine local handicrafts among them. However, it is still possible to buy items from each of the islands that is characteristic of the place. In Mallorca, these include simulated pearls, glassware, dolls and wines from the Binissalem region; in Menorca – leather goods, textiles and local gin; in Ibiza – hippy souvenirs or club clothes.

Doll in regional costume

Plate decorated with cobalt

Ceramics

Ceramic items are among the most popular souvenirs. The variety of forms and designs is staggering. Many of those on offer have not actually been produced on the islands and it is best to buy from one of the local manufacturers.

Colourful plate

Condiment container

Glass

The high-quality glassware produced on the Balearic Islands was once as popular as that made in Venice. To this day, the most popular articles of glassware are modelled on traditional designs.

"Gordioli" goblet

Leaf-shaped bowl

Pestle and mortar

Wooden Articles

Articles made of olive wood are very popular with visitors to the islands. They have a distinctive colour and are very durable. The choice is, however, limited to a few designs.

"Lafiore" pots

Traditional sandals

Leather wallet

Leather Goods

Menorca is famous for its leather goods. The factory shops sell virtually everything that can be made of leather, including wallets, coats and jackets. Many articles are made to order for large international companies.

Warm leather gloves

Woman's handbag

Hippy Jewellery

A large number of hippy products sold in Ibiza and Formentera have been produced by a flourishing cottage industry, though less authentic products are beginning to dominate. Even so, it is still worth visiting these markets, if only for their atmosphere.

Box from India

Earrings

Belt with shells

Black pearl necklace

Ring

Simulated Pearls

Simulated pearls are Mallorca's signature item. Though expensive, every item comes with a certificate of authenticity. You can buy ready-made jewellery as well as single pearls that you can use to make your own necklace or bracelet.

Necklace of simulated pearls

Wickerwork

Wickerwork is very popular with visitors to the Balearics and wickerwork items are among the most genuine Balearic products. The baskets of various shapes and sizes are particularly attractive.

Straw hat

Beach basket

Cap with "Mallorca" inscription

Clothes

Clothes, including T-shirts with a variety of slogans and original designs, such as the ones sold on Menorca with the "Ecológica de Menorca" sign, are also popular. Club clothes likewise make interesting souvenirs.

Printed T-shirts

Alcohol

A large selection of alcoholic drinks is on offer. Each island produces its own herb liqueur (hierbas). Adult visitors to Menorca might like to try these and the local gin. Connoisseurs will not miss the chance to sample Mallorcan wines, particularly the best of them – the red wine from Binissalem, but also white and rosé varieties from the same vineyards.

Herb liqueur

Almond liqueur

Local red wine

Handicrafts in the Balearic Islands

Ceramics are extremely popular in the Balearic Islands, just as in the rest of Spain. One of the most characteristic items of Mallorcan handicrafts is the *siurell* – a statuette-whistle that is made of painted clay. Sa Cabaneta, one of the Mallorcan parishes, is known as "clay country" due to the large number of pottery workshops that can be found there. Weaving and embroidery are also very popular and leather goods are plentiful, especially in Menorca. Mallorca has become famous for its production of simulated pearls.

route from Eivissa to Sant Antoni de Portmany, there are many pottery workshops producing beautiful bowls, vases and jugs based on ancient Carthaginian designs. Ceramic copies of the terracotta figurines dating from the Punic era (3rd century BC) displayed in archaeological museums in Eivissa – particularly busts of women – are popular as souvenirs from Ibiza.

Ceramic lamps on display in a market

Ceramics

The art of making pottery on the Balearic Islands goes back thousands of years. It was greatly influenced by the art of the Moors, who ruled the archipelago for several centuries.

The item you are most likely to see is the *siurell*, a statuette-whistle made of clay and painted white, with green and red decorations. It usually depicts a man sitting on a donkey or playing a guitar; but it can also be styled as a bull, a dog, a peacock, a rooster or even the devil. The origin of the *siurell* is uncertain; already known in Moorish times, it was most likely inherited from the Phoenicians. The Spanish artist Joan Miró was particularly taken with these little toy whistles and drew inspiration from them. The *siurell* was once a highly important item; a man would hand it to the lady of his choice – if she blew on it, it

meant "yes", but if she put it aside, it meant that the suitor had been rejected. The Romeria de Sant Marçal *(see p31)*, a lively fair held at the end of June in Sa Cabaneta, is dedicated to these clay whistles.

Original ceramic products with distinctive yellow and green glazing are produced in Felanitx in Mallorca. At the busy Sunday market in this small town, you can also purchase blue-and-white bowls and jugs, decorated with delicate floral or arabesque motifs.

In Pòrtol, near the small town of Santa Maria del Camí, there are a few remaining potters who produce traditional bulging pots made of red clay *(ollas)* and shallow bowls *(greixoneras)*.

In Ibiza, in the small village of Sant Rafael situated on the

Glassware

The earliest glass vessels found on the Balearic Islands date as far back as Roman times. In the 16th century, glassware from Mallorca competed successfully with popular Venetian products. Even today, the bestselling products tend to be copies of ancient designs.

There are three factories of artistic and household glass in Mallorca; the best known of these is the Can Gordiola glass museum near Algaida, on the road from Palma to Manacor. The oldest glassworks on the island, it has been run by the same family since 1719. Here, it is possible for visitors to watch the glassblowers at work. Using long, thin pipes, they can produce a variety of objects, from lovely small trinkets to large vases.

Traditional condiment pot

Clay pot production in a pottery workshop

Simulated Pearls

The production method for simulated pearls was patented in 1925 by Eduard Heusch, a German engineer. The recipe for producing a thin bead-coating layer is kept secret to this day, for obvious reasons, though it is said to contain fish scales mixed with resin.

Two factories in Manacor and Montuïri produce these simulated pearls, which are of good quality and, to the untrained eye, virtually impossible to distinguish from the real thing.

The beads are immersed repeatedly in a liquid compound, which imitates the natural process of pearl production. Afterwards, each pearl is polished by hand and weighed. The production process can be seen during a visit to the Perlas Orquidea factory. Be aware that the factory shop sells them at much lower prices than those charged by shops elsewhere.

Inside the Gordiola glass factory in Mallorca

Straw hat, popular in the islands

Wood and Wicker Products

Artifacts made of olive wood are very popular in the Balearic Islands and can be distinguished by their rich colour and unusual grain. Olivart, a factory in Palma, produces a number of basic household goods, such as bowls and mortars, as well as ornamental items and many other souvenirs.

The dwarf palm, or palmito, grows on many of the islands' mountain slopes. Its leaves are used, particularly in Artà, to weave chair seats, baskets, bags and the soles of the espadrille or alpargatas. In addition to this, local craftsmen produce a wide variety of bags and baskets woven from strong grass or jute, and hats that are popular with the locals and tourists alike.

Other Local Products

The Balearic Islands, and Menorca in particular, are famous for their production of excellent footwear. In Menorca the centre of the leather industry is Ferreries. Here, you can buy relatively inexpensive shoes, bags and leather clothes. It is worth taking a closer look at some of the sandal designs, which are unique to this island, locally known as abarcas menorquinas. In Mallorca the cheapest place to buy leather products is Inca.

Weaving and embroidery have a long local history. The traditional robes de llengues – print-decorated heavy linen fabrics – are often used to decorate Mallorcan homes, even today. They can be used for curtains and bedspreads as well as wall linings and furniture upholstery. Clothes that imitate hippy fashions from the 1960s are still very much in vogue, and designs produced in this style

An olive wood household bowl

continue to create a stir at the annual fashion shows. The fashion show Moda Ad Lib is held every June, in Eivissa, Ibiza. Clothes that are shown here can later be bought in Eivissa's fashionable boutiques – at high prices.

Traditional gold and silver jewellery has been produced by local craftsmen on the Balearic Islands for centuries. Although less fashionable now, it is still used as an addition to folk costumes. Similar to the enduringly popular fashion in clothing, the designs of gold jewellery are inspired largely by hippy culture. Silver and metal items can be bought at "hippy markets", particularly in Ibiza and Formentera.

A cobbler at work

ENTERTAINMENT IN THE BALEARIC ISLANDS

Ibiza is listed in the *Guinness Book of Records* as the world's most entertaining place. This is no doubt due to the number of nightclubs, bars and pubs packed into this small island. The other islands of the archipelago also have plenty of entertainment on offer and there are many clubs, concerts and shows to choose from. The range of entertainment available to visitors is much wider than this, however. At the height of the holiday season, the larger resorts open up casinos, concert halls, cinemas and theatres and also organize folklore, theatre and cinema festivals. On top of this, and perfect for the kids, are the many aquaparks and other amusement parks found on the islands.

Shelves of the many liqueurs on offer in a shop

Information

It is a good idea to find out what is on offer before you leave, as local tourist information offices may not always have details of forthcoming cultural events, particularly if they are held in another town. The Internet has a wealth of information on concerts, amusement parks and festivals and may sometimes include first-hand accounts of particular attractions.

Current details may often be found in the local press. Keep your eyes peeled, too, as many events are advertised on posters. Other valuable sources on what is happening are hotel reception areas.

Booking Tickets

Tickets to some of the major nightclubs in Ibiza, such as Amnesia and Privilege, can be booked before you go on holiday, over the Internet or by telephone. The same applies to concerts and music festivals,

and guided tours often require advance booking, too. The earlier you book, the better your chances of getting a ticket. However, in many cases, tickets are only sold a short time in advance. If you are unable to book tickets in advance, and are staying in a hotel, the reception will often be happy to do the booking for you. Admission to many open-air events is often free.

Nightlife

Nightlife flourishes on the islands. Ibiza is particularly famous for it (*see pp124–5*), but Mallorca also has many nightclubs (*discotecas*). The clubs usually open their doors between midnight and 1am and many remain open all night. Admission to the most famous and fashionable places in Ibiza and Mallorca is relatively expensive. Lesser-known venues tempt guests in with various gimmicks or free drinks.

Entry ticket to Jardines d'Alfàbia

Earlier in the evening you can visit bars and pubs. For those people who do not fancy the nightclubs, there are also casinos and many venues that put on artistic programmes.

Music and Theatre

Despite appearances, the cultural life on the Balearic Islands is not limited to pubs, clubs and religious festivals. Classical music, opera and theatre are all very popular with the locals, particularly on Mallorca and Menorca. Theatres and opera houses can be found in the larger towns. Their repertoire includes mainly modern Spanish drama and there are frequent performances by visiting theatre and opera companies from mainland Spain, as well as from other European countries, including Germany, Italy and the UK.

The leading theatres are the **Teatre Principal** in Palma and

Tourist information office in Sant Antoni de Portmany, Ibiza

Partygoers enjoying themselves at Amnesia, Ibiza

Fundació Teatre Principal de Maó in Menorca. During the summer season, when the theatres close, theatre festivals come to take their place. These are mostly international events. Many of these include theatre workshops, which offer plenty of opportunities for audience participation. The **Centro Cultural Andratx** hosts concerts and exhibitions. There are resident artists in the complex too, and it is well worth a visit to see them at work.

Lovers of classical music will also find something on the islands. World-class musicians and orchestras frequently appear in the concert halls, such as the Auditórium de Palma de Mallorca. In addition, many music festivals and concerts are organized during the holiday season. In Menorca, there are three major festivals during the summer season – in Maó, Ciutadella and Fornells. Festivals taking place between June and September are held in concert halls, theatres and churches. Among the important musical events in Mallorca are the classical music festivals held in Palma (Jan–Apr) and the Chopin Festival in Valldemossa (Aug). Other popular events include international festivals of music in Deià (May–Sep) and Pollença (Jul–Aug) during the summer.

Popular Music

Lovers of jazz and rock have no cause to complain in the Balearic Islands, particularly during the summer season. Occasionally, top rock groups or pop stars make an appearance. You should enquire about dates and venues in the local tourist information office. There are also numerous local regular events, such as a Rock'n'Rostoll Festival in Maria de la Salut, in Mallorca, while cities such as Palma have many live music venues.

Some events have become a permanent fixture in the islands' cultural calendar. Anyone who loves jazz may know about Sant Climent in Menorca. On Tuesdays from May to October, "jam sessions" are held here. Two extremely popular events in Mallorca are the International Jazz Festival held every year during May and June in Cala d'Or, and the Mallorca Jazz Festival during August in Sa Pobla. In Palma, the Jazz Voyeur Festival runs from September to December.

Fiestas

When visiting the islands, it is worth including one of the fiestas in your itinerary. These are held not only as celebrations of patron saints, but may also commemorate historic events (mainly Medieval events) or celebrate important harvests (such as the grape harvest festival in Binissalem and the melon festival in Vilafranca de Bonany). These colourful, bustling celebrations, accompanied by music, dancing and feasting, can continue for several days, during which time the town's business life grinds to a halt as the locals join in the fun.

Street processions with people dressed in regional costumes or their Sunday best are often spiced up by the *dimonis* – devils that personify evil, which are defeated in the end. This happens during the fiestas in Montuïri and Santa Margalida. An important element of many fiestas are the horse races and shows. The most interesting of these are held during the Sant Joan fiesta in Ciutadella (in June). The majority of fiestas, as well as other cultural and entertainment events, are held during the summer months, at the peak of the holiday season. Important events taking place outside the tourist season include the Procession of the Three Magi (Jan), the carnival (Feb) and the celebrations associated with Holy Week.

Sign for a horse show

Participants in a colourful fiesta

Shows

Once the sun goes down, there are plenty of shows to keep you entertained on the Balearics, and there is always something for everyone. As well as being a gambler's haven, the **Casino Mallorca** also offers glamorous nightly extravaganzas. **Son Amar** stages shows to rival those in Las Vegas, with a variety of dance and music artists, in a huge auditorium. **Son Martorellet**, on the other hand, puts on family-friendly dressage displays and performances that demonstrate man's strong bond with the horse.

Excursions

Those looking for an active holiday will have no trouble finding plenty of outlets able to provide details of walking or cycling trails, and even organize excursions. For anyone looking for a less strenuous excursion, there are plenty of coach tours. It is, of course, possible to hire a car and drive to some of the most interesting places around the islands. You can also ask at tourist offices about guided tours. You might, however, bear in mind that some groups may contain a number of nationalities and you should be prepared to listen to a commentary in a variety of languages.

Of all the tours and excursions on offer on the Balearic Islands, possibly the most pleasant are boat cruises. Across the Balearics, the standard cruise is in a large, motorized boat that cuts its way along the coast, dipping into coves and bays on the way. Some of the boats double as beach ferries – like the one between Port de Pollença and Platja de Formentor – while others venture out to uninhabited islets, like the little boats that bob out from Sant Elm to the Parc Natural de Sa Dragonera. Some cruises include swimming and picnic stops, others sail out to isolated

Glass-bottomed boat ride

Logo of Menorca's natural history museum

beaches where you can sunbathe from dawn to dusk. Some are equipped for coral-reef watching with glass-bottomed boats, though this can induce seasickness with remarkable speed, and some cater for snorkelling. There are more specialized boat trips along Maó's magnificent harbour, with its sprinkling of historic islets, but the most popular cruise of them all is to Sa Calobra, the box-canyon beach on Mallorca's north coast, which is best visited the day after heavy rain. In terms of distance, the longest cruise is to the rugged, sun-bleached archipelago of Cabrera, off the south coast of Mallorca – a very remote spot. **Barcos Azules** is a reliable and proficient cruise company offering a wide range of island boat trips. **Marcabrera** is a smaller boat company that arranges charming excursions out to Cabrera Island.

Children

The Spanish are famously fond of children, and kids are welcomed in restaurants, especially at lunchtimes.

In terms of attractions, Mallorca has the lion's share, with waterparks, caves and promenades for cycling. Fun shows, including mock pirate battles and jousting

tournaments, are organized for the enjoyment of younger visitors. During the high season there are also many funfairs with carousels and circus troupes featuring acrobats and magicians. Out of season, there are visits by circuses and fairs to the islands and some of the larger clubs run youth after-noons at the weekends. **Palma Aquarium**, just outside the city, makes for a great day out.

Although the other islands have fewer attractions, there is still plenty to keep children entertained. Menorca has pony rides and riding shows, for example, while Ibiza's beaches and all the associated seaside attractions, such as snorkelling, beach games and banana rides, will keep most children happily occupied for the duration of your holiday.

Another form of entertain-ment in the islands is afforded by a visit to one of the numerous caves, especially in Mallorca (see p83). Some of these have their own light and music shows.

Slides in a waterpark in Ibiza

DIRECTORY

Nightlife

BCM
Avda S'Olivera, Magaluf.
Tel 625 597 256.
w bcmplanetdance.
com
British-run entertainment
complex – the biggest
club on the island.

Menta
Avda Tucan, Alcúdia.
Tel 664 435 717.
w menta-disco.com
Two dance floors, seven
bars and an indoor pool.

Paladium Paguera
Avda 50, Paguera.
Tel 680 944 490.
A smaller club that gets
packed on the weekends.

Tito's
Paseo Marítimo, Palma.
Tel 687 570 130.
w titosmallorca.com

Theatres

Café Teatre Sans
C/C'an Sanç 5,
Palma, Mallorca.
Tel 971 727 166.

**Fundació Teatre
Principal de Maó**
C/Costa Deià 40, Maó,
Menorca.
Tel 971 355 603.
w teatremao.com
See p98 for further details.

Orfeó Maonès
C/ Verge de Gràcia 155,
Maó, Menorca.
Tel 971 363 942.

Teatre del Mar
Llucmajor 90, "Es Molinar",
Palma, Mallorca.
Tel 971 248 400.
w teatredelmar.com

**Teatre Municipal
de Manacor**
Avda del Parc s/n,
Manacor, Mallorca.
Tel 971 554 549.

Teatre Principal
Riera 2, Palma, Mallorca.
Tel 971 219 696.

Teatre de Vilafranca
Sant Martí 26, Vilafranca
de Bonany, Mallorca.
Tel 971 832 072

Trui Teatre
Camí Son Rapinya, 29,
Palma, Mallorca.
Tel 971 783 279.
w truiteatre.es

Music

Auditori d'Alcúdia
Plaça de la Porta de
Mallorca 3, Alcúdia,
Mallorca. **Tel** 971 897 185.

**Auditórium de
Palma de Mallorca**
Paseo Marítimo 18,
Palma, Mallorca.
Tel 971 734 735.
w auditoriumpalma.
com

**Auditórium
Sa Màniga**
C/ Son Galta 4, Cala Millor,
Mallorca. **Tel** 971 587 373.

**Centro Cultural
Andratx**
C/ Estanyera 2,
Andratx, Mallorca.
Tel 971 137 770.
Concerts during the
summer.

Shows

Casino Mallorca
Porto Pi Centro, Mallorca.
Tel 971 130 000.
w casinodemallorca.
com

**Club Escola
Menorquína**
Ctra Ferreries–Cala
Galdana, Menorca.
Tel 971 373 497.

Es Foguero
Highway Palma–Santanyí,
Exit No 10, Mallorca.
Tel 971 265 260.
w esfoguero.com
Flamenco, ballet & cabaret.

Son Amar
Ctra de Sóller, km 10 ,
Palmanyola, Mallorca.
Tel 971 617533 *(free)*.
w sonamar.com

Son Martorellet
Ctra Ferreries–Cala
Galdana, km 1.7 km,
Menorca.
Tel 971 373 406.
w sonmartorellet.com

Excursions

Barcos Azules
Passeig Es Través 3, Port
de Sóller, Mallorca.
Tel 971 630 170.
w barcosazules.com
Island boat trips.

Marcabrera
Colònia de Sant Jordi,
Mallorca. **Tel** 971 656 403.
w marcabrera.com

**Riding Academy
Mallorca**
Son Magraner. Cami d'
Ullastre, 39, Palma.
Tel 610 419 223.
Special courses for children.

Children

Aguamar
Platja d'en Bossa, Ibiza.
Tel 971 330 735.
Open May–Oct.

Aqua Center
Urb Los Delfines,
Calanblanes, Menorca.
Tel 971 388 705.
w aquacenter-
menorca.com

Aqualand El Arenal
Autopista Palma–S'Arenal,
exit 13, Mallorca.
Tel 971 440 000.
w aqualand.es/elarenal
One of the world's largest
water-parks, which
includes a mini-zoo.

Aquarium Cap Blanc
Ctra Cala Grassió, Sant
Antoni de Portmany,
Ibiza. **Tel** 663 945 475.
w aquariumcapblanc.
com

Aventura Park
Ángel Guimerà 11, Palma,
Mallorca. **Tel** 871 949 452.

Club Hipico Son Gual
Ctra Puigpunyent-
Establiments, km 6.2,
Mallorca.
Tel 608 532 096.
w hipicasongual.com

Golf Fantasía
C/Tenis 3, Palmanova–
Calvià, Mallorca.
Tel 971 135 040.
w golffantasia.com
Crazy golf with a choice
of three circuits.

Natura Parc
Santa Eugènia, Mallorca.
Tel 971 144 078.
w naturaparc.net

Palma Aquarium
Manuela de los Herreos i
Sorá 21, Mallorca.
Tel 902 702 902.
w palmaaquarium.com

Western Park
Ctra de Cala Figuera,
Magaluf, Mallorca.
Tel 971 131 203.
w westernpark.com
Long-established
waterpark on the edge
of town.

OUTDOOR ACTIVITIES

The warm climate and diversity of the landscape on the Balearics make them an excellent place for all types of sport. The most popular of these are, of course, water sports and you will find windsurfing, sailing and diving are all well catered for. Those looking for an activity holiday of this kind will have the chance to practise their favourite sports under professional supervision. Cycling, horse riding and golf are also popular in the islands and many travel bureaux and agents offer equipment hire, from yacht charter to bicycle rental. Some hotels also have their own facilities and can often hire out equipment.

Wind- and kite-surfers in Can Pastilla, on the west coast of Mallorca

Windsurfing

The conditions for windsurfing are not as impressive here as they are in the Canary Islands because the local winds are not strong enough for advanced surfers. As a consequence, the Balearic Islands are not popular with professionals, but this makes them a very good place for beginners to pick up some of the basic techniques.

Although the number of schools is rather limited, all of the islands have at least one school that teaches basic windsurfing and offers equipment hire. Surfing enthusiasts will also be able to find suitable spots in the Balearic Islands, but do not expect the "ultimate wave".

Sailing

Sailing is the most popular water sport in the Balearic Islands. Major international regattas include the King's Cup and the Princesa Sofia Trophy held in Mallorca. These are high-profile events and attract many of the world's leading sailors; King Juan Carlos was a frequent competitor. The Trofeo Almirante Conde de Barcelona, held in August, features regattas with classic sailing boats. Almost every coastal town has its own marina and these are visited by yachts from all over Europe. Many vessels remain here for the winter.

Of course, you do not have to own a yacht in order to cruise the Balearic Islands. Many firms offer sea-going vessels for charter. Smaller inshore catamarans can be rented by the hour on local beaches. You can also find many clubs or schools that are able to teach you the rudiments of sailing.

The popularity of sailing is so great that during the high season the marinas tend to be very busy, even though the mooring charges are extremely high. Some boats moor in sheltered bays, accessible only by sea.

Fishing

Despite the fact that the local waters teem with fish, fishing is not a popular sport here. A few agents organize trips, however. Further information is available from the **Asociación Balear de Pesca** or from the Club Nautics.

Beach Activities

During the high season, beaches employ lifeguards so it is safer to bathe and swim. Most beaches are sandy and situated in small bays. Sailing yachts and fishing boats sometimes anchor at the mouth of the bay and these are only a hazard if you swim out too close to them. The beaches can be busy and are sometimes short of space for beach sports. Nevertheless, a few of them have areas designated for volleyball, and even on busy beaches you can still find space to kick a ball around or play frisbee.

Diving and Snorkelling

The clear, clean coastal seawaters, combined with the diversity of underwater flora

Catamarans on Es Pujols beach in Formentera

Beach volleyball, popular throughout the islands

also take water-skiing lessons or (an easier option) bump along on a rubber raft, towed by a speeding boat.

Alternatively, visitors might like to join a sea trip by kayak. The most interesting routes go to the islands such as Conillera, near Ibiza, or Dragonera, off Mallorca. Equally exciting are trips to the waters of Formentor (Mallorca) and Cavalleria (Menorca).

Hiking

Hiking around the islands is extremely popular. The best area for hiking is probably the mountainous regions of Mallorca. The trails leading through the Serra de Tramuntana are difficult; however, they offer a wonderful experience and breathtaking scenery. Trekking across the mountains along rough paths requires suitable footwear and clothing and this activity should not be undertaken alone, as there are potential hazards such as sudden changes in the weather and unexpected ravines.

Menorca also offers many hiking trails. Most of these lead through the local nature reserves, of which the island has 18. The regions of S'Albufera, Cap de Favaritx and Cap de Cavalleria are truly magnificent areas for hiking. Many agents organize themed excursions, such as birdwatching trips. If setting off without a guide, you should make sure you have a good map, as many tourist trails are not signposted.

and fauna, create ideal conditions for diving, and the sport is as popular as sailing throughout the islands. Every seaside resort has at least one diving centre (centro de buceo) where you can hire equipment, go for a test dive with an instructor or enrol on a course. A one-week stay would be sufficient to complete the beginners' course in scuba diving. The organizers ensure proper supervision by a qualified instructor and provide all the necessary equipment.

People hoping to dive in deeper waters must hold a proper diving certificate, such as PADI, CUC, CMAS/FEDAS or SSI. Holders of these certificates can join expeditions, some of which explore underwater caves. One of the best places to dive is the water around Cabrera, about 18 km (11 miles) off the coast of Mallorca. In 1991, Cabrera and its surrounding waters were awarded the status of a national park – the first park of its kind in Spain. Diving here requires the permission of the park ranger.

A much cheaper but equally exciting way of getting a glimpse of underwater life is to go snorkelling. A snorkeller can observe the wonders of the deep while floating on the surface of the water almost anywhere. Perhaps the most interesting places are the small bays rarely visited by tourists, where nature has hardly been

touched by the hand of humans. A word of warning: snorkelling can be dangerous if you are distracted and collide with nearby rocks.

Motorboat with parachute waiting for the adventurous to paraglide

Other Water Sports

Other water sports that are popular with visitors include taking out a high-speed water-bike or paragliding. Paragliding behind motorboats (similar to hang-gliding) offers a wonderful way to see the islands. You can

Snorkelling in shallow waters in Menorca

Cyclists in a boulevard in Palma, Mallorca

Two-Wheeled Sport

Cycling is very popular here, and renting a bicycle from one of the numerous hire firms is inexpensive. Cycling is an excellent way to explore the towns or get to a nearby beach. On the island of Formentera it is the most popular form of transport, along with the scooter.

More ambitious cyclists may want to undertake longer trips, and all types of terrain can be encountered on the islands, from long, flat stretches of coast through to steep mountain roads. The islands also offer many interesting trails for mountain bikes, although the routes leading through the wild mountain terrains on Mallorca, or the coastal crags of Menorca, are best undertaken with a guide. Agents who organize these tours generally offer guides and equipment.

Horse Riding

Horse riding is another popular island sport and there are several riding centres on the islands that

Sea-cave diving – growing in popularity

provide facilities for beginners as well as for advanced riders. The riding areas and trails are deliberately set amid beautiful scenery, but you should not expect romantic gallops along the beach. All horse riding is done under the supervision of an instructor. There are many riding centres in Menorca and this is where they breed the famous Menorcan black horses that play such a prominent part in many fiestas. As well as riding lessons and outings, many centres also stage displays of horse breaking. For those who fancy a flutter, regular horse races are held on Mallorca and Ibiza.

Caving

Caving and associated pursuits, such as canyoning and rock climbing, are still in their infancy in the Balearics but growing in popularity.

Only a handful of Mallorca's caves, including the Drac and Hams (see p84), are open to all; most are reserved for experienced potholers. Adventurers can therefore explore the caves of the Tramuntana mountains and, on Menorca, try sea-cave diving as well. Organized caving expeditions offer anything from a half-day guided starter's cave trip, to day- and even week-long caving holidays, with all equipment provided.

The steep rocks along the coast of Mallorca and the inland regions are good places for rock climbing, too, providing various

degrees of difficulty. Companies such as **Rocksport Mallorca** offer walking, canyoning and rock climbing at beginner and advanced levels. **Diving Center Ciutadella** offers sea-cave diving training at various sites around the Menorca. Cave exploration can be dangerous and is only recommended for people who have been trained and have the proper equipment. Before embarking on any adventure sport, check your insurance cover.

Climber on a rock face near Valldemossa, Mallorca

Other Sports

The warm climate and varied terrain mean that most sports can be enjoyed somewhere in the islands. Surprisingly, for such a dry region, there are even places that are good for canoeing, a very popular sport in Spain but one that requires a high level of fitness. When planning these expeditions you should seek advice from the organizers, who will not only inform you about the best routes but will also ensure suitable supervision.

The good aerodynamic conditions on Mallorca make the island suitable for hang-gliding and paragliding *(see p175)*. These sports are not popular in the other islands of the archipelago. The best lifting currents are found in the inland regions. This is where beginners' courses are held and where you can also meet experienced hang-gliders. The islands' weather conditions are also favourable for ballooning. A number of companies and some of the more exclusive hotels on the island can organize hot-air balloon flights.

DIRECTORY

Ballooning

Mallorca Ballons
Tel 971 596 969.
w mallorcaballoons.com

Caving

Diving Center Ciutadella
Ciutadella, Menorca.
Tel 651 644 319.
w diveinnmenorca.com

Rocksport Mallorca
Tel 629 948 404.
w rocksportmallorca.com

Diving

Aqua Diving Center
Port Sant Antoni de Portmany, Ibiza.
Tel 693 045 723.
w aquadivingcenter.com

Big Blue
C/ Marti Ros García 6, Palmanova, Mallorca.
Tel 971 681 686.
w bigbluediving.net

Blue Water Scuba
Cala'n Bosch, Menorca.
Tel 971 387 183.
w bluewaterscuba.co.uk

Octopus
Canonge Oliver 13, Port de Sóller, Mallorca.
Tel 971 633 133.
w octopus-mallorca.com

Skualo
Passeig Cap d'es Toll 11, Porto Cristo, Mallorca.
Tel 971 815 094.
w skualo.com

Vellmari Formentera Diving
Marina de Formentera 14, Puerto de la Savina, Formentera.
Tel 971 322 105.
w vellmari.com

Fishing

Asociación Balear de Pesca
C/ Joan Miró, 325, Calanova, Palma, Mallorca.
Tel 971 702 088.

Federación Española de Pesca y Casting
Navas de Tolosa 3, Madrid.
Tel 915 328 352.
w fepyc.es

Hiking

Dia Complert
Passeig Marítim 41, Fornells, Menorca.
Tel 609 670 996.
w diacomplert.com

Ecoibiza
Juan Carlos 1, Edificio Transat, Eivissa, Ibiza.
Tel 971 302 347.
w ecoibiza.com

Mallorca Activa
Son Pereto 9, Palma, Mallorca.
Tel 971 783 160.
w mallorcaactiva.com

Horse Riding

Ca'n Paulino
Ctra Vieja de Algaida s/n, Llucmajor, Mallorca.
Tel 664 384 924.
w canpaulino.com

Hípica Son Gual
Ctra Puigpunyent to Establiments, km 6.2, Palma, Mallorca.
Tel 608 532 096.
w hipicasongual.com

Menorca a Cavall
Ctra Es Mercadal-Ferreries, km 24, 3 Santa Rita, Es Marcadel, Menorca.
Tel 971 374 637.
w menorcaacavall.com

Riding Academy Mallorca
See p173.

Sailing

Centro Wet Four Fun
Platja d'Es Pujols, Formentera.
Tel 609 766 084.
w wet4fun.com

Club Náutico el Arenal
C/ Roses s/n, S'Arenal, Mallorca.
Tel 971 440 142.
w cnarenal.com

Club Náutico Ciutadella
Cami de Baix s/n, Ciutadella, Menorca.
Tel 971 383 918.
w cnciutadella.com

Club Náutico Porto Cristo
C/ Vela 29, Porto Cristo, Mallorca.
Tel 971 821 253.
w cnportocristo.com

Club Náutico Sant Antoni
Paseo Marítimo s/n, Sant Antoni de Portmany, Ibiza.
Tel 971 340 645.
w esnautic.com

Escuela Balear de Náutica
C/ Aragón 28 bajos, Palma, Mallorca.
Tel 971 909 060.
w escueladenautica.com

Real Club Náutico de Palma
Muelle de Sant Pere s/n, Palma, Mallorca.
Tel 971 726 848.
w rcnp.es

Windsurfing

Cesar's Watersports
Playa S'Arganassa, Santa Eulalia del Rio, Ibiza.
Tel 971 330 919 or 670 629 961 *(mobile)*.
w watersportscesars.com

Club Náutico Sa Ràpita
Explanada del puerto s/n, Sa Ràpita, Mallorca.
Tel 971 640 001 or 971 641 535 (courses).
w cnrapita.com

Windsurf Fornells
Bahia Fornells, Menorca.
Tel 664 335 801.
w windfornells.com

Golf in the Balearics

Golf is well established in the Balearic Islands, with a growing number of modern and environmentally sensitive golf courses on Mallorca, Menorca and Ibiza. Blessed with a mild climate and boasting excellent facilities, these courses attract golfers all year round. The Federación Balear de Golf oversees a total of 26 courses on the three larger islands, as well as an ever-expanding range of competitions and trophies, training and practice facilities, and junior championships. Formentera has a ferry link that makes a round of golf on Ibiza a viable possibility.

Teeing off on one of the many courses in the Balearic Islands

General Information

The Balearic Islands' golf culture is relatively new compared to the sport's history, which means that courses have been designed to meet the demands of the modern golfer. They are also mindful of the fact that golfers are here for a holiday. In addition to training and activities (some organize tournaments, for example), all courses offer extensive leisure amenities – clubhouses, restaurants, bars and shops.

Spain's forward-thinking attitude towards the disabled has led to the active promotion of access, facilities, training and tournaments for disabled golfers at the **Real Golf de Bendinat** course in Mallorca.

There are golf tournaments every week of the golf year, although the most important date is the Baleares Doubles, held at Mallorca's **Golf Santa Ponsa II** course in June.

Green fees range from €50 to €150 a day, depending on the course and the season. Many clubs and holiday agencies offer discounts on fees and equipment hire. All of the golf courses included in the directory listings are recommended by the **Federación Balear de Golf**.

Mallorca

The first ever golf course in Spain opened on Gran Canaria in the Canary Islands only in 1891, some 200 years after St Andrews in Scotland. The first golf course in the Balearics was the **Golf Son Vida**, opened in 1964 a few kilometres outside Palma, in an idyllic valley setting with views of the sea and the Serra de Tramuntana mountains.

Most Balearic golf courses offer extensive and modern facilities, in addition to advanced grounds-maintenance technology. Already considered one of the key golf destinations in Europe, Mallorca is drawing leading course design architects such as Robert Trent Jones Jr, Bradford Benz, Falco Nardi and José Gancedo.

In 1967, Son Vida was followed by the **Golf Son Servera** course, designed by John Harris, near Artà. It was another 10 years before the next golf course opened; the first of the (now three) **Golf Santa Ponsa** courses, designed by Falco Nardi, is still the largest on the island. It was followed in 1978 by another John Harris course, **Golf de Poniente**, still regarded as one of the toughest on Mallorca. Laid out among pine and olive groves, the par-72 Poniente has 18 holes and a number of "character-building" bunkers planted along its *recorrido* (course).

The 1980s and 1990s saw another 23 courses open in quick succession in the Balearic Islands. Perhaps the ultimate so far is the exclusive **Arabella Golf**, opened in 2000 and winner of two awards for sensitive ecological course management. **Golf Son Termens** has also been praised for its sympathetic approach to pre-existing landscape in its planning.

Most courses cater to all levels of player ability, although a few are designed to put even the most experienced enthusiast through their paces. **Golf de Pollença**, for example, integrated among ancient olive groves on a gentle hill overlooking the Bahia de Pollença, admits that "none of the holes is easy", and deems most to be suitable for mid- to high-experience players and professionals. The Robert Trent

Beautiful views across Bahia de Alcúdia from Golf Alcanada

Jones Jr-designed **Golf Alcanada**, opened in 2003, is blessed with sea views of the splendid Bahia de Alcúdia from every hole, although players are advised to beware the 58 bunkers Jones has included in the design of this idyllic but testing course. **Golf de Andratx** has declared each of its holes a *reto*, or challenge, while the course at **Golf de Canyamel** is still considered the toughest on the island.

Landscape and climate make Mallorca an ideal setting for golf. It is impossible to say which golf course boasts the most impressive architecture, although Son Muntaner is the most exquisitely manicured. **Golf de Capdepera** is set in a lush valley surrounded by scenic mountains, while the Poniente is set among mature pine and olive woodlands. The most striking course is

Pula Golf, whose grounds, located in an old country estate, are shared with some of the most important talayot structures on the island.

Menorca

Menorca and Ibiza are still a considerable way behind Mallorca; however, it is only a matter of time until they catch up. Menorca's main course, **Golf Son Parc**, is an unusual course with a 69 par and an ingenious course by Dave Thomas that requires strategic thinking to negotiate rocky bunkers, several lakes, reedbeds and, not least, a resident colony of peacocks.

Ibiza

The only golf course on the island of Ibiza, **Golf de Ibiza** is something of an oddity. The old Roca Lisa nine-hole course has now been absorbed into the larger, neighbouring Golf de Ibiza, with a new 18-hole course, giving it a 27-hole total. The shorter course is said to be the easier terrain; however, all 27 holes are still described as difficult.

The challenging course of Golf de Ibiza

DIRECTORY

General Information

Federación Balear de Golf

Camí Son Vida 38, 07013 Palma de Mallorca.
Tel 971 722 753.
W **fbgolf.com**

Mallorca

Arabella Golf

Ctra Son Vida, 07013 Palma.
Tel 971 783 000.
W **arabellagolf mallorca.com**

Golf Alcanada

Carretera del Faro s/n, 07400 Puerto de Alcúdia.
Tel 971 549 560.
W **golf-alcanada.com**

Golf de Andratx

Carrer Cromlec 1, 07160 Camp de Mar.
Tel 971 236 280.
W **golfdeandratx.com**

Golf de Canyamel

Avda des Cap Vermell s/n, 07589 Capdepera.
Tel 971 841 313.
W **canyamelgolf.com**

Golf de Capdepera

Carretera Artà–Capdepera, km 3.5, 07570 Artà. **Tel** 971 818 500.
W **golfcapdepera.com**

Golf in Mallorca

W **golfinmallorca.com**

Golf de Pollença

Carretera Palma–Pollença, km 49.3, 07460 Pollença.
Tel 971 533 216.
W **golfpollensa.com**

Golf de Poniente

Carretera Cala Figuera s/n, 07182 Magaluf.
Tel 971 130 148.
Fax 971 130 176.
W **ponientegolf.com**

Golf Santa Ponsa I, II & III

Av. Golf s/n, 07180 Santa Ponsa.
Tel 971 690 211.
W **golf-santaponsa. com**

Golf Son Servera

Urbanización Costa de los Pinos, 07550 Son Servera.
Tel 971 840 096.
Fax 971 840 160.
W **golfsonservera.com**

Golf Son Termens

Carretera S'Esglaieta, km 10, 07110 Bunyola.
Tel 971 617 862.
Fax 971 617 895.
W **golfsontermens.com**

Golf Son Vida

Urbanización Son Vida, 07013 Palma.
Tel 971 791 210.
Fax 971 791 127.
W **sonvidagolf.com**

Pula Golf

Carretera Son Servera–Capdepera, km 3, 07550 Son Servera.
Tel 971 817 034.
Fax 971 817 035.
W **pulagolf.com**

Real Golf de Bendinat

C/ Campoamor s/n, Urb Bendinat, 07181 Calviá.
Tel 971 405 200.
Fax 971 700 786.
W **realgolfbendinat. com**

Vall d' Or Golf

Ctra. cala d'Or Portocolom, km 7.7, 07669 S'Horta (Felantix).
Tel 971 837 001.
W **valldorgolf.com**

Menorca

Golf Son Parc

Urbanización Son Parc s/n, 07740 Es Mercadal, Menorca.
Tel 971 188 875.
W **golfsonparc menorca.com**

Ibiza

Golf de Ibiza

Carretera Jesús a Cala Llonga s/n, 07840 Santa Eulària des Riu.
Tel 971 196 052.
Fax 971 196 051.
W **golfibiza.com**

SURVIVAL
GUIDE

PRACTICAL INFORMATION

The Balearic Islands are one of Europe's most popular holiday destinations. The islands have invested heavily in tourism and are geared up to receive multitudes of visitors. Hotel and catering facilities are extensive and there are plenty of attractions for the whole family to enjoy. In general, the islands are safe for visitors, although, as with any other busy resort destination, holidaymakers are vulnerable to crimes such as bag-snatching. Such crimes can often be avoided if you take sensible precautions. A well-developed information service, especially on the Internet, makes researching and planning a trip here a relatively straightforward business. During the peak period, tour operators tend to snap up the available accommodation, so be sure to book in advance. In the off-season, reservations are not as essential.

When to Visit

Each season has something to offer. Nevertheless, the tourist season is at its busiest from July until September. It peaks in August, which coincides with the hottest weather on the islands. The hotels, bars and restaurants fill up, beaches are full of sun-lovers and the clubs are crowded. At the height of the season you are more likely to hear German or English being spoken than Spanish or Catalan.

Anyone who dislikes crowds should plan their visit for the period before the high season or when things begin to quieten down. In May, June, late September and early October, the weather is still warm enough for sunbathing. Springtime is between February and April. This is the best time

West End in Sant Antoni de Portmany, Ibiza

for hiking, as the flowers are in bloom, although there can be heavy rain and storms at this time of year. The islands are quietest during the autumn months and December.

Visas

Regulations covering admission to the Balearic Islands are the same as for the rest of Spain. Nationals of all the European Union member states do not require a visa to enter the Balearic Islands. People from many other non-EU countries, including Australia, Canada, Israel, Japan, New Zealand and the USA, are likewise not required to obtain a visa before entry for tourist visits of up to 90 days. If in doubt, you should contact the Spanish Embassy or seek advice from a travel agent. Anyone who does require a visa must apply in person at the consulate in their own country.

Travel Safety Advice

Visitors can get up-to-date travel safety information from the **Foreign and Commonwealth Office** in the UK, the **State Department** in the US and the **Department of Foreign Affairs and Trade** in Australia.

Customs Regulations

Customs regulations state in detail the limits on goods imported to and exported from the Balearic Islands. Such information may be obtained from Spanish Embassies and travel agents. Specific customs queries may be referred to the *Departamento de Aduanas e Impuestos Especiales* (Customs and Excise Department) in Madrid. Remember that only adults are entitled to export alcohol and cigarettes in the quantities allowed by the regulations.

Nationals of non-EU countries may apply for VAT refunds on goods purchased in any of the islands' shops bearing the sign "Tax Free Shopping". The refund is

Strolling through Ciutadella, Menorca

◀ Bicycles parked by Ses Illetes beach, Formentera

worked out on the basis of the *formulari* (Global Refund Cheque), stamped by the Customs Officer at the point of departure before checking the luggage. The refund can be claimed at the airport, at any Cash Refund desk, or on returning home, by post or via bank transfer.

Language

The official joint languages of the Balearic Islands are Catalan and Spanish (Castilian). For many locals, however, the everyday language is Catalan. This bilingual culture can be felt when using local maps, where the names of places may be given in one or the other language. Catalan, in its turn, is divided into variants specific to each of the islands. In Mallorca it is known as *Mallorquín*, in Menorca as *Menorquín* and in Ibiza as *Eivissenc*.

During Franco's dictatorship, Catalan was banned in all public arenas. Nevertheless, the local population has never abandoned its use, and learning a few courtesy phrases in Catalan is a good way to win over the locals.

In tourist areas English and German are readily understood. Information signs and restaurant menus are generally multilingual. Greater problems with communication may be experienced away from the busiest areas. But even in the provinces, increasing numbers of people can speak at least one major European language as well as Spanish.

Tourist Information

You will find Tourist Information offices *(Informació turística)* in all of the larger towns and resorts on the islands. These offer free maps and information packs; they also have details

Horse-cab ride in Palma, Mallorca

of current cultural events, entertainment and available accommodation. However, the information they provide may be somewhat general in nature and it is usually limited to the town where the tourist office is located or to its immediate vicinity. A valuable source of information is the Internet. Individual islands, towns, tourist offices, hotels, car hire firms and museums all have their own websites. They usually include photographs with text written in several languages. It is therefore much simpler to do your research on a specific town before leaving home rather than once you are already there.

Signposts on Menorca

Youths/Students

The Balearics are an ideal destination for young holidaymakers. The fine weather, great beaches and clubs attract thousands of young people from all over Europe. Some also come in search of seasonal employment, combining work with pleasure. Holders of the International Student Identity Card (ISIC) and the Euro under-26 card are entitled to many benefits when visiting the Balearic Islands. They can get discounts on ferry travel, entrance charges to museums and galleries, and tickets to some of the other tourist attractions.

Children

As with much of Spain, children are welcome in most places except the big clubs, which, of course, have age restrictions for obvious reasons. Most hotels can provide cots; some have all-day care, babysitting and special entertainment for youngsters. It is nevertheless worth checking in advance what facilities are available at any given hotel.

Restaurants in hotels and in towns are also good at providing for the needs of children. They have highchairs and have special menus for children. When hiring a car, you should have no problem getting a child seat.

Children visiting one of Menorca's historic sights

Stall holders at the market in Inca, Mallorca, offering a range of locally grown produce

Facilities for the Disabled

The Balearic Islands are not particularly well equipped to deal with the needs of disabled people. Most hotels and restaurants are not adapted to serve guests who use wheelchairs, although new restaurants and hotels have to offer access by law. Many public places – such as museums, galleries and shops – are also often inaccessible. When planning a visit, it is wise to use the services of an organization that deals with the issues of disabled people. **Handisport Mallorca** is a good first stop for advice. Or you can approach **COCEMFE** (the Spanish Association for the Disabled). Another helpful agency is **Viajes 2000**.

Public transport also presents a number of issues for people with limited mobility, and travelling from town to town can be difficult. Disabled visitors to Mallorca are able to use the services of a specialized company, such as EMT Special Bus Service.

Excursions

Travel agents who sell holidays to the Balearic Islands usually also offer a choice of excursions for an additional fee. These are mostly day-long sightseeing trips, cruises, safaris, or visits to casinos, theatres or clubs. However, the prices you pay for these may be higher than those quoted by local tourist agents, and it is worth browsing through leaflets displayed at the hotel reception desk, or calling in at one or two local tourist offices to check what is on offer.

Parking sign for the disabled

Island Time

All the islands are 1 hour ahead of Greenwich Mean Time (GMT), 6 hours ahead of Eastern Standard Time and 9 hours ahead of Pacific Standard Time. The change-over to summertime, as with mainland Spain, takes place on the last Sunday in March. The clocks are put back on the last Sunday in October.

In terms of vocabulary, the word used to describe the early hours after midnight is *la matinada*. *El mati* means morning (up to 1pm); late afternoon and evening are translated as *la tarda*, while night is referred to as *la nit*.

Opening Hours

Museums and historic monuments in the Balearics are generally open from Tuesday to Sunday, from 10am to 2pm and again from 4pm to 6pm. As with most offices, they close for public holidays and fiestas. Tourist information offices have similar opening hours.

Some sectors of business have started to reassess their traditional opening hours. Big department stores, for example, and hypermarkets tend to forgo the siesta and are generally open until 9pm or 10pm, though most still close on Sundays.

Tourists taking a break from sightseeing in Dalt Vila, in Eivissa

Theme parks and gardens are open seven days a week and they do not close for siesta. Most clubs open their doors late at night and stay open until morning. Many offices associated with tourism work shorter hours during the winter, and some close altogether.

Electrical Supply

The mains voltage on the islands is 220V AC. A three-tier standard travel convertor will enable you to use foreign equipment. Mains sockets require the European-style two-pin, round-pronged plugs.

Religion

Like the rest of Spain the Balearic Islands are Roman Catholic and religion plays an important part in community life. All religious festivals are lavishly celebrated and at these times the offices in town remain closed. Church opening hours vary. Some, like the cathedral church in Eivissa, have set sightseeing hours. Others, including Palma cathedral, expect a donation or charge an admission fee. Many churches are open only for services, that is early mornings or evenings (6–9pm).

When planning to visit a particular religious building,

Statue on top of a church

you should check its opening hours in advance. Hotel reception desks and tourist information centres can sometimes provide details.

Customers relaxing at a café in Palma

DIRECTORY

Embassies in Mainland Spain

Australia
Paseo de la Castellana 259D, 28046 Madrid.
Tel 913 536 600. .

United Kingdom
Paseo de la Castellana 259D, 28046 Madrid.
Tel 917 146 300.

Consulates

France
Mallorca: C/Caro 1, 1st floor G, 07002, Palma.
Tel 971 730 301.

Ibiza: Avda. Bme. Vte Ramón 10, 07800, Ibiza.
Tel 971 312 031.

Germany
Mallorca: C/Porto Pi 8, 3rd floor D, 07015 Palma.
Tel 971 707 737.
Menorca: C/Des Negres 32, 07703 Maó.
Tel 971 361 668.
Ibiza: C/D'Antoni Jaume 2, 2–9th floor, 07800 Eivissa.
Tel 971 315 763.

The Netherlands
Mallorca: C/San Miquel 36, 6th floor, 07002 Palma.
Tel 971 716 493.

United Kingdom
C/Convent dels Caputxins 4, Edif Orisba B, 4th floor D, 07002 Palma.
Tel 902 109 356.

Ibiza: Avda/ Isidoro Macabich 45, 1st floor, 07800 Eivissa.
Tel 902 109 356.

Travel Safety Advice

Australia
Department of Foreign Affairs and Trade
W dfat.gov.au
W smartraveller.gov.au

UK
Foreign and Commonwealth Office
W gov.uk/foreign-travel-advice

USA
Department of State
W travel.state.gov

Organizations for the Disabled

COCEMFE
Luis Cabrera 63, Madrid.
Tel 917 443 600.
W cocemfe.es

Handisport Mallorca
Tel 971 132 268.
W handisportmallorca.org

Viajes 2000
W viajes2000.com

Tourist Information

Formentera
Port de la Savina.
Tel 971 322 057.

Ibiza
Passeig Vara de Rey 1, Eivissa.
Tel 971 301 900.
Fax 971 301 740.

Passeig de ses Fonts, Sant Antoni de Portmany.
Tel 971 343 363.

Mallorca
Plaça de la Reina 2, Palma.
Tel 971 173 990.
Av. Argentina 1, Palma.
Tel 902 102 365.

Menorca
Muelle de Llevant 5, Maó.
Tel 902 929 015.
Plaça des Born, Ciutadella.
Tel 971 484 155.

Tourist Information Websites

W balearweb.com
W caib.es
W illesbalears.es
W spain.info

Formentera
W formentera.es
W formenteraonline.net
W guiaformentera.com
W visitformentera.com

Ibiza
W descubreibiza.com
W ibiza-online.com
W ibiza-spotlight.com
W ibiza.travel

Mallorca
W infomallorca.net
W visitmallorca.com

Menorca
W menorca.es
W menorca.net
W visitmenorca.com

Personal Security and Health

The crime level on the Balearic Islands is lower than in most regions of Europe. Thefts do occur in the most crowded places and even in hotels, but they can be minimized by taking sensible precautions. Credit cards and money are best hidden away. Never leave anything visible in your car when you park it. It is also advisable to avoid carrying excessive amounts of cash. When in need, you can always ask a policeman for help. Basic medical help and advice is usually provided by a pharmacist. Holders of valid medical insurance can receive treatment in public hospitals and clinics.

Lifeguard on duty at Sant Elm beach, Mallorca

Personal Property

Before travelling abroad it is wise to make sure you have adequate holiday insurance in order to protect yourself financially from the loss or theft of your property. Even so, it is also advisable to take common-sense precautions against loss or theft in the first place. If you have two credit cards, do not carry them together and make sure you keep a separate note of credit card cancellation numbers. Particular care should be exercised in crowded places such as airports and bus stations. Patrolling policemen often remind visitors about the need to be careful. There are also cases of tourists falling victim to theft when drunk. Never leave a bag or handbag unattended and do not put a mobile phone, purse or wallet on a tabletop in a café. The moment you discover a loss or theft, report it to the local police. The police will give you a *denuncia* (written statement), which you will need to make an insurance claim. If you have your passport lost or stolen, report it to your consulate.

Beach notice board in Cala Millor

Spanish Police

The island police are friendly towards tourists. They are always ready to give advice and help. However, in case of any infringement of the law, they can be very firm and it is best not to try to argue with them.

As in the rest of Spain there are three types of police on the islands. The *Policía Nacional* (state police), the *Policía Municipal*, also known as the *Policía Local* (local police), and the *Guardia Civil* (National Guard). The force encountered most frequently by tourists is the *Policía Municipal*. Their officers are mostly found in small towns, and patrol the streets of crowded tourist resorts; they have a separate branch for traffic. The *Policía Nacional* wear dark-blue uniforms. They deal with more serious incidents and matters concerning foreign dignitaries; they also guard various important buildings in large cities. The *Guardia Civil*, dressed in green uniforms, patrol rural areas. You can see them while travelling the roads and wild areas of the Balearic Islands.

State police car or *Policía Nacional*, frequently seen around the islands

Beaches

During the high season most beaches have lifeguards. Many beaches have swimming areas marked by buoys, although this does not mean that swimming outside these areas is prohibited. Many beaches have Red Cross stations. Notice boards at the entrance to the beach give information on facilities such as showers or wheelchair access. Many smaller beaches do not have lifeguards. Nevertheless, swimming is usually safe, as beaches are generally situated in small coves with calm waters.

The majority of the Balearic Islands' beaches are sandy. However, those along the northern shores of the islands are often rocky. You should exercise special care when swimming off rocky beaches. It is also recommended that you use footwear when entering the water and that you watch out for underwater rocks when snorkelling.

The sun should be taken seriously while on the beach. Between noon and 6pm it is best not to stay exposed for too long. It can take only minutes to get sunburned and children are especially vulnerable. Be sure to apply a high-factor sunblock cream and also make use of an umbrella. Deckchairs and umbrellas can often be hired for a fee. Drink plenty of water to avoid dehydration.

Medical Care

The UK Foreign Office advises all travellers to buy medical insurance. However, visitors from EU countries are entitled to free national health treatment if they travel with a European Health Insurance Card (EHIC), which can be obtained in the UK from the Department of Health or from a post office before you travel. Note that Spanish health care does not cover all expenses, such as the cost of dental treatment. Having private health insurance can also avoid time-wasting bureaucracy. Visitors from outside the EU should always carry valid medical insurance.

In case of illness, you should report to a hospital or clinic. At night, patients are seen by the *Urgencias* (Emergency).

Pharmacies

Pharmacies have the same opening hours as other shops. They carry a green or red cross with the word *farmàcia*, or sometimes *apotecaria*. Details about those open at night and on public holidays can be found in the windows of all pharmacies. Most pharmacists in large towns speak at least one foreign language. This is

Ambulance on Formentera

important, since when dealing with minor medical problems pharmacists are entitled to give advice and even dispense necessary medicines. In this instance, consulting a pharmacist may be enough.

Decorative pharmacy sign

Pharmacies on the Balearic Islands sell several medicines over the counter that in other countries are available only on prescription. Away from the big towns, a *farmàcia* may be found in any small town or village. Here, opening hours may be shorter, and they are not often open over the weekends. In addition, in smaller towns and villages the pharmacist may be less used to dealing with foreign tourists, and communication may be more problematic as a result.

Fire Hazards

The Balearic Islands have a dry Mediterranean climate, with mild winters and hot summers. The summer heat often causes droughts since rain falls only sporadically between October and February. This creates conditions where fire can spread extremely quickly. Parched woodlands, combined with the general layout of the land, make firefighting very difficult. Often fire fighting necessitates aeroplanes and

helicopters dropping vast amounts of water. It is vital, therefore, when travelling on the islands or using picnic facilities, to remember to take great care to prevent a fire from starting. Before leaving, carefully check the remains of any bonfire and be sure to pick up glass, particularly bottles, that may also cause fire. It goes without saying that you should be especially careful when extinguishing cigarettes in country areas.

The island firefighters are called *Bomberos*, and as elsewhere in the world, they have a simple emergency telephone number.

DIRECTORY

Emergency Numbers

Police, Guardia Civil, Red Cross, Ambulance & Fire Brigade
Tel 112.

Pharmacies

Formentera
Juan Torres Quetglas.
C/ Santa Maria,
Sant Francesc.
Tel 971 322 419.

Ibiza
Farmacia Ferrer,
C/ Formentera,
8, Figueretas, Eivissa.
Tel 971 302 737.

Mallorca
Farmacia La Rambla C B Rambla
Ducs de Palma 14,
Palma de Mallorca.
Tel 971 711 511.

Menorca
Farmacia Segui Puntas,
Avda Vives Llull 16, Maó.
Tel 971 360 993.

Firefighting aeroplane on Ibiza

Communication and Banks

The quality of telephone services in the Balearic Islands is high for both landlines and mobile phones. The banking services on the islands are equally efficient and many foreign banks, mainly German, have branches here. The Spanish postal system functions quite well, but it may take a week or longer for a letter posted in the Balearic Islands to reach its destination. When communicating with Spanish companies, it is best to use email.

Bright and easy-to-spot post box belonging to the Spanish *correos*

Telephones and Mobile Phones

You will be able to enjoy good mobile-phone reception in all but the most remote corners of Mallorca and Menorca, with the network fixed at GSM900/1800, the band used in the rest of Europe, Australia and New Zealand. Mobile phones purchased in North America will need to be adjusted to this GSM band.

Rather than using your own mobile phone, you may find it cheaper to buy a local SIM card. Bear in mind, however, that this can get complicated: many mobiles will not permit you to swap SIM cards, and the connection instructions for the replacement SIM card may be in Spanish only. If you overcome these problems, you can buy SIM cards at high-street phone companies, which offer myriad deals beginning at about €5 per SIM card.

Tourist navigating the streets of the islands with a digital tablet

When dialling a number you should remember that in Spain you must always dial the full nine-digit number, even if you are in the same area. The code for the Balearic Islands is 971. Making a call from Mallorca to Menorca will cost the same as one from Palma to Andratx.

When telephoning the Balearic Islands from the UK, Ireland and New Zealand, you must first dial 0034 (the country code for Spain) followed by the subscriber's number starting with the area code (971). When calling a mobile phone number you should dial the country code, followed by the subscriber's number. To phone the UK from the Balearic Islands dial 0044, then the area code (minus the 0), then the number; to phone Ireland dial 00353, then the area code (minus the 0), then the number; to phone the US or Canada dial 001, then the area code, then the number.

Logo of Movistar

Internet

All hotels and airports, plus a large number of bars, on the Balearic Islands have Internet hot spots, but be aware that sometimes they will charge you a small fee for access, and you will usually need to ask for a password. Cafés with free Wi-Fi are mainly found in the city centres. Nearly all hotels have at least one computer for guests to send emails.

Postal Service

The Spanish postal system is now quite efficient, and postcards and letters sent from the islands take a couple of days to reach the addressee. It is also possible to send express (*urgente*) or registered (*certificado*) mail.

Post offices are open between 8:30am and 2:30pm Mondays to Fridays (main offices are open to 8:30pm), and between 9:30am and 1pm Saturdays. If you only want stamps, note that these are also sold at kiosks bearing the sign *timbre* or at tobacconists; or, ask at your hotel reception. Postal charges depend on where the item is being sent to and fall into bands that include the EU, the rest of Europe, the USA and the rest of the world. Post offices also accept telegrams, registered mail and parcels. Letters and cards can be mailed in a yellow post box.

Currency

The euro (€) is the common currency of the European Union. It went into general circulation on 1 January 2002, initially for 12 participating countries. Spain was one of those 12 countries, and the Spanish peseta was phased out in January 2002. Euro notes, in denominations of €5 to €500, are identical throughout the Eurozone countries, while the coins have one side identical (the value side), and one side with an image unique to each country.

Banks and Cash Dispensers

The easiest way to get cash is from a cash dispenser, or ATM, and these are ubiquitous across the Balearic Islands. Note that most major credit and debit cards are accepted. However, with credit cards you will be charged a supp-lementary fee; this is not the case with debit cards. For changing currency, most banks are open from 8am until 2pm.

One of the many cash dispensers available on the islands

Debit and Credit Cards

The most widely accepted credit cards on the Balearic Islands are Visa and MasterCard. However, most cash dispensers, as well as shops, hotels and restaurants, will also accept American Express or Diners. When you pay with a card,

staff will usually pass your card through a reading machine. Sometimes you may be asked to punch in your PIN number. Some smaller places, such as market stalls and independent shops may not accept credit cards.

Radio and Television

Numerous pubs and cafés have a television and it is easy to watch major sporting events live, including many English and German league soccer matches. Hotels have a larger selection of TV channels. Besides Spanish national TV, such as TVE1 and TVE2, there are a number of local channels including Catalan TV3 and Canal 33. These broadcast mainly Spanish news and light entertainment shows..

You can tune into the BBC's World Service 24 hours a day online or through audio channels offered by local TV providers in some hotels.

Newspapers

Several local newspapers are published on each of the islands. These cover mainly local issues and they can also be valuable sources of information for visitors who want to find out about forthcoming cultural and sporting events. They also publish useful addresses and telephone numbers. Some of the local newspapers have foreign-language supplements.

Popular dailies published in the Balearic Islands

In many towns, kiosks and hotels sell Spanish national papers as well as British and German newspapers and magazines. The majority of popular publications from other EU countries arrive on the Balearic Islands with a minimum delay.

DIRECTORY

Post Offices

Ibiza
Avda Isidor Macabich 67,
Eivissa.
Tel 902 197 197.

Mallorca
Constitucio 5,
Palma.
Tel 971 721 095.

Menorca
C/Bon Aire 15, Maó.
Tel 971 356 629.
Pl Borne 9, Ciutadella.
Tel 971 380 081.

Lost or Stolen Credit Cards

American Express
Tel 1273 696 933.

Diners Club
Tel 1273 696 933.

MasterCard
Tel 900 971 231.

Visa
Tel 900 991 216.

Kiosks selling papers in Passeig d'es Born in Palma, Mallorca

TRAVEL INFORMATION

Most visitors arrive on the Balearic Islands by air. This is not only the fastest, but often also the cheapest, way of getting here. The airports are on Mallorca, Menorca and Ibiza. Provided by international airlines, these flights are a mixture of charter and regular scheduled flights from a wide range of European countries. Alternatively, you can fly to mainland Spain and change planes. During peak season, Palma's airport is one of the busiest in Europe. Sea links are equally convenient, but you must first get to the Spanish coast. The routes from Barcelona, Dénia and Valencia to the Balearic Islands are served by large ferries that may carry cars, and also by fast catamarans.

Palma airport's departure hall, Mallorca

Multilingual information sign at Palma's airport

Air Travel

Regular links between large Spanish cities and the Balearic Islands are provided by the Spanish carriers **Iberia**, **Vueling** and **Aireuropa**. There are also regular flights between the Balearic Islands (mainly Mallorca) and countries that provide the greatest numbers of visitors, such as Germany and Britain, as well as Austria, Switzerland, France and the Netherlands.

The Balearic Islands are featured by a wide range of European tour operators – ask your travel agent for advice. Package holidays operate year-round and feature both scheduled and charter flights. Palma, Ibiza and Menorca are also served by low-cost airlines, including **easyJet** and **Ryanair**, with flights from London Gatwick, Stansted, Luton, Bristol, East Midlands, Manchester, Liverpool, Newcastle and Glasgow. Flights from the UK take under 3 hours. These relatively short flight times mean that the islands are popular for annual holidays as well as "mini-breaks". Flights from the US require changing planes in London, Barcelona or Madrid.

Flights Between the Islands

The main carrier providing flights between the islands is **Iberia**. The flight from Mallorca to Menorca takes only 30 minutes. For that reason this is a convenient way of travelling. Before island-hopping, it is a good idea to find out what type of aircraft you are going to fly in. Some are quite small and you may not be able to take large hand luggage. Travelling in a small, packed and stuffy light aircraft can be a little unpleasant for anybody who suffers from claustrophobia or other health problems. Even in the best of weather, the flight may be bumpy and a small aircraft makes this more noticeable. However, flying between the islands will not only save you time but will also give you the chance to see magnificent views of the archipelago.

Airports

Son Sant Joan airport on Mallorca is situated on the outskirts of Palma, around 11 km (7 miles) from the centre of the island's capital. The nearby motorway provides a fast road link to Palma. The airport has many shops, car hire agents and a tourist information centre.

Over the last few years, the airport has been constantly extended for the needs of tourists. Despite its size, it is difficult to get lost here. There is only one terminal, where check-ins are made on the second floor, and boarding is on the fourth floor. Individual zones are well signposted, but be prepared for long walks when making your way from one sector of the airport to another. **Menorca**'s airport is near the island's capital – Maó. This is the smallest of the Balearic airports. **Ibiza**'s airport is a dozen or so kilometres from Eivissa and is far busier. The traffic increases

Colourful aircraft at Ibiza's airport

Ferries in Maó's harbour, Menorca

particularly during weekends, when club-goers from all over Europe arrive for the Saturday–Sunday revel. The aircraft touching down here are often painted in the most fantastic designs. When taking off or landing in Eivissa, you get a bird's-eye view of the town and of Dalt Vila. Frequent bus services operate from all the main airports and can take you straight to the city centres.

Ferries

Anyone who plans to take their own car or motorcycle to the islands must use a ferry. There are frequent and regular services between large towns on the Spanish mainland and the harbours of Mallorca, Menorca and Ibiza. Journey times are quite reasonable; it takes 7 hours by ferry from Barcelona to Palma for example.

Logo of Balearia ferry lines

The large ferries operated by **Trasmediterranea** sail from Barcelona and Valencia to Palma and Maó. They also provide transport to Ibiza. The latter may be reached from Barcelona (10 hours) or Valencia (about 4 hours). **Balearia**, a smaller ferry company, also has services to the islands. If you're in a hurry, you can also use Trasmediterranea's high-speed ferry service, which carries up to 900 passengers and 265 cars and can take you from Valencia to Ibiza in 3 hours. Inter-island services are equally diverse. You can choose a fast Trasmediterranea catamaran or a slower ferry. Both of them have bars for passengers.

Using ferries to hop from island to island will often be cheaper than flying and it can be a very pleasant option. Arriving by sea and catching your first glimpse of Maó's ancient harbour is an unforgettable experience. Some islands can only be reached by sea. These include Cabrera, Formentera and Dragonera. A journey by ferry from Ibiza to Formentera takes about 1 hour; by catamaran it takes about 30 minutes. Ticket prices for ferries providing links between the islands are reasonable, but going by a catamaran will cost you more. Price differences between the competing companies are greater for longer routes, but prices depend mostly on the time of year. The lowest prices can be obtained after high season, from October until December, and again from the end of January until the end of March. In the period from Easter until the beginning of July – known as the "half-season" – the ferry prices tend to go up again. Children up to the age of 12 are entitled to a 50 per cent reduction, and infants travel free.

Party boat leaving the port of Mallorca with revellers on board

Getting Around the Islands

The Balearic Islands have only two railway lines, both of which are in Mallorca. The first is an historic line travelling from Palma to Sóller (*see p74*); the other links Palma with Manacor, via Inca. To explore the more remote parts of the island, as well as the remaining islands of the archipelago, you will need a car, a scooter or a bicycle. On Formentera, a scooter and bicycle are the best means of transport. When travelling round the islands, you should pay particular attention to the numerous motorbike riders.

Scenic, winding road leading to Sa Calobra, Mallorca

Roads

Roads and signage on the Balearic Islands are generally good, although there is a shortage of hard shoulders. As a consequence, stopping along the road in order to admire the scenery can be difficult and dangerous and is not recommended. The only major motorway runs along the coast of Badia de Palma, encircling Mallorca's capital. Its second segment links Palma with Inca. There is also a toll levied to use the tunnel on the main road from Palma to Sóller. During the morning and afternoon rush hour in the areas around Palma and other industrial towns like Inca or Manacor, you may experience traffic jams.

Take great care when you are trying to reach some beaches or sights off the beaten track. The roads leading to them can be narrow, steep and winding. Problems can arise when two cars try to pass each other. Some beaches and sights inland can only be reached along unmade, bumpy roads and to travel to these requires a four-wheel drive vehicle.

Maps

When hiring a car you will normally be given an outline road map of the island. It will show the main roads on which it is safe to drive. Unfortunately the maps are not always up to date and it is advisable to buy one of the maps sold in bookshops, souvenir shops or petrol stations. The folding B&B maps are particularly good. Please note that town and street signs now appear in Catalan rather than Spanish (Castilian), so make sure you get a map marked in Catalan.

Car and Scooter Hire

It is easy to rent a car as soon as you have landed in the Balearic Islands, as all the major car hire companies, **Avis, Hertz** and **Europcar** have their desks at the airports. It is, however, worth taking your time to search for a small local firm that may offer you a better price than the international companies.

The price of car hire varies depending on the time of year, the size of the car and the length of hire. Advance booking can also affect the price. It is worth not only comparing the prices quoted by the various companies but checking exactly what the quote includes.

When hiring a car, you will be asked to show your passport and valid driver's licence. You should also carefully check the conditions regarding insurance and any restrictions about driving on rough tracks or taking the car from one island to another. Be sure to inspect the condition of the car, as you will have to return it in the same condition or pay a fine. The terms and conditions of hire can vary greatly from company to company. Check carefully before signing any contract.

Scooters are a very popular form of transport, particularly on the islands of Formentera and Ibiza. Hire rates for these are much lower and they can transport you to places that cars cannot reach. Many people learn to ride a scooter during their holidays.

Car and bike rental service in Ibiza

Petrol station run by the Cepsa chain

Rules of the Road

Driving on the Balearic Islands is no different to driving in any other European country. You should remember the speed limits, which are 120 km/h (74 mph) on motorways, 90 km/h (56 mph) on major roads and 40 km/h (25 mph) in towns. The fines for breaking the speed limits are high, just as they are for drunken driving. The highest permitted blood alcohol level is 0.025 per cent.

Buying Petrol

Petrol station pumps are generally operated by the staff. Only a few are automatic and open 24 hours. Menorca, Ibiza and Formentera have very few petrol stations. The same applies to the Serra de Tramuntana region of Mallorca. When touring these areas you should remember that a car uses more fuel on mountainous terrain than on a flat road. It is therefore worth filling the tank before setting off.

Town Driving

If at all possible, you should avoid driving in large town centres and popular resorts. Many streets in historic towns are narrow, with one-way traffic. Cars parked alongside pavements make driving conditions even more difficult. Popular resorts are always crowded and it can be hard to find a parking space.

Most car parks charge fees, and there are fines for non-payment. Paid car parking spaces along pavements are marked with a blue line. Generally, the parking fees apply from 9am to 1pm and from 5pm to 8pm on weekdays, and from 9am to 1pm on Saturdays. In many towns, such as Eivissa, parking in these spaces is limited to a set time. A yellow line painted along the pavement means that parking is prohibited. In Palma and Maó, use one of the underground car parks. Here, there is no time limit on parking, but you may have to wait in a long queue.

Sign for a parking meter

Buses

Bus links between major towns as well as between large and small towns are very good. Links between small towns and villages are less frequent. Of the large towns, only Palma and Maó have their own municipal bus network. Bear in mind that during weekends bus services are less frequent. When planning a further journey, particularly on Mallorca, check your options for the return journey.

Ibiza has a special night bus service during high season, taking guests to the most popular clubs and ferrying them between Sant Antoni de Portmany and Eivissa.

Taxis

For travelling around town, it is best to hire a taxi. Most taxis in Palma have a black-and-cream colour scheme. The driver is obliged to turn on the meter at the start of the journey, and the sum displayed is the one you pay.

For disabled people, taxi transport is by far the most convenient, as you can order a specially adapted vehicle. Taxis to the airport charge an additional airport and luggage fee.

For taxis on Mallorca, call 971 755 440; on Menorca, call 971 367 111; and on Ibiza, call 971 398 483.

Bicycle and "quadcycle" on a promenade

General Index

Acknowledgments

Dorling Kindersley would like to thank the following people whose contributions and assistance have made the preparation of this book possible.

Consultant Chris Rice

Factcheckers Paula Canal, Bernat Fiol, John Gill

Proofreaders Stewart Wild, Nikky Twyman

Indexer Helen Peters

Additional Contributors Tony Kelly, Jeffrey Kennedy, Andrew Valente

Additional Photography Ian Aitken, Simon Bracken, Joe Cornish, Neil Lucas, Ian O'Leary, Coline Sinclair

Revisions and Relaunch Team Tora Agarwala, Claire Baranowski, Sonal Bhatt, Subhadeep Biswas, Emma Brady, Paula Canal, Jo Cowen, Gadi Farfour, Rebecca Flynn, Anná Freiberger, Lydia Halliday, John Gill, Sumita Khatwani, Phil Lee, Bhavika Mathur, Alison McGill, Caroline Mead, Sonal Modha, Marianne Petrou, Mani Ramaswamy, Alice Reese, Sands Publishing Solutions, Farah Sheikh, Azeem Siddiqui, Rituraj Singh, Lucinda Smith, Susie Smith, Priyansha Tuli, Hugo Wilkinson, Conrad Van Dyk, Ajay Verma, Richa Verma

Senior Editor Jacky Jackson

Managing Editor Helen Townsend

Publishing Manager Kate Poole

Special Assistance

Wiedza i Życie would like to thank the following people for their help in creating this guide.

Martin & Toni Cornell, Zbigniew Dybowski, Joanna Egert-Romanowska, Christiane Hagen, Martin Hagmüller, Javier Lopez Silvosa, Barbara Sudnik.

The publisher would also like to thank the people and institutions who allowed photographs of their property to be reproduced, as well as granting permission to use photographs from their archives:

AENA, Gabinete de Comunicación-Aeropuertos de Baleares; Aeropuerto de Palma de Mallorca (Elisabet Royo Romero); AFP in Warszawie (Piotr Ufnal); Aguamar in Platja d'en Bossa; Amic Hotels in Palma (Andreu Llabrés); Amnesia in Sant Rafael (Stéphane Schweitzer, Aymeric Huot-Marchand); Banys Àrabs in Palmie (Doña Pilar); National Library in Warsaw (Iwona Grzybowska); Centre Perles in Palma (Lluc Antonio Bibiloni, Carolina Gato); Corbis – Agencja Free in Warsaw (Gabriela Ściborska); Coves de Campanet (Maria Antònia Siquier); Eden in Sant Antoni de Portmany (Gemma); El Divino in Eivissa; Els Calders (Javier Marqués); Es Paradis in Sant Antoni de Portmany; Fundació Pilar i Joan Miró in Cala Major (Núria Sureda, Joan Insa); Grupo Aspro-Ocio (Omar García Melcon); Ibatur (Esteve Rigo Ribas); La Granja (Manuel Moragues Marqués); La Residencia in Deià (Arantza Zamora); La Reserva Puig de Galatzó (Heike Killisch); Modas Leather in Ferreries (Suzanne Sparkes-Keeble); Museu d'Art Espanyol Contemporani in Palma (Antonio Barcelo); Museu de Lluc in Monasteri de Luc (Elvira González); Museu de Mallorca in Palma (Guillem Rosselló Bordoy); Museu de Menorca in Maó (Anna Fernandez); Naviera Universal Española, S.L. in Barcelona (Núria Alvarez); paulunderhill.com (Paul Underhill); Safari-zoo Mallorca (Miquel Brunet Alós)

Picture Credits

a–above; b–below/bottom; c–centre; f-far; l–left; r–right; t–top.

Works of art have been reproduced with the permission of the following copyright holders: *Personage and Bird* and *Mosaic* in Parc de la Mar, Palma Joan Miró © Succession Miró/ADAG, Paris and DACS, London 2011: 62c/52bl; *La Eustacia* Guillermo Perez Villalta © DACS, London 2011 60tl.

The publisher is grateful to the following individuals, companies and picture libraries for permission to reproduce their photographs:

4Corners Images: Sime/Schmid Reinhard 13bl, 10cla; **Aena:** 190cla; **AFP** 187bl; **Alamy Images:** AA World Travel Library 114bc; age fotostock 110c, 124br, 125bc, 157br; Paul Bourdice 154cla; Ian Canham 125c; CFimages 191br; City Image 166cb; colau 32cla; Rainer Drexel 40crb; Greg Balfour Evans 116; Xavier Fores-Joana Roncero 128–9; Tony French 147c; imagebroker/White Star/Monica Gumm 179cr; LOOK Die Bildagentur der Fotografen GmbH 146bc; Mark Bolton Photography 22b; Chris Mattison 27bc; nagelestock. com 11cr; David Pearson 124tr; Superstock 71cl; The Geoff Williamson Image Collection 178tr; travelstock44 124cla; WENN UK 23tl; Westend61 GmbH 98ca; Wolfgang Pölzer 176bl; **Amnesia:** 171tl.

Celda de Frederic Chopin y George Sand: Cartuja de Valldemossa 71bc; **Club de Golf Alcanada:** 178bl; **Corbis:** 38c, 39br, Franz-Marc Frei 33cra; Roger Halls 115tr; Hans Georg Roth 95b; James A Sugar 25bl, 33cl; Cueva des Hams 83tl; Werner Forman 8-9.

Depositphotos Inc: mjth 188bl; **Dreamstime.com:** Alessandro0770 15tc; Artesiawells 174cla; Bojan Bokic 93cra; Emanuel Corso 192br; Foxirisha 15br; Veronika Galkina 5cl; Carmen Vicedo Giner 23br, Jpmora 106-7; Karol Kozlowski 93tl; Lunamarina 2-3, 4crb, 36tl, 47b, 137b, 180-1; Anna Lurye 92cla; Juan Moyano 4ca; Pstedrak 92bl; Schlenger86 65tc; Tamas 5cra; Victor Pelaez Torres 14cl; Xantana 41crb; Xoriguer 136. **Es Forn de Tore Soli Nou:** 159tc.

Fosh: 153cl, 158t; **Fotolia:** nito 18; **Fundació Pilar i Joan Miró:** 62b; **Getty Images:** Gonzalo Azumendi 46; Michele Falzone 94; Doug Pearson 144–5; Stringer / Jaime Reina 27br; **La Granja:** 69bc; Grupo Aspro-Ocio: 45bl, 91tr, 92clb, 93bl; **Hell's Kitchen:** 158bc; **Hemispheres Images:** Michel Gotin 12bl; **Ibatur:** 30br, 31c, 171br; **Ibiza Gran Hotel:** 151bl; **iStockphoto.com:** cinoby 92tr, Jan-Otto 93br.

Piotr Kiedrowski: 153bc, 157c; **Restaurante Jardin:** 155bl; **Juan y Andrea:** Iris Esteve 153br; **Julius and Hanna Komarniccy:** 24c, 30cl, 167la; **Wesley Kutner:** 21bl, 23tl, 152c. **Andrzej Lisowski:** 21tr, 25br, 32b, 100ca, 124cb, 133br, 175tl, 182bl, 183br, 184br, 190br; **Carlos Minguel:** 28clb, 28bl, 29c, 29cb, 29bl, 29br; **Pawel Murzyn:** 16c, 16b, 19b, 24bl, 24br, 29tl, 33bl, 44cla, 63cb, 123b, 132c, 170cl, 182cra; **Museu de Mallorca:** 56c, 56bc, 56tr, *Paris i Helena* Ca. 1665 Mattia Preti 56cla, 57bl, 57c, 57crb, *Cabeza de Mercurio* Jaume and Rafael Blanquer Ca 1630–1650 57ca.

La Paloma: 162br; **Robert Pasieczny:** 26clb, 38br, 41bl, 45tl, 49br, 68tr, 68cla, 70tl, 72br, 74c, 172tr; **La Reserva Puig de Galatzó:** 65c; **La Residencia:** 148br, 156br; **Santi Taura:** 156tl; **Biel Salas Servera:** 27c, 27ca, 27cb, 28tr, 28br, 29tc, 88clb, 89tl; **Soleado:** 161br; **Son Granot:** 150tc; **Restaurant Stay:** 152cl; **Superstock:** Album/Oronoz/Album 39cr; **Telefonica:** 188c; **Andrzej Zygmuntowicz and Ireneusz Winnicki:** 105br, 152bc, 153tc.

Front Endpaper: Alamy Images: Greg Balfour Evans Lcla; **Dreamstime.com:** Xoriguer Lbr; **Getty Images:** Gonzalo Azumendi Rbl; Michele Falzone Rcr.

Cover images: Front and spine: **Getty Images:** Douglas Pearson. Back: **Dreamstime.com:** Lunamarina

All other images © Dorling Kindersley
For further information see: www.dkimages.com

English–Catalan Phrase Book

In Emergency

Help!	Auxili!	ow-**gzee**-lee
Stop!	Pareu!	pah-**reh**-oo
Call a doctor!	Telefoneu un metge!	teh-leh-fon-**eh**-oo oon meh-djuh
Call an ambulance!	Telefoneu una ambulància!	teh-leh-fon-**eh**-oo oo-nah ahm-boo-**lahn**-see-ah
Call the police!	Telefoneu la policia!	teh-leh-fon-**eh**-oo lah poh-lee-**see**-ah
Call the fire brigade!	Telefoneu els bombers!	teh-leh-fon-**eh**-oo uhlz boom-**behs**
Where is the nearest telephone?	On és el teléfon més proper?	on-ehs uhl tuh-leh-fon mehs proo-**peh**
Where is the nearest hospital?	On és l'hospital més proper?	on-ehs looss-pee-tahl mehs proo-**peh**

Communication Essentials

Yes	Sí	see
No	No	noh
Please	Si us plau	sees plah-oo
Thank you	Gràcies	**grah**-see-uhs
Excuse me	Perdoni	puhr-**thoh**-nee
Hello	Hola	oh-lah
Goodbye	Adéu	ah-they-**oo**
Good night	Bona nit	bo-nah neet
Morning	El matí	uhl mah-**tee**
Afternoon	La tarda	lah **tahr**-thuh
Evening	El vespre	uhl **vehs**-pruh
Yesterday	Ahir	ah-ee
Today	Avui	uh-voo-**ee**
Tomorrow	Demà	duh-**mah**
Here	Aquí	uh-**kee**
There	Allà	uh-**lyah**
What?	Què?	keh
When?	Quan?	kwahn
Why?	Per què?	puhr keh
Where?	On?	ohn

Useful Phrases

How are you?	Com està?	kom uhs-**tah**
Very well, thank you.	Molt bé, gràcies.	mol beh **grah**-see-uhs
Pleased to meet you.	Molt de gust.	mol duh **goost**
See you soon.	Fins aviat.	feenz uhv-**yat**
That's fine.	Està bé.	uhs-**tah** beh
Where is/are …?	On és/són…?	ohn ehs/sohn
How far is it to…?	Quants metres/ kilòmetres hi ha d'aquí a …?	kwahnz meh-truhs/kee-loh-muh-truhs yah dah-**kee** uh
Which way to …?	Per on es va a …?	puhr on uhs bah ah
Do you speak English?	Parla anglès?	par-luh an-**glehs**
I don't understand.	No l'entenc.	noh luhn-**teng**
Could you speak more slowly, please?	Pot parlar més a poc a poc, si us plau?	pot par-lah mehs pok uh pok sees plah-oo
I'm sorry.	Ho sento.	oo **sehn**-too

Useful Words

big	gran	gran
small	petit	puh-**teet**
hot	calent	kah-**len**
cold	fred	fred
good	bo	boh
bad	dolent	doo-**len**
enough	bastant	bahs-**tan**
well	bé	beh
open	obert	oo-**behr**
closed	tancat	tan-**kat**
left	esquerra	uhs-**kehr**-ruh
right	dreta	dreh-tuh
straight on	recte	rehk-tuh
near	a prop	uh prop
far	lluny	lyoonyuh
up/over	a dalt	uh dahl
down/under	a baix	uh bah-eeshh
early	aviat	uhv-yat
late	tard	tahrt
entrance	entrada	uhn-**trah**-thuh
exit	sortida	soor-tee-thuh
toilet	lavabos/ serveis	luh-**vah**-boos/ sehr-**beh**-ees
more	més	mess
less	menys	menyees

Shopping

How much does this cost?	Quant costa això?	kwahn kost ehs-**shoh**
I would like …	M'agradaria …	muh-grad-uh-**ree**-ah
Do you have…?	Tenen…?	tehn-un
I'm just looking, thank you	Només estic mirant, gràcies.	noo-mess ehs-**teek** mee-**rahn** **grah**-see-uhs
Do you take credit cards?	Accepten targes de crèdit?	ak-**sehp**-tuhn tahr-**zhuhs** duh kreh-deet
What time do you open?	A quina hora obren?	ah keen-uh oh-ruh oh-bruhn
What time do you close?	A quina hora tanquen?	ah keen-uh oh-ruh tan-kuhn
This one.	Aquest.	ah-ket
That one.	Aquell.	ah-kehl
expensive	car	kahr
cheap	bé de preu/ barat	beh thuh preh-oo/ bah-rat
size (clothes)	talla/mida	tah-lyah/mee-thuh
size (shoes)	número	noo-mehr-oo
white	blanc	blang
black	negre	neh-gruh
red	vermell	vuhr-mel
yellow	groc	grok
green	verd	behrt
blue	blau	blah-oo
antique store	antiquari/botiga d'antiguitats	an-tee-kwah-ree/ boo-tee-gah/dan-tee-ghee-tats
bakery	el forn	uhl forn
bank	el banc	uhl bang
book store	la llibreria	lah lyee-bruh-ree-uh
butcher's	la carnisseria	lah kahr-nee-suh-ree-uh
pastry shop	la pastisseria	lah pahs-tee-suh-ree-uh
chemist's	la farmàcia	lah fuhr-**mah**-see-ah
fishmonger's	la peixateria	lah peh-shuh-tuh-ree-uh
greengrocer's	la fruiteria	lah froo-ee-tuh-ree-uh
grocer's	la botiga de queviures	lah boo-**tee**-guh duh keh-vee-oo-ruhs
hairdresser's	la perruqueria	lah peh-roo-kuh-ree-uh
market	el mercat	uhl muhr-kat
newsagent's	el quiosc de premsa	uhl kee-ohsk duh prem-suh

post office	l'oficina de correus	loo-fee-**see**-nuh duh koo-**reh**-oos
shoe store	la sabateria	lah sah-bah-tuh-**ree**-uh
supermarket	el supermercat	uhl soo-puhr-muhr-**kat**
tobacconist's	l'estanc	luhs-**tang**
travel agency	l'agència de viatges	la-**jen**-see-uh duh vee-**ad**-juhs

Sightseeing

art gallery	la galeria d'art	lah gah-luh **ree**-yuh **dart**
cathedral	la catedral	lah kuh-tuh-**thrahl**
church	l'església/ la basílica	luhz-gleh-**zee**-uh/ lah buh-zee-lee-kuh
garden	el jardí	uhl zhahr-**dee**
library	la biblioteca	lah bee-blee-oo-**teh**-kuh
museum	el museu	uhl moo-**seh**-oo
tourist information office	l'oficina de turisme	loo-fee-**see**-nuh thuh too-**reez**-muh
town hall	l'ajuntament	luh-djoon-tuh-**men**
closed for holiday	tancat per vacances	tan-**kat** puh bah-**kan**-suhs
bus station	l'estació d'autobusos	luhs-tah-see-**oh** dow-toh-**boo**-zoos
railway station	l'estació de tren	luhs-tah-see-**oh** thuh **tren**

Staying in a Hotel

Do you have a vacant room?	¿Tenen una habitació lliure?	teh-**nuhn oo**-nuh ah-bee-tuh-see-**oh lyuh**-ruh
double room with double bed	habitació doble amb llit de matrimoni	ah-bee-tuh-see-**oh doh**-bluh am **lyeet** duh mah-tree-**moh**-nee
twin room	habitació amb dos llits/ amb llits individuals	ah-bee-tuh-see-**oh** am **dohs** lyeets/ am **lyeets** in-thee-vee-thoo-**ahls**
single room	habitació individual	ah-bee-tuh-see-**oh** een-dee-vee-thoo-**ahl**
room with a bath	habitació amb bany	ah-bee-tuh-see-**oh** am **bah**nyuh
shower	dutxa	**doo**-chuh
porter	el grum	uhl **groom**
key	la clau	lah **klah**-oo
I have a reservation.	Tinc una habitació reservada.	ting oo-nuh ah-bee-tuh-see-**oh** reh-sehr-**vah**-thah

Eating Out

Have you got a table for…?	Tenen taula per…?	teh-**nuhn tow**-luh puhr
I would like to reserve a table.	Voldria reservar una taula.	vool-**dree**-uh reh-sehr-**vahr oo**-nuh **tow**-luh
The bill please.	El compte, si us plau.	uhl **kohm**-tuh sees plah-oo
I am a vegetarian.	Sóc vegetarià/ vegetariana.	sok buh-zhuh-tuh-ree-**ah** buh-zhuh-tuh-ree-**ah**-nah
waitress	cambrera	kam-**breh**-ruh
waiter	cambrer	kam-**breh**
menu	la carta	lah **kahr**-tuh
fixed-price menu	menú del dia	muh-**noo** thuhl **dee**-uh
wine list	la carta de vins	lah **kahr**-tuh thuh **veens**
glass of water	un got d'aigua	oon **got** dah-ee-gwah

glass of wine	una copa de vi	oo-nuh **ko**-pah thuh **vee**
bottle	una ampolla	oo-nuh am-**pol**-yuh
knife	un ganivet	oon gun-ee-**veht**
fork	una forquilla	oo-nuh foor-**keel**-yuh
spoon	una cullera	oo-nuh kool-**yeh**-ruh
breakfast	l'esmorzar	les-moor-**sah**
lunch	el dinar	uhl dee-**nah**
dinner	el sopar	uhl soo-**pah**
main course	el primer plat	uhl pree-**meh plat**
starters	els entrants	uhlz ehn-**tranz**
dish of the day	el plat del dia	uhl **plat**duhl **dee**-uh
coffee	el cafè	uhl kah-**feh**
rare	poc fet	pok fet
medium	al punt	ahl **poon**
well done	molt fet	mol **fet**

Menu Decoder

l'aigua mineral	**lah**-ee-gwuh mee-nuh-**rahl**	mineral water
sense gas/ amb gas	sen-zuh gas/ am gas	still/sparkling
al forn	ahl **forn**	baked
l'all	lahlyuh	garlic
l'arròs	lahr-**roz**	rice
les botifarres	lahs boo-tee-fah-rahs	sausages
la carn	lah **karn**	meat
la ceba	lah **seh**-buh	onion
la cervesa	lah-sehr-**ve**-sah	beer
l'embotit	lum-boo-**teet**	cold meat
el filet	uhl fee-**let**	sirloin
el formatge	uhl for-**mah**-djuh	cheese
fregit	freh-**zheet**	fried
la fruita	lah froo-**ee**-tah	fruit
els fruits secs	uhlz froo-**eets** seks	nuts
les gambes	lahs **gam**-bus	prawns
el gelat	uhl djuh-**lat**	ice cream
la llagosta	lah lyah-**gos**-tah	lobster
la llet	lah **lyet**	milk
la llimona	lah lyee-**moh**-nah	lemon
la llimonada	lah lyee-moh-**nah**-thuh	lemonade
la mantega	lah mahn-**teh**-gah	butter
el marisc	uhl muh-**reesk**	seafood
la menestra	lah muh-**nehs**-truh	vegetable stew
l'oli	**loll**-ee	oil
les olives	lahs oo-**lee**-vuhs	olives
l'ou	**loh**-oo	egg
el pa	uhl **pah**	bread
el pastís	uhl pahs-**tees**	pie/cake
les patates	lahs pah-**tah**-tuhs	potatoes
el pebre	uhl **peh**-bruh	pepper
el peix	uhl **pehsh**	fish
el pernil salat serrà	uhl puhr-**neel** suh-lat sehr-**rah**	cured ham
el plàtan	uhl **plah**-tun	banana
el pollastre	uhl poo-**lyah**-struh	chicken
la poma	lah **poh**-mah	apple
el porc	uhl **pohr**	pork
les postres	lahs **pohs**-truhs	dessert
rostit	rohs-**teet**	roast
la sal	lah **sahl**	salt
la salsa	lah **sahl**-suh	sauce
les salsitxes	lahs sahl-**see**-chuhs	sausages
sec	**sehk**	dry
la sopa	lah **soh**-puh	soup
el sucre	uhl-**soo**-kruh	sugar
la taronja	lah tuh-**rohn**-djuh	orange
el te	uhl **teh**	tea
les torrades	lahs too-**rah**-thuhs	toast

la vedella	*lah veh-**theh**-lyuh*	*beef*
el vi blanc	*uhl **bee blang***	*white wine*
el vi negre	*uhl **bee neh**-gruh*	*red wine*
el vi rosat	*uhl bee roo-**zaht***	*rosé wine*
el vinagre	*uhl bee-**nah**-gruh*	*vinegar*
el xai/el be	*uhl **shah**ee/ uhl **beh***	*lamb*
el xerès	*uhl shuh-**rehs***	*sherry*
la xocolata	*lah shoo-koo-**lah**-tuh*	*chocolate*
el xoriç	*uhl shoo-**rees***	*red sausage*

Numbers

0	**zero**	*seh-roo*
1	**un** (*masc*)	*oon*
	una (*fem*)	*oon-uh*
2	**dos** (*masc*)	*dohs*
	dues (*fem*)	*doo-uhs*
3	**tres**	*trehs*
4	**quatre**	*kwa-truh*
5	**cinc**	*seeng*
6	**sis**	*sees*
7	**set**	*set*
8	**vuit**	*voo-eet*
9	**nou**	*noh-oo*
10	**deu**	*deh-oo*
11	**onze**	*on-zuh*
12	**doce**	*doh-dzuh*
13	**tretze**	*treh-dzuh*
14	**catorze**	*kah-**tohr**-dzuh*
15	**quinze**	*keen-zuh*
16	**setze**	*set-zuh*
17	**disset**	*dee-**set***
18	**divuit**	*dee-voo-**eet***
19	**dinou**	*dee-**noh**-oo*
20	**vint**	*been*
21	**vint-i-un**	*been-tee-**oon***
22	**vint-i-dos**	*been-tee-**dohs***

30	**trenta**	*tren-tah*
31	**trenta-un**	*tren-tah **oon***
40	**quaranta**	*kwuh-**ran**-tuh*
50	**cinquanta**	*seen-**kwahn**-tah*
60	**seixanta**	*seh-ee-**shan**-tah*
70	**setanta**	*seh-tan-tah*
80	**vuitanta**	*voo-ee-**tan**-tah*
90	**noranta**	*noh-**ran**-tah*
100	**cent**	*sen*
101	**cent un**	*sent oon*
102	**cent dos**	*sen dohs*
200	**dos-cents** (*masc*)	*dohs-**sens***
	dues-centes (*fem*)	*doo-uhs **sen**-tuhs*
300	**tres-cents**	*trehs-senz*
400	**quatre-cents**	*kwah-**truh**-senz*
500	**cinc-cents**	*seeng-senz*
600	**sis-cents**	*sees-senz*
700	**set-cents**	*set-senz*
800	**vuit-cents**	*voo-**eet**-senz*
900	**nou-cents**	*noh-oo-**cenz***
1,000	**mil**	*meel*
1,001	**mil un**	*meel oon*

Time

one minute	**un minut**	*oon mee-**noot***
one hour	**una hora**	*oo-nuh oh-ruh*
half an hour	**mitja hora**	*mee-juh oh-ruh*
Monday	**dilluns**	*dee-**lyoonz***
Tuesday	**dimarts**	*dee-**marts***
Wednesday	**dimecres**	*dee-**meh**-kruhs*
Thursday	**dijous**	*dee-**zhoh**-oos*
Friday	**divendres**	*dee-**ven**-druhs*
Saturday	**dissabte**	*dee-**sab**-tuh*
Sunday	**diumenge**	*dee-oo-**men**-juh*